JESUS THROUGH THE CENTURIES

JAROSLAV PELIKAN

JESUS
THROUGH THE
CENTURIES

His Place in the History of Culture

Harper & Row, Publishers, New York
Grand Rapids, Philadelphia, St. Louis, San Francisco
London, Singapore, Sydney, Tokyo, Toronto

First PERENNIAL LIBRARY edition published 1987.

Library of Congress Cataloging-in-Publication Data

Pelikan, Jaroslav Jan, 1923–
    Jesus through the centuries.

    Reprint. Originally published: New Haven [Conn.]: Yale University Press, © 1985.
    Bibliography: p.
    Includes indexes.
    1. Jesus Christ—History of doctrines. 2. Jesus Christ—Influence. I. Title.
BT198.P44   1987   232.9'04   86-45679
ISBN 0-06-097080-4 (pbk.)

94 95 MPC 10 9

To the Benedictines
of Saint John's Abbey
Collegeville, Minnesota

nihil amori Christi praeponere

Contents

Illustrations

Initial crosses: *Introduction, Russian Orthodox; 1, Passover; 2, Alpha
and Omega; 3, Light and Life; 4, Labarum of Constantine; 5, Universe; 6,
Golgotha; 7, Byzantine; 8, Monogram of Charlemagne; 9, Right Hand of*

Our Lord; 10, *Christus Noster*; 11, *Cross of Peter*; 12, *Branch*; 13, *The Evangelists*; 14, *Crusaders*; 15, *Latin cross*; 16, *Fleur-de-lis*; 17, *Jerusalem*; 18, *Rainbow*.

Preface

I think I have always wanted to write this book. Having described, in *The Christian Tradition*, the history of the significance of the person and work of Jesus Christ for the faith and teaching of the Christian church, I am turning here to the other half of the story: his place in the general history of culture.

Clemenceau once remarked that war was entirely too important a matter to be left to the military. So also, Jesus is far too important a figure to be left only to the theologians and the church. And the invitation to deliver the William Clyde DeVane Lectures at Yale, public lectures in an academic setting, gave me just the opportunity I needed to write the book I had always wanted to write. The audiences at the lectures represented both town and gown—all ages, social backgrounds, educational levels, and religious persuasions. That is as well the kind of audience for whom the book is intended. Therefore I have sought, in citing my sources, to make use, if at all possible, of generally available editions, adopting and adapting earlier translations (including my own) without a pedantic explanation each time; biblical quotations are usually from the Revised Standard Version.

I have been greatly aided by listeners and students, colleagues and critics, to all of whom I am pleased to express my thanks. Special thanks are due my editors, John G. Ryden and Barbara Hofmaier, for bringing a sensitive ear and an impeccable taste to the improvement of my manuscript and for saving me from inelegancies and howlers.

The dedication is the expression of my fraternal devotion to my *fratres* at the Abbey of Saint John the Baptist in Collegeville, Minnesota, of whose Benedictine family I am proud to be an adopted son.

JESUS THROUGH THE CENTURIES

Introduction
The Good, the True, and the Beautiful

From his fulness have we all received, grace upon grace.

 Regardless of what anyone may personally think or believe about him, Jesus of Nazareth has been the dominant figure in the history of Western culture for almost twenty centuries. If it were possible, with some sort of super-magnet, to pull up out of that history every scrap of metal bearing at least a trace of his name, how much would be left? It is from his birth that most of the human race dates its calendars, it is by his name that millions curse and in his name that millions pray.

"Jesus Christ is the same yesterday and today and for ever. Do not be led away by diverse and strange teachings" (Heb. 13:8–9). With these words the anonymous (and still unknown) author of the first-century document that has come to be called the Epistle to the Hebrews admonished his readers, who were probably recent converts from Judaism to Christianity, to remain loyal to the deposit of the authentic and authoritative tradition of Christ, as this had come down to them through the apostles of the first Christian generation, some of whom were still living.

"The same yesterday and today and for ever" eventually came to have a metaphysical and theological significance, as "the same" was taken to mean that Jesus Christ was, in his eternal being, "the image of the unchangeable God, and therefore likewise unchangeable."[1] But

1

for the purposes of this book, it is the historical, not the metaphysical or theological, import of this phrase that must chiefly engage our attention. For, as will become evident in great and perhaps even confusing detail before this history of images of Jesus through the centuries is finished, it is not sameness but kaleidoscopic variety that is its most conspicuous feature. Would we not find it more accurate to substitute for the first-century formula "the same yesterday and today and for ever" the twentieth-century words of Albert Schweitzer? "Each successive epoch," Schweitzer said, "found its own thoughts in Jesus, which was, indeed, the only way in which it could make him live"; for, typically, one "created him in accordance with one's own character." "There is," he concluded, "no historical task which so reveals someone's true self as the writing of a *Life of Jesus*."[2]

This book presents a history of such images of Jesus, as these have appeared from the first century to the twentieth. Precisely because, in Schweitzer's words, it has been characteristic of each age of history to depict Jesus in accordance with its own character, it will be an important part of our task to set these images into their historical contexts. We shall want to see what it was that each age brought to its portrayal of him. For each age, the life and teachings of Jesus represented an answer (or, more often, *the* answer) to the most fundamental questions of human existence and of human destiny, and it was to the figure of Jesus as set forth in the Gospels that those questions were addressed. If we want to comprehend the answers these previous centuries found there, we must penetrate to their questions, which in most instances will not be our own questions and in many instances will not even be explicitly their own questions. For, in the provocative formula of Alfred North Whitehead,

> When you are criticizing [or, one may add, interpreting] the philosophy of an epoch, do not chiefly direct your attention to those intellectual positions which its exponents feel it necessary explicitly to defend. There will be some fundamental assumptions which adherents of all the variant systems within the epoch unconsciously presuppose. Such assumptions appear so obvious that people do not know what they are assuming because no other way of putting things has ever occurred to them. With these assumptions a certain limited number of types of philosophic systems are possible.[3]

During the past two thousand years, few issues if any have so persistently brought out these "fundamental assumptions" of each epoch as has the attempt to come to terms with the meaning of the figure of Jesus of Nazareth.

For that very reason, however, the converse of the relation between what Whitehead calls "the philosophy of an epoch" and its picture of Jesus will also hold true: the way any particular age has depicted Jesus is often a key to the genius of that age. We who seek, whether as professional or as amateur students of history, to understand and appreciate any segment of the past are continually frustrated not only by the inaccessibility of many of the most revealing monuments of that experience (since only small fragments, and not necessarily the most representative ones, have come down to us), but also by our lack of a proper antenna for picking up the signals of another time and place. We cannot, and we must not, trust our own common sense to give us the right translation of the foreign languages of the past— all of whose languages are by definition foreign, even when the past speaks in English. A sensitivity to that frustration is the necessary prerequisite, but it may also become the occupational disease, of the historian, who can end up despairing of the effort and becoming a victim of what has been called "the paralysis of analysis."

One element of any method for coping with such frustration must be to inquire after instances of continuity within the change and variety, and if possible to find issues or themes that document both the change and the continuity at the same time. The point can be illustrated by reference to a field of historical research far removed from the concerns of this book. Without interruption since the days of the Hebrew Bible and of Homer, olive oil has been a major constituent of the diet, the pharmacopoeia, and the trade of the peoples surrounding the Mediterranean Sea, so that one of the most distinguished of contemporary social and economic historians, Fernand Braudel, is able to define the Mediterranean geographically as the "region [that] stretches from the northern limit of the olive tree to the northern limit of the palm tree. The first olive tree on the way south marks the beginning of the Mediterranean region and the first compact palm grove the end."[4] But even a comparison of Homer and the Hebrew Bible will show some of the variety in both the literal and the metaphorical use of olive oil. If, therefore, one were to study its history as condiment and cosmetic, culture and commodity, one would probably be able to discover many of the continuities—and many of the discontinuities—in the past three millennia of the Mediterranean world.

Similarly, the history of the images of Jesus illustrates the continuities and the discontinuities of the past two millennia simultaneously. Arthur O. Lovejoy, founder of the history of ideas as a distinct discipline in modern American scholarship, used it to illustrate only the discontinuities. "The term 'Christianity,' " he wrote in *The Great Chain of Being*, "is not the name for any single unit of the type for which the historian of specific ideas looks." For Lovejoy saw the history of Christianity as not such a single unit at all, but rather as "a series of facts which, taken as a whole, have almost nothing in common except the name." Although he was willing to acknowledge, as that series of facts obliged him to acknowledge, that the one thing they did hold in common was "the reverence for a certain person," the person of Jesus Christ, he went on to add that his "nature and teaching . . . have been most variously conceived, so that the unity here too is largely a unity of name."[5] Yet Lovejoy would also have been obliged to acknowledge that each of the almost infinite—and infinitely different—ways of construing that name has been able to claim some warrant or other somewhere within the original portrait (or portraits) of Jesus in the Gospels. And so there is continuity in this history, yes; but no less prominent a characteristic of the ways of describing the meaning of Jesus Christ has been their discontinuity.

One consequence of the discontinuity is the great variety and unevenness in the concepts and terms that have been used to describe this meaning, from the most naive and unsophisticated to the most profound and complex. According to the Gospels, Jesus prayed, "I thank thee, Father, Lord of heaven and earth, that thou hast hidden these things from the wise and understanding and revealed them to babes" (Luke 10:21). These words have served to remind theologians and philosophers that "man's discernment is so overwhelmed that it is hindered from attaining the mysteries of God, which have been 'revealed to babes alone.' "[6] But the words of Jesus in the very next verse make the declaration "All things have been delivered to me by my Father; and no one knows who the Son is except the Father, or who the Father is except the Son and any one to whom the Son chooses to reveal him" (Luke 10:22). It took centuries of speculation and controversy by some of the most "wise and understanding" minds in the history of thought to probe the implications of that declaration.[7]

The outcome was a metaphysical tradition that, from Augustine to Hegel, interpreted the Trinity as the most profound of all the mysteries of being. Some of the images to be described here, therefore, will be quite clear and simple, others rather subtle and difficult to grasp; but chapters about both must be part of the history. In a favorite metaphor of the church fathers, the Gospels are a river in which an elephant can drown and a gnat can swim. For some of the same reasons, moreover, the images in later chapters of the book will often be considerably more diffuse than earlier ones; for the second millennium of this history is the period during which the prestige of institutional Christianity gradually declined in Western society. But it was, paradoxically, a period in which, far beyond the borders of the organized church, the stature of Jesus as an individual increased and his reputation spread.

Whatever blurring of his image the welter of portraits of Jesus may create for the eyes of a faith that wants to affirm him as "the same yesterday and today and for ever," that very variety is a treasure trove for the history of culture, because of the way it combines continuity and discontinuity. Nor is the portrait of Jesus in any epoch confined to the history of faith, central though it is for that history. It is, of course, appropriate (or, in the familiar terminology of the *Book of Common Prayer*, "meet, right, and salutary") that the history of faith, and specifically the history of the faith in Jesus Christ, should form the subject matter for scholarly research and exposition in its own right. The rise of the history of Christian doctrine at the beginning of the nineteenth century as a historical discipline in its own right— distinct from the history of philosophy, from the history of the Christian church, and from doctrinal theology, though continually related to all three of these fields—forms an important chapter in the history of modern scholarship.[8] But a narrative of the complex evolution of the doctrine of Christ, defined as "what the church of Jesus Christ believes, teaches, and confesses on the basis of the word of God,"[9] does not even begin to exhaust the history of the meaning that Jesus has had for the development of human culture. For, in the words of the Gospel of John, "from his fulness [*plērōma*] have we all received, grace upon grace" (John 1:16)—a fulness that has proved to be inexhaustible as well as irreducible to formulas, whether dogmatic or antidogmatic. To borrow the distinction of Werner Elert, alongside the "dogma of Christ" there has always been the "image of Christ."[10]

Jesus through the Centuries is a history of the "image [or images] of Christ."

This is, then, neither a life of Jesus nor a history of Christianity as a movement or an institution. The invention of a genre of biographical literature known as the *Life of Jesus* is, strictly speaking, a phenomenon of the modern period, when scholars came to believe that by applying the methodology of a critical historiography to the source materials in the Gospels they would be able to reconstruct the story of his life; Albert Schweitzer's *Quest of the Historical Jesus* remains the standard account of the growth of that literature from the eighteenth to the twentieth century. Naturally, the reconstructions of the life of Jesus in any period, beginning with the reconstructions in the Gospels themselves, will serve as indispensable artifacts of this history of Jesus through the centuries. But we shall be concerned here with more than the history of ideas, whether theological ideas or nontheological ideas— or, for that matter, antitheological ideas. For example, the efforts to portray the person of Jesus in visual form are likewise "artifacts" for our story. They will perform that function not only when, as in the Byzantine empire of the eighth and ninth centuries and again in the Reformation of the sixteenth century, the legitimacy of such efforts became a subject of intense discussion, with far-reaching implications for the history of art and aesthetics as well as for the history of European politics East and West. But in each chapter the portrayals of Christ in such works of art as roadside crosses in Anglo-Saxon Northumbria or Carolingian miniatures or Renaissance paintings will also provide us with the raw material for a cultural history of Jesus, and we shall usually concentrate on one example of such portrayals. Similarly, we shall throughout the book be drawing over and over upon works of literature, from the Old English *Dream of the Rood* through the *Divine Comedy* to Dostoevsky's tale of the Grand Inquisitor in *The Brothers Karamazov*, in order to assess the impact of Jesus on culture.

Yet the term *culture* in the subtitle "His Place in the History of Culture" does not refer here exclusively to what has now come to be called "high culture," seen as what poets, philosophers, and artists create. Would it not be ironic if the one who was attacked by his contemporaries for associating with the outcasts of polite and respectable society were to be interpreted solely on the basis of his contribution to the enhancement and beautification of the life and thought of the rich and educated classes? As *culture* is used here, however, it has almost the significance it has in anthropology, including as it does the life of society and of the state no less than literature, philosophy, and the fine arts. For we shall also be paying attention to the political, social, and economic history of the interpretation of Jesus, and we must incorporate into our recital instances of the ongoing practice of invoking the name of Jesus to legitimate political activity, as this practice becomes visible in the history of both radical and reactionary movements.

The most inclusive conceptual framework for this range of images is provided by the classical triad of the Beautiful, the True, and the Good, which has itself played a significant role in the history of Christian thought.[11] Corresponding to that classical triad, though by no means identical with it, is the biblical triad of Jesus Christ as the Way, the Truth, and the Life, as he is described as having identified himself in the Gospel of John (John 14:6). This formula from the Gospel of John became the motif for a striking image of Jesus in the Archiepiscopal Chapel at Ravenna: "EGO SUM VIA VERITAS ET VITA."[12] As one ancient Christian writer had put it in an earlier century, "He who said 'I am the Way' . . . shapes us anew to his own image," expressed, as another early author had said, in "the quality of beauty";[13] Christ as the Truth came to be regarded as the fulfillment and the embodiment of all the True, "the true light that enlightens every man" (John 1:9); and Christ as the Life was "the source" for all authentic goodness.[14] The Ravenna mosaic, therefore, summarized Christ as the Way, the Truth, and the Life, and at the same time it epitomized Christ as the Beautiful, the True, and the Good.

In a set of public lectures delivered at the University of Berlin in the academic year 1899–1900, that university's most renowned scholar, Adolf von Harnack, undertook to answer the question "What is Christianity?" The book that came out of his lectures has achieved a circulation of well over one hundred thousand copies in the original version, has been translated into more than a dozen languages, and is still in print both in German and in English.[15] Harnack's introduction opens with words that can well form the conclusion of this introduction:

The great English philosopher, John Stuart Mill, once commented that "mankind can hardly be too often reminded that there was once a man named Socrates." That is correct; but it is even more important to remind mankind that a man named Jesus Christ once stood in their midst.[16]

The images in this book represent a series of such reminders "through the centuries."

1

The Rabbi

*A light for glory to
thy people Israel.*

The study of the place of Jesus in the history of human
culture must begin with the New Testament. This is not
simply for the self-evident reason that all representations
of him since the first century have been based—or, at any
rate, have claimed to be based—on the New Testament,
although of course they have. But we shall not understand the history
of those subsequent representations unless we begin by considering
the nature and literary form of the sources that have come down to
us in the four Gospels. For the presentation of Jesus in the New
Testament is in fact itself a representation: it resembles a set of paintings more closely than it does a photograph.

Even without settling all the thorny problems of authorship and of
dating, we must recognize that in the several decades between the
time of the ministry of Jesus and the composition of the various
Gospels, the memory of what he had said and done was circulating
among the various Christian congregations, and probably beyond
them, in the form of an oral tradition. Thus the apostle Paul, writing
to one such congregation at Corinth in about the year 55 C.E. (hence
about twenty years or so after the life of Jesus), was able to remind
them that during his visit to Corinth a few years before, probably in
the early fifties, he had orally "delivered to you as of first importance
what I also received" still earlier, thus perhaps in the forties, con-

cerning the death and resurrection of Jesus (1 Cor. 15:1–7) and the institution of the Lord's Supper (1 Cor. 11:23–26). But it is noteworthy that, except for the words of the institution of the Lord's Supper themselves, Paul does not in any of his epistles quote the exact words of any of the sayings of Jesus as we now have them in the Gospels. Nor does he mention a single event in the life of Jesus—again except for the institution of the Lord's Supper—between his birth and his death on the cross. From the writings of Paul we would not be able to know that Jesus ever taught in parables and proverbs or that he performed miracles or that he was born of a virgin. For that information we are dependent on the oral tradition of the early Christian communities as this was eventually deposited in the Gospels, all of which, in their present form at any rate, probably appeared later than most or all of the epistles of Paul.

Everyone must acknowledge, therefore, that Christian tradition had precedence, chronologically and even logically, over Christian Scripture; for there was a tradition of the church before there was ever a New Testament, or any individual book of the New Testament. By the time the materials of the oral tradition found their way into written form, they had passed through the life and experience of the church, which laid claim to the presence of the Holy Spirit of God, the selfsame Spirit that the disciples had seen descending upon Jesus at his baptism and upon the earliest believers on the fiftieth day after Easter, in the miracle of Pentecost. It was to the action of that Spirit that Christians attributed the composition of the books of the "new testament," as they began to call it, and before that of the "old testament," as they referred to the Hebrew Bible. Because the narrative of the sayings of Jesus and of the events of his life and ministry had come down to the evangelists and compilers in this context, anyone who seeks to interpret one or another saying or story from the narrative must always ask not only about its place in the life and teachings of Jesus, but also about its function within the remembering community. Although there is no warrant for the extreme skepticism of those who maintain that the historical figure of Jesus, if indeed there even was one, is irretrievably lost behind the smoke screen of the preaching of the early Christian church, it is necessary nevertheless to begin with the caution that every later picture of Jesus is in fact not a picture based on an unretouched Gospel original, but a picture of what in the New Testament is already a picture.

It is obvious—and yet, to judge by much of the history of later centuries, including and especially the twentieth century, it is anything but obvious—that according to the earliest portrayals Jesus was a Jew. Therefore the first attempts to understand and interpret his message took place within the context of Judaism, and it is likewise there that any attempt to understand his place in the history of human culture must begin. Although the New Testament was written in Greek, the language that Jesus and his disciples spoke was Aramaic, a Semitic tongue related to Hebrew but by no means identical with it.[1] For the use of Hebrew was by this time largely restricted to worship and scholarship, while the spoken tongue among Palestinian Jews was Aramaic, and in many instances Greek in addition. Meanwhile, many of the Jews of the Diaspora, in places like Alexandria, apparently could not even speak Aramaic, much less Hebrew, but only Greek, and are therefore sometimes called Hellenists.[2] There are Aramaic words and phrases, transliterated into Greek, scattered throughout the Gospels and the other books of the early Christian community, reflecting the language in which various sayings and liturgical formulas had presumably been repeated before the transition to Greek became complete in Christian teaching and worship. These include such familiar words as Hosanna, as well as the cry of dereliction of Jesus on the cross, *"Eloi, Eloi, lama sabachthani?"* "My God, my God, why hast thou forsaken me?" which in the original Hebrew of Psalm 22 would have been *"Eli, Eli, lama azavtani?"*[3]

There are, among these Aramaic words that appear in the New Testament, at least four titles for Jesus, which can provide a convenient set of labels for our consideration of the Jewish idiom and Jewish framework of reference in which the earliest followers of Jesus spoke about him: Jesus as *rabbi* or teacher; Jesus as *amen* or prophet; Jesus as *messias* or Christ; and Jesus as *mar* or Lord.

The most neutral and least controversial of these titles is probably *rabbi*, together with the related *rabbouni*.[4] Except for two passages, the Gospels apply the Aramaic word only to Jesus;[5] and if we conclude, as we seem to be justified in concluding, that the title "teacher" or "master" (*didaskalos* in the Greek New Testament) was intended as a translation of that Aramaic name, it seems safe to say that it was as a rabbi that Jesus was known and addressed by his immediate followers and by others. Yet the Gospels, by a superficial reading at any rate, usually seem to be accentuating the differences, rather than the similarities, between Jesus and the other rabbis as teachers. As the scholarly study of the Judaism contemporary or nearly contemporary to Jesus has progressed, however, both the similarities and the differences have become clearer. On the one hand, scholars of the relation between the Gospels and rabbinic sources have, as their "first basic observation," come to the conclusion that "Jewish material has been taken over by the Christian tradition and ascribed to Jesus"; on the other hand, the comparison has shown that many passages that sound like borrowings from the rabbis are in fact "something new in distinction from Judaism."[6] A good illustration of both characteristics is the anecdote with which, in the story line of the Gospel of Luke, the preaching ministry of Jesus as rabbi is reported to have been launched (Luke 4:16–30).

Luke tells us that after the baptism of Jesus and his temptation by the devil, which taken together are an inauguration into his ministry according to Matthew and Mark as well, he "came to Nazareth, where he had been brought up, and he went to the synagogue, as his custom was, on the sabbath day. And he stood up to read." Following the customary rabbinical pattern, he took up a scroll of the Hebrew Bible, read it, presumably provided an Aramaic translation-paraphrase of the text, and then commented on it. The words he read were from the sixty-first chapter of the Book of Isaiah:

> The Spirit of the Lord is upon me,
> because he has anointed me to preach good news to the poor.
> He has sent me to proclaim release to the captives
> and recovering of sight to the blind,
> to set at liberty those who are oppressed,
> to proclaim the acceptable year of the Lord.

But instead of doing what a rabbi was normally expected to do, which was to provide an exposition of the text that compared and contrasted earlier interpretations and then applied the text to the hearers, he proceeded to declare: "Today this scripture has been fulfilled in your hearing." Although the initial reaction even to this audacious declaration was said to be wonderment "at the gracious words which proceeded out of his mouth," his further explanation produced the opposite reaction, and everyone was "filled with wrath."

Behind the many such scenes of confrontation between Jesus as rabbi and the representatives of the rabbinical tradition, the affinities are nevertheless clearly discernible in the very forms in which his teachings appear in the Gospels. One of the most familiar forms is that of question and answer, with the question often phrased as a teaser. A woman had seven husbands (in series, not in parallel); whose wife will she be in the life to come? Is it lawful for a devout Jew to pay taxes to the Roman authorities? What must I do to inherit eternal life? Who is the greatest in the kingdom of heaven?[7] In the Gospel narratives the one who puts each of these questions acts as a kind of straight man. Sometimes, in the so-called controversy dialogues, it is an opponent of Jesus who is the straight man; at other times it is one of his followers. This sets up the opportunity for Rabbi Jesus to drive home the point, often by standing the question on its head. There is an old story about a rabbi who was asked by one of his pupils: "Why is it that you rabbis so often put your teaching in the form of a question?" To which the rabbi answered: "So what's wrong with a question?" A striking illustration of such rabbinic pedagogy in the Gospels, and one that is pertinent to several of the issues of affinity and difference with which we are dealing here, is the following story:

> And when he entered the temple, the chief priests and the elders of the people came up to him as he was teaching, and said, "By what authority are you doing these things, and who gave you this authority?" Jesus answered them, "I also will ask you a question; and if you tell me the answer, then I also will tell you by what authority I do these things. The baptism of John [the Baptist], whence was it? From heaven or from men?" And they argued with one another, "If we say, 'From heaven,' he will say to us, 'Why then did you not believe him?' But if we say, 'From men,' we are afraid of the multitude; for all hold that John was a prophet." So they answered Jesus, "We do not know." And he said to them, "Neither will I tell you by what authority I do these things." (Matt. 21:23–27)

To the writers of the New Testament, however, the most typical form of the teachings of Jesus was the parable: "All this," Matthew tells us, "Jesus said to the crowds in parables; indeed he said nothing to them without a parable" (Matt. 13:34). But this word "parable" (parabolē in Greek) was taken from the Septuagint, where it had been used by the Jewish scholars who translated the Hebrew Bible into Greek to render the Hebrew word mashal. Thus here, too, the evangelists' accounts of Jesus as a teller of parables make sense only in the setting of his Jewish background. Recent interpretations of his parables on the basis of that setting have fundamentally altered conventional explanations of the point being made in many of these comparisons between the kingdom of God and some incident from human life, often rather homely in its outward appearance.[8] One example is the familiar parable of the prodigal son (Luke 15:11–32), which in some ways might better be called the parable of the elder brother. For the point of the parable as a whole—a point frequently overlooked by Christian interpreters, in their eagerness to stress the uniqueness and particularity of the church as the prodigal younger son who has been restored to the father's favor—is in the closing words of the father to the elder brother, who stands for the people of Israel: "Son, you are always with me, and all that is mine is yours. It was fitting to make merry and be glad, for this your brother was dead, and is alive; he was lost, and is found." The historic covenant between God and Israel was permanent, and it was into this covenant that other peoples, too, were now being introduced. This parable of Jesus affirmed both the tradition of God's continuing relation with Israel and the innovation of God's new relation with the church—a twofold covenant.

That oscillation between tradition and innovation, between describing the role of Jesus as a rabbi and attributing to him a new and unique authority, made it necessary to find additional titles and categories to describe his ministry. Of these, the next one up on the scale was the title of prophet, as in the acclamation that appears in the story of Palm Sunday, "This is the prophet Jesus from Nazareth of Galilee" (Matt. 21:11). Probably the most intriguing version of this designation is, once again, in Aramaic: "The words of the *Amen*, the faithful and true witness, the beginning of God's creation" (Rev. 3:14). Ever since the Hebrew Bible, the word Amen had been the formula of affirmation to conclude a prayer; for example, in the mighty chorus of the recitation of the law in the closing charge of Moses to the people of Israel, each verse concludes: "And all the people shall say, 'Amen' " (Deut. 27:14–26). Amen continued to perform that function in early Christianity. Thus Justin Martyr, describing the liturgy of the second-century Christian community for his pagan Gentile readers, says that at the end of the prayers, "all the people present express their assent by saying 'Amen.' " "This word 'Amen,' " Justin explains, "corresponds in the Hebrew language to 'So let it be!' "[9]

But a further extension of the meaning of Amen becomes evident for the first time in the New Testament in the best-known message (or compilation of messages) in the Gospels, the so-called Sermon on the Mount. There it appears as what grammarians call an asseverative particle: *"Amēn legō hymin,* Truly, I say to you." It is used as such some seventy-five times throughout the four Gospels, but exclusively in the sayings of Jesus, to introduce an authoritative pronouncement. As the one who had the authority to make such pronouncements, Jesus was a prophet. Despite our English usage, the word *prophet* does not mean here only or even chiefly one who *foretells,* although the sayings of Jesus do contain many predictions, but one who *tells forth,* one who is authorized to speak on behalf of Another. That is the basis of the title in the Book of Revelation, "the Amen, the faithful and true witness"; and that is also why the Amen-formula begins to make its appearance in the Sermon on the Mount, which is a document of the oscillation, even in the earliest pictures of Jesus, between rabbinic tradition and prophetic innovation.

The comparisons that both Jewish and Christian scholars have made between the method of interpretation at work in the Sermon on the Mount and the literature of rabbinic Judaism have documented that oscillation. For it is in the Sermon on the Mount that, after the introductory pronouncements called the Beatitudes, Jesus is quoted as asserting: "Think not that I have come to abolish the law and the prophets; I have come not to abolish them but to fulfil them. For truly [*amēn*], I say to you, till heaven and earth pass away, not an iota, not a dot, will pass from the law until all is accomplished" (Matt. 5:17–18). That ringing affirmation of the permanent validity of the law of Moses as given to the people of Israel on Mount Sinai is followed by a series of specific quotations from the law. Each of these quotations is introduced with the formula "You have heard that it was said to the men of old"; and each such quotation is then followed by a commentary opening with the magisterial formula *"But I say to you."*[10] The sense of the commentary is an intensification of the commandment, to include not only its outward observance but the inward spirit and motivation of the heart. All these commentaries are an elaboration of the warning that the righteousness of the followers of Jesus must exceed that of those who followed other doctors of the law (Matt. 5:20).

In confirmation of the special status of Jesus as not only rabbi but also prophet, the conclusion of the Sermon on the Mount reads: "And when Jesus finished these sayings, the crowds were astonished at his teaching, for he taught them as one who had authority, and not as their scribes. When he came down from the mountain, great crowds followed him" (Matt. 7:28–8:1). Then there come several miracle stories. As a recent study has noted, in such stories "Matthew has sought to make an important point that once more recalls the function of miracle in the rabbinic tradition: to lend authority to Jesus' activity, and especially to his interpretation of the Law."[11] The New Testament does not attribute the power of performing miracles only to Jesus and his followers, for Jesus defends himself against the accusation of being in conspiracy with Beelzebul, prince of devils, by retorting: "And if I cast out demons by Beelzebul, by whom do your sons cast them out?" (Matt. 12:27). But it does cite the miracles as substantiation of his standing as rabbi-prophet. (It should be noted, in relation to our examination of Aramaic titles, that there are also Aramaic formulas by which Jesus performs some of the miracles: "*Ephphatha*, that is, 'Be opened,' " to heal a deaf man; and "*Talitha cumi*, which means, 'Little girl, I say to you, arise,' " to raise a child from the dead.)[12]

The identification of Jesus as prophet was a means both of affirming his continuity with the prophets of Israel and of asserting his superiority to them as *the* prophet whose coming they had predicted and to whose authority they had been prepared to yield. In the Pentateuch (Deut. 18:15–22) the God of Israel tells Moses, and through him the people, that he "will raise up a prophet from among you," to whom the people are to pay heed. In the context, this is the authorization of Joshua as the legitimate successor of Moses; but already within the New Testament itself, and then at greater length in later Christian writers such as Clement of Alexandria around the year 200, the promise of the prophet to come is taken as a reference to Jesus, who had the same name as Joshua.[13] He is portrayed as the one prophet in whom the teaching of Moses was simultaneously fulfilled and superseded, as the one rabbi who both satisfied the law of Moses and transcended it. For, in the words of the Gospel of John (John 1:17), "The law was given through Moses; grace and truth came through Jesus Christ." To describe such a revelation of grace and truth, the categories of rabbi and prophet, while necessary, were not sufficient. Studies of the descriptions of Jesus in the Jewish tradition after the age of the New Testament have shown that it sought to accommodate him within those categories, but in its disputes with Judaism Christianity insisted that he had broken out of that entire categorial system. And so, by the time Islam came along to identify him as a great prophet, greater in many ways than Moses but still a prophet who had acted as a forerunner to Mohammed, that was, for such anti-Muslim Christian apologists as John of Damascus in the eighth century, not adequate and therefore not even accurate.[14] Consequently, the potential significance of the figure of Jesus as a meeting ground between Christians and Jews, and between Christians and Muslims, has never materialized.

For the rabbi and the prophet both yielded to two other categories, each of them likewise expressed in an Aramaic word and then in its Greek translation: *Messias*, the Aramaic form of "Messiah," translated into Greek as *ho Christos*, "Christ," the Anointed One;[15] and *Marana*, "our Lord," in the liturgical formula, *Maranatha*, "Our Lord, come!" translated into Greek as *ho Kyrios* and quoted by the apostle Paul and in a very early liturgical prayer.[16] The future belonged to the titles "Christ" and "Lord" as names for Jesus, and to the identification of him as the Son of God and the second person of the Trinity. It was not merely in the name of a great teacher, not even in the name of the greatest teacher who ever lived, that Justinian built Hagia Sophia in Constantinople and Johann Sebastian Bach composed the *Mass in B-Minor*. There are no cathedrals in honor of Socrates. But in the process of establishing themselves, *Christ* and *Lord*, as well as even *Rabbi* and *Prophet*, often lost much of their Semitic content. To the Christian disciples of the first century the conception of Jesus as a rabbi was self-evident, to the Christian disciples of the second century it was embarrassing, to the Christian disciples of the third century and beyond it was obscure.   *why embarrassing?*

The beginnings of the transformation, what Dix has labeled the "de-Judaization of Christianity,"[17] are visible already within the New Testament. For with the decision of the apostle Paul to "turn to the Gentiles" (Acts 13:46) after having begun his preaching in the synagogues of the Mediterranean world, and then with the sack of Jerusalem by the Roman armies under Titus and the destruction of the temple in the year 70 C.E., the Christian movement increasingly became Gentile rather than Jewish in its constituency and in its outlook. In that setting, as we shall have several occasions to note in this and in subsequent chapters, the Jewish elements of the life of Jesus grew increasingly problematical and had to be explained to the Gentile readers of the Gospels. The writer of the Gospel of John, for instance, found himself obliged to account for the jars of water changed by

Jesus into wine at the wedding in Cana by stating that they were intended to be used "for the Jewish rites of purification" (John 2:6), which any Jewish reader would have been expected to know without being told. And the Book of the Acts of the Apostles can be read as a kind of "tale of two cities": its first chapter, with Jesus and his disciples after the resurrection, is set in Jerusalem, for "he charged them not to depart from Jerusalem"; but its last chapter, and thus the book as a whole, reaches its climax with the final voyage of the apostle Paul, in the simple but pulse-quickening sentence "And so we came to Rome."

The apostle Paul often appears in Christian thought as the one chiefly responsible for the de-Judaization of the gospel and even for the transmutation of the person of Jesus from a rabbi in the Jewish sense to a divine being in the Greek sense. Such an interpretation of Paul became almost canonical in certain schools of biblical criticism during the nineteenth century, especially that of Ferdinand Christian Baur, who saw the controversy between Paul and Peter as a conflict between the party of Peter, with its "Judaizing" distortion of the gospel into a new law, and the party of Paul, with its universal vision of the gospel as a message about Jesus for all humanity.[18] Very often, of course, this description of the opposition between Peter and Paul, and between law and gospel, was cast in the language of the opposition between Roman Catholicism (which traced its succession to Peter as the first pope) and Protestantism (which arose from Luther's interpretation of the epistles of Paul). Luther's favorite among those epistles, the letter to the Romans, became the charter for this supposed declaration of independence from Judaism.

Since then, however, scholars have not only put the picture of Jesus back into the setting of first-century Judaism; they have also rediscovered the Jewishness of the New Testament, and particularly of the apostle Paul, and specifically of his Epistle to the Romans. They have concluded, in the words of Krister Stendahl, that "in this letter Paul's focus really is the relation between Jews and Gentiles, not the notion of justification or predestination and certainly not other proper yet abstract theological topics." For such a reading of the epistle, moreover, "the climax of Romans is actually chapters 9–11, i.e., his reflections on the relation between church and synagogue, the church and the Jewish *people*—not 'Christianity' and 'Judaism,' not the attitudes of the gospel versus the attitudes of the law."[19] Chapters 9–11 of the Epistle to the Romans are Paul's description of his struggle over that relation between church and synagogue, concluding with the prediction and the promise: "And so all Israel will be saved"— not, it should be noted carefully, converted to Christianity, but *saved*, because, in Paul's words, "as regards election they are beloved for the sake of their forefathers. For the gifts and the call of God are irrevocable" (Rom. 11:26–29).

"It is stunning to note," Stendahl has observed, "that Paul writes this whole section of Romans (10:18–11:36) without using the name of Jesus Christ." Yet if one accepts this reading of the mind of Paul in Romans, his many references to the name of Jesus Christ in the remainder of the epistle acquire a special significance: from "descended from David according to the flesh . . . , Jesus Christ our Lord," in the first chapter to "the preaching of Jesus Christ," which "is now disclosed and through the prophetic writings is made known to all nations," in the final sentence of the final chapter. The Jesus Christ of the Epistle to the Romans is, as Paul says of himself elsewhere, "of the people of Israel . . . , a Hebrew born of Hebrews" (Phil. 3:5). The very issue of universality, which has been taken to be the distinction between the message of Paul and Jewish particularism, was for Paul what made it necessary that Jesus be a Jew. For only through the Jewishness of Jesus could the covenant of God with Israel, the gracious gifts of God and his irrevocable calling, become available to all people in the whole world, also to the Gentiles, who thus "were grafted in their place to share the richness of the olive tree," the people of Israel (Rom. 11:17).

During later centuries it repeatedly became necessary to return to this theme, even as many other ways of portraying Jesus were developed that came to make more sense to those centuries than did the picture of him as Rabbi. But no one can consider the topic of Jesus as Rabbi and ignore the subsequent history of the relation between the synagogue and the church, between the people to whom Jesus belonged and the people who belong to Jesus. It is important, in considering that history, to take to heart the recent reminder that "we have no license to judge the distant past on the basis of our present perception of events of more recent times."[20] Nevertheless, the religious, moral, and political relations between Christians and Jews do run like a red line through much of the history of culture. Even as we heed the warning against rashly judging the quick and the dead, since ultimately there is another Judge who will do so and who will judge us as well, we who live in the twentieth century do have a unique responsibility to be aware of that red line, above all as we study the history of the images of Jesus through the centuries.

One such image from the twentieth century, Marc Chagall's *White Crucifixion*, has made this point forcefully. The crucified figure in Chagall's painting wears not a nondescript loincloth, but the *tallith* of a devout and observant rabbi. His prophecy, "They will put you out of the synagogues; indeed, the hour is coming when whoever kills you will think he is offering service to God" (John 16:2), is seen as having been fulfilled, in a supreme irony, when some who claimed to be his disciples regarded the persecution of Jews as service to God. And the central figure does indeed belong to the people of Israel, but he belongs no less to the church and to the whole world—precisely because he belongs to the people of Israel.

For the question is easier to ask than it is to answer, and it is easier to avoid than it is to ask in the first place. But ask it we must: Would there have been such anti-Semitism, would there have been so many pogroms, would there have been an Auschwitz, if every Christian church and every Christian home had focused its devotion on icons of Mary not only as Mother of God and Queen of Heaven but as the Jewish maiden and the new Miriam, and on icons of Christ not only as Pantocrator but as *Rabbi Jeshua bar-Joseph*, Rabbi Jesus of Nazareth, the Son of David, in the context of the history of a suffering Israel and a suffering humanity?

2

The Turning Point of History

When the time had fully come,
God sent forth his Son, born of
woman, born under the law.

The contemporaries of Jesus knew him as a rabbi, but this was a rabbi whose ministry of teaching and preaching had as its central content "the gospel of God: 'The time is fulfilled, and the kingdom of God is at hand; repent, and believe in the gospel' " (Mark 1:14–15). Many of his early followers found it unavoidable to describe him as a prophet, but further reflection led them to specify what was distinctive about his prophetic mission: "In many and various ways God spoke of old to our fathers by the prophets; but in these last days he has spoken to us by a Son, whom he appointed the heir of all things, through whom also he created the world. He reflects the glory of God and bears the very stamp of his nature, upholding the universe by his word of power" (Heb. 1:1–3).

"The time is fulfilled . . . in these last days": it is obvious from these and other statements of the early generations of Christian believers that as they carried out the task of finding a language that would not collapse under the weight of what they believed to be the significance of the coming of Jesus, they found it necessary to invent a grammar of history. Categories of the cosmos and of space, and not only categories of history and of time, were pressed into service for this task; and before the task was finished, the followers of Christ had managed to transfigure the systems of metaphysics that they had inherited from Greek philosophy. "But," as Charles Norris Cochrane, one of the most provocative and profound analysts of this process, has suggested, "the divergence between Christianity and Classicism was in no respect more conspicuously or emphatically displayed than with regard to history." "In a very real sense indeed," he concludes, "it marked the crux of the issue between the two."[1] It likewise marked the crux of the issue between the church and the synagogue. Calling itself the new Israel and the true Israel, the church appropriated the schema of historical meaning that had arisen in the interpretation of the redemption of Israel accomplished by the exodus from Egypt, and adapted this schema to the redemption of humanity accomplished by the resurrection of Jesus Christ from the dead.

Like every other portrait in the history of the depictions of Jesus, then, this one had its origins in Jewish tradition. In language redolent of Ezekiel, Daniel, and later Jewish apocalyptic writings, one of his early followers, who heard Jesus call himself "the first and the last," that is, the Lord of history, declared:

> Then I turned to see the voice that was speaking to me, and on turning I saw seven golden lampstands, and in the midst of the lampstands one like a son of man, clothed with a long robe and with a golden girdle round his breast; his head and his hair were white as white wool, white as snow; his eyes were like a flame of fire, his feet were like burnished bronze, refined as in a furnace, and his voice was like the sound of many waters; in his right hand he held seven stars, from his mouth issued a sharp two-edged sword, and his face was like the sun shining in full strength. (Rev. 1:12–20)

Except for some details (such as the shoes instead of "feet like burnished bronze"), Albrecht Dürer's *Vision of the Seven Candlesticks*, with its "sense of fantastic unreality," in which "the three-dimensionality of space is stressed and denied at the same time,"[2] looks almost as though it could have served as the basis for these words of the Apocalypse, rather than the other way around. The majestic figure in Dürer's woodcut truly is the Lord of history, sovereign over heaven and earth, over eternity and time, and is both "the Alpha and the Omega, the beginning and the end."[3]

From contemporary Jewish sources we know that the proclamation of Jesus himself about the kingdom of God, as well as such proclamations of his followers about him, resounded with the accents of

Albrecht Dürer, *Vision of the Seven Candlesticks*, woodcut, c. 1498, from the *Apocalypse*.

Jewish apocalypticism, the fervid expectation that the victory of the God of Israel over the enemies of Israel, so long promised and so often delayed, was now at last to break. The generation to which Jesus, and before him John the Baptist, addressed that proclamation was, we are told, a generation standing on tiptoes "in expectation" (Luke 3:15). The Book of Acts describes the disciples of Jesus, even after the events of Good Friday and Easter, as inquiring of him just before he withdrew his visible presence from them, "Lord, will you at this time restore the kingdom to Israel?" to which Jesus replies, "It is not for you to know about times or seasons which the Father has fixed by his own authority" (Acts 1:6–7).

It would, however, be too easy an evasion of the deepest problems connected with the Jewish and the early Christian expectation of the coming kingdom of God to leave it at that. For particularly in the twentieth century, New Testament scholarship has forced consideration of the place that apocalyptic expectation held not only for the hearers of Jesus but in the message of Jesus himself.[4] Repeatedly in the message of Jesus the call for repentance and the summons to ethical change took as its ground the promise of the Parousia: that the coming of the Son of Man in the clouds of glory would soon put an end to human history and would usher in the new order of the kingdom of God. Specifically, the moral teachings of the Sermon on the Mount, such as the command about turning the other cheek, which have so often seemed (except, of course, to Tolstoy) to be an utterly impractical code of ethics for life in the real world, came as the announcement of what his followers were to do in the brief interim between his earthly ministry and the end of history. "You will not have gone through all the towns of Israel," Jesus said to his disciples according to Matthew, "before the Son of man comes"; and all three of the Synoptic Gospels quote him as saying near the end of his ministry, "Truly, I say to you, this generation will not pass away till all these things take place. Heaven and earth will pass away, but my words will not pass away."[5]

But that generation did not live to see it all: the Son of Man did not come, and heaven and earth did not pass away. It has even been suggested that "the whole history of 'Christianity' down to the present day, that is to say, the real inner history of it, is based on the delay of the Parousia, the non-occurrence of the Parousia, the abandonment of eschatology.'"[6] What did this disappointment of the apocalyptic hope of the Second Coming mean for the promise "My words will not pass away"? How could, and how did, the person of Jesus retain hold on an authority whose validity had apparently depended on the announcement of the impending end of history? Twentieth-century scholars have sought to identify a crisis brought on by the disappointment as the major trauma of the early Christian centuries and the source for the rise of the institutional church and of the dogma about the person of Jesus. Somewhat surprisingly, however, this hypothesis of a trauma caused by the "delay of the Parousia" finds very little corroboration in the sources of the second and third centuries themselves. What those sources disclose instead is the combination, side by side in the same minds, of an intense apocalyptic expectation that history will end and of a willingness to live with the prospect of a continuance of human history—both of these finding expression in an increasing emphasis on the centrality of Jesus.

The North African thinker Tertullian, the first important Christian writer to use Latin, may serve as an illustration of such a combination at the end of the second century.[7] Warning his fellow believers against attending the degrading shows and spectacles of Roman society, Tertullian urged them to wait for the greater spectacle of the great day coming, when the victorious Christ would return in triumphal procession like a Roman conqueror and would lead in his train, as prisoners, the monarchs and governors who had persecuted his people, the philosophers and poets who had mocked his message, the actors and other "ministers of sin" who had ridiculed his commandments. "And so," he wrote elsewhere, "we never march unarmed. . . . With prayer let us expect the angel's trumpet."[8] Yet this same Tertullian could declare, in response to the charge of treason against the Roman empire: "We also pray for the emperors, for their ministers and for all in authority, for the welfare of the world, for the prevalence of peace, *for the delay of the final consummation.*"[9] Such statements about the Roman emperors were in some sense a preparation for the rise, in the fourth century, of the notion of a Christian Roman emperor, reigning in the name and by the power of Jesus Christ; but in the present context we must address the assertion that Christians were praying for the postponement of the second coming of Jesus Christ.

For that assertion of Tertullian represents nothing less than a new understanding of the meaning of history, an understanding according to which Jesus was not simply going to be the end of history by his second coming in the future, as a naive and literalistic apocalypticism had viewed him, but already was the Turning Point of History, a history that, even if it were to continue, had been transformed and overturned by his first coming in the past. Tertullian is likewise remembered as a major figure in the history of the development of the dogmas of the Trinity and of the person of Christ, anticipating in his theological formulas much of the ultimate outcome of the debates that were to occupy the third and fourth centuries. During those centuries, however, it was not only the theological and dogmatic significance of Jesus as the Son of God that was worked out in the clarification of the dogma of the Trinity, but also the cultural significance of Jesus as the hinge on which history turned and therefore as the basis both for a new interpretation of the historical process and for a new historiography.

The new interpretation of the historical process began with the history of Israel, whose principal goal was now taken to be the life, death, and resurrection of Jesus. That made itself evident in the interpretation—and the manipulation—of the *prophetic* tradition of the Jewish Scriptures. Describing the exodus of the children of Israel from captivity, the prophet Hosea had said, speaking in God's name, "When Israel was a child, I loved him, and out of Egypt I called my son" (Hos. 11:1); but in the hands of the Christian evangelist, these words became a prediction of the flight to Egypt by the Holy Family to escape the murderous plot of King Herod (Matt. 2:15). The so-called enthronement psalms identified God as the true king of Israel, even when Israel had earthly kings like David, and Psalm 96 declared, "The Lord reigns!"; but Christian philosophers and poets added to the text an explicit reference to the cross of Christ, so that it now became "The Lord reigns *from the tree*," words which they then accused the Jews of having expunged.[10] Christians ransacked the Hebrew Bible for references to Christ, compiling them in various collections and commentaries.[11] The prophets of Israel had found their aim, and their end, in Jesus.

So it was as well with the *kingdom* of Israel, which Christians saw as having now become the authentic kingdom of God, over which the Crucified reigned "from the tree." Israel had been changed into a kingdom with the reign of King Saul; but "when he was rejected and laid low in battle, and his line of descent rejected so that no kings should arise out of it, David succeeded to the kingdom, whose son

Christ is chiefly called." King David, who "was made a kind of start-ing-point and beginning of the advanced youth of the people of God," established Jerusalem as the capital of his kingdom; yet even as king of that "earthly Jerusalem," he was "a son of the heavenly Jerusalem." He received the promise that "his descendants were to reign in Je-rusalem in continual succession."[12] But David as king had looked beyond himself and his own kingdom to the kingship of Jesus Christ, declaring in Psalm 45, which, according to the Christian reinterpre-tation of history, had been addressed to Christ as king:

> Your throne, O God, endures for ever and ever.
> Your royal scepter is a scepter of equity;
> You love righteousness and hate wickedness.
> Therefore God, your God, has anointed you
> [in the Greek of the Septuagint, *echrisen se*, has made you Christ]
> with the oil of gladness above your fellows.
>
> (Ps. 45:6–7)

Thus David had called him God in the first line, and then had identified him as both king and Christ, the authentic king anointed to be "much superior to, and differing from, those who in days of old had been symbolically anointed."[13] A review of the entire history of the divided kingdoms of Judah and Israel on the basis of what "the providence of God either ordered or permitted" showed that although the kings beginning with Rehoboam, the son of Solomon, did not "by their enigmatic words or actions prophesy what may pertain to Christ and the church," they did nevertheless point forward to Christ. For when the divided kingdoms were eventually reunited under one prince in Jerusalem, this was intended to anticipate Christ as the one and only king; and yet their kingdom no longer possessed any au-thority and sovereignty of its own, for "Christ found them as tribu-taries of the Romans."[14]

The history of the changes and successive forms of the *priesthood* of Israel also made sense, according to the Christian argument, only when viewed from the perspective of Jesus as its turning point. The Levitical priesthood of Aaron had been temporary, nothing more than a shadow, whose substance had now at last appeared in the true high priest, Jesus Christ; for "he holds his priesthood permanently, be-cause he continues for ever" (Heb. 7:24). The threat and prophecy addressed to Eli the high priest (1 Sam. 2:27–36), "I will raise up for myself a faithful priest, who shall do according to what is in my heart and in my mind," was not fulfilled in the priesthood and the priests of Israel, all of whom had been temporary, but had "come to pass through Christ Jesus" as the eternal high priest.[15] Although in the New Testament itself the term *priest* does not ever refer explicitly to the ministers of the Christian church, nor even to the apostles of Jesus in their ministry, but only to Christ himself as priest or to the priests of the Old Testament or to all believers as priests, the church soon took over the term for its ordained clergy.[16] The history of priesthood, therefore, was seen as having begun with the shadowy figure of Melchizedek, who "offered bread and wine," and then as acquiring a definite form with Aaron, the brother of Moses; but it all led to Jesus Christ, from whom, in turn, it led to the priesthood of the New Testament church and to the sacrifice of the Mass.[17]

Thus the entire history of Israel had reached its turning point in Jesus as prophet, as priest, and as king.[18] After the same manner, he was identified as the turning point in the entire history of all the nations of the world, as that history was encapsulated in the history of the "mistress of nations," the Roman empire. Although this was in fact a leitmotiv of the third, fourth, and fifth centuries, the most massive and most influential monument of that identification was what the author himself called in his preface his "great and arduous task," Augustine's *City of God*.[19] For this task of locating Jesus within world history, as indeed for the entire enterprise of interpreting the person and the message of Jesus to the Gentile world, the New Testament, as a book written chiefly by Jewish Christians, offered far less explicit guidance than it did for the specification of his locus within the history of Israel. But it did speak of his having come only in the fulness of time.[20]

Echoing this Pauline language, one early Christian writer, in an attempt to explain why God had waited so long, divided the history of the world into two "times" or "epochs," on the basis of the "pattern" that was both disclosed and established in Jesus.[21] Others, too, made an effort to establish some connection between the coming of Jesus and the history of Rome, beginning as early as the first chapters of the Gospel of Luke, with their language about "the decree [that] went out from Caesar Augustus that all the world should be enrolled" and about "the fifteenth year of the reign of Tiberius Caesar."[22] But the catalyst for a thoroughgoing examination of that connection was the accusation that the substitution of Christ for the gods of Rome had brought their wrath and punishment down upon the city and had caused Rome to fall. For, Augustine contended, "not only before Christ had begun to teach, but even before he was born of the Virgin," the history of Rome was characterized by the "grievous evils of those former times," evils that had, moreover, become "intolerable and dreadful" not when Rome suffered military defeat but when it achieved military victory.[23] Indeed, "when Carthage was destroyed and the Roman republic was delivered from the great reason for its anxiety, then it was that a host of disastrous evils immediately resulted from the prosperous condition of things," above all the concentration of the "lust of rule" in the hands of the "more powerful few," while the "rest, worn and wearied" were subjected to its yoke.[24] It was not defeat and depression that Rome could not handle, but prosperity and victory. Therefore the expansion of the Roman empire, which accusers were blaming Christ for having reversed, was not automatically of any obvious benefit to the human race; for, in an oft-quoted maxim of Augustine, "If justice has been abolished, what is empire but a fancy name for larceny [*grande latrocinium*]?"[25]

On the other hand, the many undoubtedly great achievements of Rome could be traced, according to Augustine, to what the Roman historian Sallust had identified as its ambition and its "desire for glory" and prestige, which functioned as a restraint on vice and immorality.[26] The God who had acted and become known in Christ made use also of these qualities in carrying out the purposes of history, which were the result not of luck or fortune or the power of the stars, but of an "order of things and times, which is hidden from us, but thoroughly known to [God, who] . . . rules as lord and appoints as governor."[27] This concept of an "order of things and times," what the Bible called a "series of generations," Augustine vigorously defended against the theory that history repeats itself, that "the same temporal event is reenacted by the same periodic revolutions" and cycles.[28] And the clinching argument against the theory of cycles in history was the life and person of Jesus Christ: Because "Christ died for our sins once and for all, and, rising from the dead, dies no more," it also had to be true that Plato had taught in the Academy at only one point in history, not over and over again "during the countless cycles that are yet to be."[29] It was the consideration of the life, death, and resurrection of Christ, as an event that was single and unrepeatable and yet at the same time as a message and "mystery announced from the very beginning of the human race,"[30] that made it possible for Christopher Dawson to call Augustine, with only slight exaggeration, "not only the founder of the Christian philosophy of history," but "actually the first man in the world to discover the meaning of time."[31]

Time and history were, then, crucial for Augustine—crucial in the literal sense of *crucialis*, as pertaining to the *crux Christi*, the cross of Christ (a usage of the word *crucialis* for which there is not any classical or even patristic precedent, our English word being apparently a coinage of Sir Francis Bacon):[32] the history of the cross of Christ was both his work for redemption and his example for imitation.[33] But the events of the life of Jesus, seen as the turning point of history, did not affect merely the interpretation of that history; they were also responsible for a revitalized and transformed interest in the writing of history. Although Augustine not only composed many different kinds of literature but in his *Confessions* even created a literary genre for which there is no genuine precedent, classical or Christian, he himself never put his hand to narrative history, except perhaps for one or two of his works of controversy which did have marks of such history. But two Greek Christian authors from the century before Augustine, Eusebius of Caesarea and Athanasius of Alexandria, may serve as documentation for this new historiography, inspired by the person of Jesus Christ. That they happened to be on opposing sides of the great debate of the fourth century touching the relation of the person of Jesus Christ to the Godhead makes their common contribution to historiography all the more noteworthy.

Although Eusebius has sometimes been accused of excessive optimism and even of dishonesty,[34] his work as a historian of the first three centuries makes him indispensable to any understanding of the period: if one were to take any modern church history of that period and delete from it the data that come from Eusebius, only bits and pieces would be left. As the author of two books intended to be an apologia for the Christian message, *The Preparation of the Gospel* and *The Demonstration of the Gospel,* and as the principal historian of earlier apologias during those preceding centuries, Eusebius was critical of his predecessors for concentrating on "arguments" rather than on "events."[35] In his *Ecclesiastical History* he set out to rectify that imbalance, and to do so concretely in the way that he would write history in the light of the life of Jesus.

In the preface to the work he stated two objections made by pagan critics of Christ and Christianity: that Christ was "a recent arrival in human history," and that the nation of Christ was "hidden away in some corner of the world somewhere," in short, that Christ was both "novel and outlandish." His answer to these objections was, first and foremost, to describe the history of Jesus himself.[36] According to Eusebius, this history extended all the way to the beginnings of the human experience, for all those to whom God had appeared could be called Christians "in fact if not in name."[37] But the history also extended forward into the author's own time; for like the historians of classical antiquity, Eusebius concentrated on contemporary events. Yet there was this fundamental difference: according to Eusebius the decisive event in the history he was narrating had not been in his own lifetime, but had taken place in the life of Jesus Christ. As one scholar has put it, "his interest was directed toward grasping, on the basis of the plan of God for the world, the universal-historical implications of the entry of Jesus into the world."[38] To set forth these implications, he presented not arguments but events: he wrote a historical account whose turning point was the "principate of Augustus," when Jesus Christ was born.[39]

The contemporary and sometime adversary of Eusebius, Athanasius bishop of Alexandria, is remembered chiefly for his works of dogmatic and polemical theology. Yet in many ways the most influential book he ever wrote dealt with dogmatics and polemics only incidentally. It was *The Life of Antony*, a biography of the founder of Egyptian Christian monasticism, which even the harshest critics of Athanasius are compelled to admire.[40] Apparently the work was written at least partly for a Western readership and was translated during the author's own lifetime from Greek into Latin, in which form it seems to have played a part in Augustine's conversion.[41] For our present purposes *The Life of Antony* stands as a prime example of the new historiography and new biography inspired by the life of Jesus in the Gospels.

To be sure, there are many affinities between it and various pagan Greek biographies. The well-known *Parallel Lives* of Plutarch presents some similarities, although the differences are far more striking. One of the most meticulous studies of the literary form of the Greek *Lives of the Saints*, that of Karl Holl, has pointed especially to the biographies of Posidonius and of Apollonius of Tyana as models.[42] Although the purpose of the book is to present Antony as the embodiment of an ideal, that does not prevent Athanasius from describing his life in concrete terms as an existential struggle, and a struggle that never ends until death. Throughout, it is an effort to describe Antony's life as "the work of the Savior in Antony."[43] It is clear that Antony chose the monastic life because here he was able to obey the teachings of Jesus the most effectively.[44] *The Life of Antony* is replete with miracle stories, as well as detailed in its recital of the sermons against heresy that Antony delivered. Johannes Quasten, our leading historian of early Christian literature, has accurately summarized the place of Athanasius's *Life of Antony* in the history of biography:

> There cannot be any doubt that the ancient classical model of the hero's [*Vita*] as well as the newer type of the *Vita* of the sage served as inspiration for Athanasius. But it remains his great achievement that he recast these inherited expressions of popular ideals in the Christian mold and disclosed the same heroism in the imitator of Christ aided by the power of grace. Thus he created a new type of biography that was to serve as a model for all subsequent Greek and Latin hagiography.[45]

Such a medieval biography as Bede's *Life of Cuthbert* is an outstanding example of the tradition established by *The Life of Antony*; as a recent study has observed, "It is commonplace to observe that a holy man like Cuthbert imitated the lives of Christ and the saints, but we tend to forget the reality and the implications of such imitation when we talk about biography."[46] The life of Jesus in the Gospels was a turning point both for the life of Cuthbert (the life that he lived) and for *The Life of Cuthbert* (the life that Bede wrote).

Eventually the very calendar of Europe, which then became the calendar for most of the modern world, evolved into a recognition of this view of the significance of the figure of Jesus as the turning point of history, the turning point both of history as process and of history as narrative. As we have noted, Christian historians from Luke to Eusebius and beyond retained the Roman system of dating events by the reigns of the emperors. The dates of the imperial reigns were in turn cited according to a chronology, computed from the legendary date of the founding of Rome by Romulus and Remus, as A.U.C., *Ab Urbe Condita* (the actual title of the work of Livy which we now call *The History of Rome*). The persecutions of the church under the emperor Diocletian, who ruled from 284 to 305, led some Christian groups to date their calendars from the so-called Age of the Martyrs. For example, the fourth-century *Index to the Festal Letters of Athanasius* is arranged according to the Egyptian calendar of months and days within each year, but it identifies the year of the first *Festal Letter* as "the forty-fourth year of the Diocletian Era," that is, A.D. 327.[47] This is a calendrical system still retained by the Christian Copts of Athanasius's Egypt and by the Christians of Ethiopia.

But in the sixth century a Scythian monk living in Rome, Dionysius Exiguus ("Little Denis"), proposed a new system of reckoning. It was to be named not for the pagan myth of the founding of Rome by Romulus and Remus, nor for the persecutor Diocletian, but for the incarnation of Jesus Christ, specifically for the day of the annunciation of his birth to the Virgin Mary by the angel Gabriel, 25 March, in the year 753 A.U.C. For reasons that seem still to be somewhat obscure, Dionysius Exiguus miscalculated by four to seven years, producing the anomaly by which it is sometimes said that Jesus was born in 4 B.C. Such trifles aside, however, Dionysius's identification of "the Christian era" gradually established itself, even though the process of establishing it required many centuries, and is now universal.[48] Henceforth the dates of history and biography are marked as A.D. and B.C., according to "the years of Our Lord." Even the life of an Antichrist is dated by the dates of Christ; biographies of his enemies have to be written this way, so that we speak of Nero as having died in A.D. 68 and of Stalin as having died in A.D. 1953. In this sense at any rate, and not only in this sense, everyone is compelled to acknowledge that because of Jesus of Nazareth history will never be the same.

3

The Light of the Gentiles

He did not leave himself without
witness.

"Nothing is so incredible," Reinhold Niebuhr has said, "as an answer to an unasked question."[1] He went on to use that epigram as a basis to divide human cultures into those "where a Christ is expected" and those "where a Christ is not expected." But the disciples of Jesus, in their effort to explain the meaning of his message and work to their world during the first three or four centuries, carried out their mission on the growing assumption that there was no culture "where a Christ is not expected" and that therefore, in his person and in his teaching, in his life and in his death, Jesus represented the divine answer to a question that had in fact been asked everywhere, the divine fulfillment of an aspiration that was universal, in short, what one of the earliest of them called "the ground for hoping that [all of humanity] may be converted and win their way to God," through Jesus the Christ, "our common name and our common hope."[2]

In addressing the message of that common hope to the Gentile world, they sought to discover in Greco-Roman culture the questions to which that common name of Jesus Christ was the answer; as had been prophesied of him in his infancy,[3] he was

thy salvation
which thou hast prepared in the presence of all peoples,

> a light for revelation to the Gentiles,
> and for glory to thy people Israel.

By analogy with the techniques that seemed to be working so successfully, beginning with the New Testament, in using the Hebrew Bible to interpret Jesus as the glory of the people of Israel, there were discovered several methods for interpreting him also as the light for revelation to the Gentiles. These methods may usefully be grouped under three headings: non-Jewish prophecies of a Christ; Gentile anticipations of the doctrine about Jesus; and pagan foreshadowings or "types" of the redemption achieved by his death.

While messianic hope and messianic prophecy had been the peculiar feature of the history of the Jewish people, they were not the exclusive possession of Israel. "Even in other nations," Augustine said, "there were those to whom this mystery was revealed and who were also impelled to proclaim it."[4] Job, Jethro the father-in-law of Moses, and Balaam the prophet were three such "Gentile saints," spoken of in the Hebrew Bible, with whose existence both the rabbis and the church fathers had to come to terms.[5] Armed with such biblical warrant, Christian apologists found in Gentile literature other evidence of messianic prophecy that pointed forward to Jesus.

Perhaps the most dramatic and almost certainly the most familiar was the prophecy of the Roman poet Vergil in the fourth of his *Eclogues*.[6] It predicted the breaking in of a "new order of the ages"; for "now the virgin is returning [*jam redit et virgo*]," and "a new human race is descending from the heights of heaven." What would bring about this change would be "the birth of a child [*nascenti puero*], with whom the iron age of humanity will end and the golden age begin." His birth would achieve a transformation of human nature; for

> Under your guidance, whatever vestiges remain of our ancient wickedness,
> Once done away with, shall free the earth from its incessant fear.

There would even be changes in nature:

> For your sake, O child, the earth, without being tilled,
> Will freely pour forth its gifts.
> ....
> Your very cradle shall pour forth for you
> Caressing flowers. The serpent too shall die.

And therefore:

> Assume your great honors, for the time will soon be at hand,
> Dear child of the gods, great offspring of Jove!
> See how it totters—the world's vaulted might,
> Earth, and wide ocean, and the depths of heaven,
> All of them, look, caught up in joy at the age to come!

It is not surprising that these words—which are translated here from Latin into as neutral, that is, nonbiblical, an English as possible—should have been seized upon by early Christians as evidence for a messianic hope also outside the boundaries of the people of Israel. They seemed especially close to the prophecies in the Book of Isaiah, but they appeared to echo other biblical accents as well: they anticipated "a new heaven and a new earth"; they looked forward to a new human race, one whose citizenship would be of heaven, not of earth; they predicted the abolition of the ancient and hereditary blight of wickedness that clung to human nature in this fallen world; they even described the crushing of the serpent, the old evil foe of humanity, as the consolation given to Adam and Eve in the Garden of Eden had promised—all of this brought about by the coming of the wondrous Virgin and by the birth of the divine Child, who would be the very progeny of the Most High.[7]

As was perhaps appropriate (though somewhat ironically so) for a poem written to celebrate the emperor Augustus, the *Fourth Eclogue* was claimed as a prophecy of Jesus by the emperor Constantine, in a Good Friday *Oration to the Saints* delivered perhaps in 313; he quoted Vergil in a Greek translation and provided a Christian commentary on the *Eclogue*, line by line.[8] Although Jerome was not prepared to accept the messianic interpretation of Vergil, Augustine, like Constantine, maintained that "it is of [Christ] that this most famous poet speaks."[9] A setting of the Mass of Saint Paul, sung at Mantua until the end of the Middle Ages, contained the legend that the apostle had visited the grave of Vergil in Naples and had wept over not having come soon enough to find him alive.[10] But the most unforgettable application of the *Fourth Eclogue* to the coming of Jesus is in the twenty-second canto of the *Purgatorio*,[11] where Dante quotes the verses of Vergil in Italian translation,

> Secol si rinova;
> torna giustizia e primo tempo umano,
> e progenie scende da ciel nova,

and then adds a salute to Vergil:

Per te poeta fui, per te cristiano
[Through you I became a poet, through you a Christian].

The standing of Vergil's *Fourth Eclogue* as a prophecy about Jesus was enhanced for his Christian interpreters by his reference to the authority of the Greco-Roman prophetess Cuma, the Cumean Sibyl; Vergil spoke of her also in the *Aeneid* as she "sang frightening riddles [*horrendas canit ambages*]."[12] There were several collections of visions and sayings of the various Sibylline oracles, one of the most important of which was destroyed by a fire in the Capitol in the year 83 B.C.E. That provided an irresistible opportunity over the next several centuries for various groups—pagan, Jewish, and Christian—to tamper with the new collections of oracles, and entire books of Christian (or Christianized) sayings were interpolated into them.

"Instead of calling Jesus the Son of God," wrote one of the most important early critics of Christianity, "it would be better to give that honor to the Sibyl." But the Christians were using the Sibyls to back up their claims about Jesus as the Son of God, and we know from the same source that Christians were quoting the Sibylline Oracles, albeit in a heavily doctored version.[13] They cited them as prophetic books with an authority derived from their inspiration by the Holy Spirit, which deserved to be equated with the authority of the Hebrew Bible itself.[14] The Sibyl was "at once prophetic and poetic."[15] In the *Oration to the Saints* Constantine also appealed to the Sibyl, finding in her a poem whose first letters spelled the Greek words "Jesus Christ, Son of God, Savior, cross,"[16] which in turn were an acrostic for *ichthys*, the Greek word for fish, a symbol of Christ[17]—all of this predicted, so it was assumed, by a pagan Roman prophetess (though actually, of course, by some anonymous Christian forger).

In addition to providing this supposedly ancient Roman prophecy of the coming of Christ, and even of his very name, the Sibylline tradition was especially useful as a source of verification concerning the coming of Christ to judgment at the end of the world. For already in their unalloyed pagan form, the sayings of the Sibyl had apparently contained threats and warnings about a divine punishment to come. In Jewish and then especially in Christian hands, these threats became both more extensive and more explicit. To substantiate the prophecy of the creed that Jesus was to come a second time as judge of the quick and the dead, apologists for the Christian creed quoted the Sibyl's prophecy that everything changeable and corruptible was going

to be destroyed by God in the Last Judgment, and quoted her as proof
that God was the source of famines, plagues, and all other dire pun-
ishments.[18] Especially in this function as a prophecy of the second
coming of Christ to judge the quick and the dead, the oracles of the
Sibyl enjoyed wide favor both in the theology and in the folklore of
the Middle Ages, but also in medieval art, especially in the Italian art
of the late Middle Ages and the Renaissance.[19]

This reached its artistic climax when, along the left and right walls
of the Sistine Chapel, Michelangelo's ceiling frescoes depicted five of
the Sibyls and five of the prophets of the Old Testament in alternating
figures. Despite differences of emphasis that Charles de Tolnay sees
in Michelangelo's treatment of them, "the correlation of Prophets and
Sibyls," he suggests, "reverts to an old literary and artistic tradition,"
in which "Sibyls had always been depicted as predicting the advent
and passion of Christ."[20] Although de Tolnay argues that "Michelangelo conceived the Sibyls as a contrast to the Prophets," both their
size and their placement by Michelangelo can be taken to mean that
he was in substantial agreement with the tradition in depicting the
Delphic Sibyl and the prophet Isaiah as occupying jointly the position
of witnesses who predicted the first and second comings of Christ.
As such a prediction about Christ, the sayings of the Sibyl were
permanently enshrined in the words of the "Dies irae" of Thomas of
Celano, sung at countless Requiem Masses (at least until the Second
Vatican Council):

> Dies irae, dies illa,
> solvet saeclum in favilla,
> teste David cum Sibylla.

> The day of wrath, that dreadful day
> Shall the whole world in ashes lay,
> As David and the Sibyl say.

A second method for portraying Jesus as the light of the Gentiles
was to find in Gentile thought anticipations of the Christian doctrines
about him. The most complete formulation of this method comes from
Clement of Alexandria at the end of the second century. He had read,
widely if not always deeply, in classical Greek literature, especially
in Homer and Plato, but he consistently saw himself as a faithful pupil
of Jesus, the divine Tutor, whom he described in his book *Paidagogos*,
or *Tutor*, as follows:

? How could Jesus be passionless

Our Tutor is like God his Father, whose Son he is—sinless, blameless, and with a soul devoid of passion; God in the form of man, stainless, the minister of his Father's will, the Word [Logos] who is God, who is in the Father, who is at the Father's right hand, and with the form of God is God. He is to us a spotless image; to him we are to try with all our might to assimilate our souls.[21]

That is as explicit and as complete a confession of what came to be acknowledged as the orthodox faith about Jesus in his relation to God as can be found in any thinker of the time. And again:

Where he came from and who he was, he showed by what he taught and by the evidence of his life. He showed that he was the herald, the reconciler, our saviour, the Word, a spring of life and peace flooding over the whole face of the earth. Through him, to put it briefly, the universe has already become an ocean of blessings.[22]

Or, as Eric Osborn has paraphrased the latter passage, "The Lord, despised in his humility, was divine Word, true God made known, equal to the Lord of all things. He took flesh and acted out the drama of man's salvation."[23]

But at the same time, as Osborn points out, "this high and lyrical enthusiasm [about the person of Jesus] is combined with a Platonism in which the Son is the highest excellence, most perfect, holy, powerful, princely, regal and beneficent."[24] For this devout and orthodox advocate of the person of Jesus was, at the same time and without any final sense of contradiction, an advocate of Platonic philosophy, to which he assigned a high and holy mission. "Before the advent of the Lord [Jesus]," he maintained, "philosophy was necessary to the Greeks for righteousness." It could perform this role because one and the same "God is the cause of everything that is good"—of the revelation of Christ given in the Old and in the New Testament, of course, but also of the illumination given to the Greeks in their philosophy. "Perhaps," he was willing to suggest, "philosophy was given to the Greeks [by God] directly and primarily," although not permanently, but "until the Lord should call the Greeks." The apostle Paul had said, in the Epistle to the Galatians, that the law of Moses was a kind of tutor or "custodian until Christ came." In somewhat the same way, Clement maintained, "philosophy was a preparation, paving the way for the one who is perfected in Christ," in short, "a tutor to bring the Hellenic mind to Christ."[25] In sum, as Henry Chadwick puts it, for Clement "both the Old Testament and Greek philosophy are alike tutors to bring us to Christ and are both tributaries of the one great river of Christianity."[26]

Most scholarly commentators on this passage from Clement, whether they have commended him or condemned him, have concentrated on what he says about philosophy, often not noting with equal care that philosophy was intended, according to him, "to bring the Hellenic mind *to Christ*": "the real philosophy" as the Greeks had discovered it would lead to "the true theology" as Christ had disclosed it.[27] Among the many philosophical anticipations of the Christian doctrine of Christ to which Clement and other early Christian philosophers laid claim, the most important is probably the *Timaeus* of Plato, with its description of how the creation of the world had been accomplished. The statements in the *Timaeus* about the creator as "father" and about the three levels of divine reality were, for Clement, evidence for "nothing else than the Holy Trinity."[28] This dialogue is, with the *Laws*, one of the two great works of his last years, and it was also to be for many centuries the best known of the Platonic dialogues in the Latin Middle Ages.[29] In it Plato declared that "the maker and father of this universe it is a hard task to find, and having found him, it would be impossible to declare him to all mankind." But he asserted that the most fundamental of all questions, "which, it is agreed, must be asked at the outset of inquiry concerning anything," was: "Has it always been, without any source of becoming; or has it come to be, starting from some beginning?" To which Plato replied: "It [the universe] has come to be; for it can be seen and touched and it has body, and all such things are sensible." The main body of the dialogue described the emergence of order from chaos as having been achieved by the action of creation. The creator, "being without jealousy . . . desire[d] that all things should come as near as possible to being like himself"; "this is," he added, "the supremely valid principle of becoming and of the order of the world."[30] Such "becoming" took place through the action of an intermediary agent of creation, less than the supreme God but more than creatures, the Demiurge, who brought order and rationality out of primal chaos and thus gave "form" to "matter."

Clement quoted extensively from the *Timaeus* of Plato, including several of the passages just cited, as proof that "the philosophers, having heard so from Moses, taught that the world was created."[31] Since he was sure that it was from Moses that Plato had learned this,

Clement found it legitimate to interpret the *Timaeus* on the basis of the first chapters of Genesis—which meant, at the same time of course, to interpret Genesis on the basis of Plato. The key to that interpretation was Jesus as the Son of God; for Plato had said in the *Timaeus* that it was possible to understand God only on the basis of the "descendants" of God, and Jesus had said the same: "No one knows the Father except the Son and any one to whom the Son chooses to reveal him."[32] Therefore the Demiurge of Plato's *Timaeus* was the creating Word of God of the Genesis story and the prologue to the Gospel of John, according to which all things had come to be through the Word or Logos of God. As the preexistent Demiurge and Logos, the Word and the Reason of God, Jesus had brought order and rationality out of primal chaos, and man in his rationality was created, according to both Genesis and *Timaeus*, in the image of God; for, Clement explains, Jesus himself was "the Image of God as the divine and royal Logos, the man who could not suffer; and the image of that Image is the human mind," human reason patterned after divine Reason, which was Jesus Christ.[33]

A third technique for identifying Jesus as the light of the Gentiles no less than as the glory of the people of Israel was to look in classical history and literature for persons and events that could be interpreted as "types" and prefigurings of Jesus and of redemption through him. "A type," according to the definition of Origen of Alexandria in the third century, "is a figure that came before us in the [Old Testament] fathers, but is fulfilled in us." For example, when Joshua conquers Jericho, this deed of the first Joshua, the son of Nun, foreshadows the redemption accomplished by the second Joshua, Jesus, the son of Mary; for in Aramaic and in Greek the two names are the same.[34] Thus "as Moses lifted up the [bronze] serpent in the wilderness, so must the Son of man be lifted up [on the cross], that whoever believes in him may have eternal life."[35]

In his presentation of the arguments for Jesus to a rabbi named Trypho (who may have been the well-known Rabbi Tarphon mentioned in the Mishnah), Justin Martyr maintained that wherever wood or a tree appeared in the Old Testament, this could be a type or figure of the cross. But when he turned to present the arguments for Jesus to a Roman emperor, Antoninus Pius, he drew upon non-Jewish sources and examples to set forth the case for the cross as "the greatest symbol of the power and rule" of Jesus.[36] In the *Timaeus*, invoking what Iris Murdoch has called one of "the most memorable images in European philosophy,"[37] Plato had taught that in the creation of the universe the Demiurge had "split [the soul-stuff] into two halves and [made] the two cross one another at their centers in the form of the letter Chi."[38] Repeating the standard charge of Jewish and Christian apologists that Plato had borrowed from the Hebrew Bible, Justin insisted that Plato, misunderstanding Moses "and not apprehending that it was the figure of the cross," had nevertheless said that the Logos, "the power next to the first God, was placed crosswise in the universe."[39]

Among the examples of the cross in Justin's catalogue, one of the most intriguing is his symbol of the cross as a mast, without which it would be impossible to traverse the sea. For that symbolism, of which sailors have been reminded throughout Christian history, provided the interpreters of the person of Jesus to the Gentiles with the occasion for discovering at the very fountainhead of classical literature a "type" of the cross to correspond to the pole on which Moses had lifted up the bronze serpent, the story of Odysseus at the mast.[40] The story is taken from book 12 of Homer's *Odyssey*,[41] where Odysseus addresses his companions, relaying the instructions of the divine Circe:

> First of all she tells us to keep away from the magical
> Sirens and their singing and their flowery meadow, but only I,
> she said, was to listen to them, *but you must tie me hard in
> hurtful bonds, to hold me fast in position upright against the
> mast*, with the ropes' end fastened around it; but if I
> supplicate you and implore you to set me free, then you must tie
> me fast with even more lashings.

Although some of the early Christian writers, including Justin and Tertullian, repeated Plato's criticisms of Homer,[42] even Tertullian was obliged to acknowledge him as "prince of poets, the very billow and ocean of poetry."[43] Once again, however, it was Clement of Alexandria who made the most effective and profound use of the image of Odysseus at the mast as a foreshadowing of Jesus. Circe's instructions to Odysseus and his band were twofold: to avoid the allurements of the Sirens by stopping up their ears, and to tie Odysseus to the mast so that he alone would hear the call of the Sirens but would triumph over it. Both parts applied to Christian believers. They were to avoid sin and error "as we would a dangerous headland, or the threatening Charybdis, or the mythic Sirens"; as Odysseus ordered his helmsman,[44]

> You must keep her clear from where the smoke and the breakers are, and make hard for the sea rock lest, without your knowing, she might drift that way, and you bring all of us into disaster.

But they could do this because of Jesus, the Logos and Word of God, the Christian Odysseus:

> Sail past their music and leave it behind you, for it will bring about your death. But if you will, you can be the victor over the powers of destruction. Tied to the wood [of the cross], you shall be freed from destruction. The Logos of God will be your pilot, and the Holy Spirit will bring you to anchor in the harbor of heaven.[45]

During the Byzantine period various Christian commentaries on both the *Iliad* and the *Odyssey* carried out this image and in the process helped to protect the ancient classics against the misplaced zeal of religious bigotry.[46] And a fourth-century Christian sarcophagus, made of marble and now preserved in the Museo delle Terme in Rome, shows Odysseus at the mast, which rises to the yardarm to form a cross.[47] As a later Byzantine sermon was to put it, "O man, do not fear the loudly roaring waves in the sea of this life. For the cross is the pattern of a strength that cannot be broken, so that you may nail your flesh to that unlimited reverence for the Crucified One and so with great pain arrive at the haven of rest."[48] The story of Odysseus at the mast became a permanent component of the Gentile "types of Christ."

In using the Hebrew Bible and the Jewish tradition to explain the meaning of Jesus, Christians had applied all three of these methods—foreshadowings of the cross, anticipations of doctrine, and prophecies of the coming of Christ—to their interpretation of Moses. His description of the binding and sacrifice of Isaac became one of the most pervasive figures of redemption: God, like Abraham, had willingly offered his own first-born Son as a sacrifice.[49] Moses' narrative of the creation of the world through the word of God was fundamental to the Christian identification of Jesus as the Logos or Word of God who had been with God forever and who interpreted the will of God to the world of creatures.[50] And his prophecy that another prophet, Joshua-Jesus, was to arise as his legitimate successor gave Christians a basis for declaring that "Moses prophetically, giving place to the

Logos as the perfect Tutor, predicts both the name and the office of the Tutor."[51]

When they addressed the message of Jesus to the Gentiles, on the other hand, Socrates performed a function similar to that of Moses.[52] He was himself a type and forerunner of Christ. The divine Logos, the same that was to appear in Jesus, had been active in Socrates, denouncing the polytheism and devil-worship of the Greeks. As one who "lived reasonably, viz., in accordance with the Logos [*meta Logou*]," Socrates was "a Christian before Christ," and like Christ he was put to death by the enemies of reason and the Logos. "Socrates," Justin said, "was accused of the very same crimes as we are" and as Jesus was.[53] The teachings about Jesus Christ could likewise justly lay claim to Socrates as one who had anticipated Christian doctrine, preeminently the Christian doctrine of life eternal. For while the New Testament had asserted that Jesus "abolished death and brought life and immortality to light through the gospel," most early Christian thinkers (except for a few such as Tatian of Syria) did not take this to mean that there had not been any awareness of immortality before him.[54] On the contrary, quoting the Book of Psalms and Plato's *Republic* on the Final Judgment, Clement could conclude, "It follows from this that the soul is immortal," a doctrine on which Scripture and philosophy were agreed.[55]

But Socrates and Plato could also serve the interpreters of Christ as the source for prophecy about Jesus—not only, as in the case of Vergil, about the birth of the Child, but even about his death on the cross. In the course of listing various pagan prophecies about creation, the Sabbath, and other biblical themes, Clement came to one prophecy in which, he said, "Plato all but predicts the history [*oikonomia*] of salvation." This remarkable passage is from the dialogue between Socrates and Glaucon in book 2 of Plato's *Republic*.[56] Drawing a distinction between righteousness and unrighteousness, Glaucon postulates that, instead of beings who are both righteous and unrighteous, as most of us are most of the time, there would arise one unrighteous man who is entirely unrighteous and one righteous man who is entirely righteous. Let this one "righteous man, in his nobleness and simplicity, one who desires, in the words of Aeschylus, to be a good man and not merely to give the impression of being a good man," now be accused of being in fact the worst of men. Let him, moreover, "remain steadfast to the hour of death, seeming to be unrighteous and yet being righteous." What will be the outcome? The answer, for whose gruesomeness Glaucon apologizes in advance to Socrates, must be (and, to preserve once again the neutrality of language, this translation is that of Gilbert Murray) nothing other than the following: "He shall be scourged, tortured, bound, his eyes burnt out, and at last, after suffering every evil, shall be impaled or crucified."[57]

As Paul, the apostle of Jesus Christ, had said to the Greeks about "the Unknown God," so the successors of Paul went on to say to the Greeks and to all the Gentiles about "the Unknown Jesus": "What therefore you worship as unknown, this I proclaim to you."[58]

4

The King of Kings

The kingdom of the world has be-
come the kingdom of our Lord and
of his Christ, and he shall reign
for ever and ever.

 Even before Jesus was born, the Gospels inform us, the angel of the annunciation told his mother: "The Lord God will give to him the throne of his father David, and he will reign over the house of Jacob for ever; and of his kingdom there will be no end" (Luke 1:32–33). After his birth there came wise men from the East, asking, "Where is he who has been born king of the Jews?" (Matt. 2:2) The entry into Jerusalem on Palm Sunday reminded his followers of the words of the prophet, "Behold, your king is coming to you, humble and mounted on an ass" (Matt. 21:5). When he died on the cross on the last day of that same week, Pontius Pilate had placed over his head an inscription in three languages: "Jesus of Nazareth, the King of the Jews" (John 19:19). The last book of the New Testament, employing a title that had also been claimed by earthly monarchs, hailed him as "Lord of lords and King of kings" (Rev. 17:14).

And yet Pontius Pilate could ask him (John 18:37), "So you are a king?"

Pilate's question could be, and has been, answered in many different ways. For the title "king" did not remain on the cross; it moved out into the world of nations and of empires. And the cross itself moved out to decorate the crowns and flags and public buildings of empires and of nations—as well as the graves of those who died in their wars: as Augustine said, "That very cross on which he was derided, he has now imprinted on the brows of kings."[1] Before the entire process of the enthronement of Jesus as King of kings was finished, it had transformed the political life of a large part of the human race. As we shall see repeatedly in later chapters, much of the "divine right of kings" and of the theory of "holy war" rested on the presupposition that Jesus Christ was King, and so did much of the eventual rejection both of all war and of the divine right of kings. To trace the historical variations and permutations of the kingship of Jesus in its interaction with other political themes and symbols is to understand a large part of what is noble and a large part of what is demonic in the political history of the West: even the Nazi swastika, though older than Christianity in its form, was used as an obscene parody of the cross of Christ, as is evident from its very name, *Hakenkreuz*. "So you are a king?"—Pilate's question has continued to be a very good question indeed.

Accompanying the image of Jesus as King of kings was the expectation that he was about to establish his kingdom here on earth, in which the saints would rule with him for a thousand years; the classic statement of that expectation was the twentieth chapter of the Book of Revelation. The prophecy of Daniel about the four kingdoms that would perish from the earth (Dan. 7:17–27) was now to be fulfilled, and the fourth of the kingdoms was the Roman empire.[2] Declaring that Christ "shall destroy temporal kingdoms and introduce an eternal one," several writers of the early church went on to describe in great detail the changes both in human life and in nature itself that the coming of Christ as King would accomplish.[3] In substantiation of this millenarian hope for the coming kingdom, the writer of the Apocalypse heard voices in heaven shouting: "The kingdom of the world has become the kingdom of our Lord and of his Christ, and he shall reign for ever and ever" (Rev. 11:15). Yet we should note, as various exponents of the millenarian hope themselves did, that this literal expectation of the reign of Christ was by no means universal among Christians even in the second century. Thus Irenaeus admitted that there were some, with whom he did not agree, who interpreted it all as an allegory of eternal life in heaven, while Justin Martyr acknowledged that although he "as well as many others" held to a literal expectation of the earthly kingdom of Christ, there were "many who belong to the pure and pious faith and are true Christians [who] think otherwise."[4]

Both the millenarians and the antimillenarians, moreover, would have answered Pilate's question by saying with Justin that "truly Christ is the everlasting King."[5] Coming as it did from the representative of Tiberius Caesar, Pilate's question was to be echoed many times in the following centuries by the representatives of other Caesars. It is clear, for example, from the account (which has been shown to be authentic) of the martyrdom of seven men and five women at Scillium in North Africa in the year 180 that the title "King of kings" when applied to Jesus meant, to the Christian martyrs and to their pagan persecutors alike, an opposition to Caesar's claims to be supreme king.[6] Thus the representatives of Caesar asked Polycarp of Smyrna at about the same time: "What harm is there in saying 'Caesar is Lord [*Kyrios Kaisar*],' and offering incense and saving your life?" But he replied, according to *The Martyrdom of Polycarp*: "For eighty-six years I have been the servant [of Jesus Christ], and he never did me any injury. How then can I blaspheme my King who saved me?"[7] A similar story told in *The Martyrdom of Ignatius*, which—if it is authentic—may be even earlier, has Ignatius telling the emperor Trajan to his face, "I have Christ the King of heaven [within me], . . . May I now enjoy his kingdom."[8]

Alongside such pledges of allegiance to Jesus as the heavenly King over all earthly kings, however, there stand the repeated reassurances by the apologists for Christianity that this did not make the followers of Jesus disloyal to their earthly kings. "When you hear that we are looking for a kingdom," they said to the Roman emperor himself, "you suppose, without making any further inquiry, that we are speaking about a human kingdom." In fact, they insisted, they were not speaking about a political kingdom at all, but about a kingdom "that is with God." For if it had been a this-worldly and a political kingdom, they would not have hesitated to make the political compromises necessary to buy their safety by denying Christ. Rather, Jesus Christ was "the King of glory," who made an ultimate claim upon human life. In response to that ultimate claim, "we render worship to God alone, but in other things we gladly serve you, acknowledging you as kings and rulers."[9] They cited as evidence of their loyalty the prayers "for the safety of our princes" that were being offered in

Christian worship "to the eternal, the true, the living God, whose favor, beyond all others, they must themselves desire. . . . We pray for security to the empire, for protection to the imperial house." What they refused to do was to treat the emperor as divine, to say "Kyrios Kaisar," and to swear by his "genius."[10] The kingdoms of this present age had been established by God, not by the devil as some heretics maintained, and therefore were worthy of obedience under God.[11] In short, "as far as the honors due to kings and emperors are concerned," the command was obedience, but obedience short of idolatry: "Render therefore to Caesar the things that are Caesar's, and to God the things that are God's."[12] But since Caesar, even when he called himself lord, was only king and emperor while Jesus was King of all kings and Lord of all lords, not simply one in a series of lords,[13] there was nothing due to Caesar that was not due also, and first, to God.

Thanks to the careful work of recent social and political historians of late antiquity, we are beginning to understand better the complex of political, social, economic, psychological, and ideological factors that, along with the religious factors, underlay the Roman persecutions of Christians.[14] Nevertheless, as those scholars have also shown, it does remain necessary to conclude that the image of Jesus as King and Lord repeatedly came into conflict with the sovereignty of Caesar as king and lord. Christians did not look upon Jesus as the leader of a political revolution "from below" that would mean the end of the empire and its replacement by still another political system. And yet, despite the sincerity of their protestations that they prayed for the delay of the end of the world and for the health of the empire, they were all awaiting the second coming of Christ, which would "from above" bring the end of the world and therefore of the empire. The continuance of the Roman empire was the final obstacle to the end; for when Rome fell, the world would fall.

One of them summarized this complex position with simple eloquence:

> Do you think that [Jesus] was sent [by God], as might be supposed, to establish some sort of political sovereignty [*tyrannis*], to inspire fear and terror? Not so. But in gentleness and meekness has He sent him, as a king would send a son who is himself a king. He sent him, as [God] sending God. . . . And He will send him [again] in judgment, and who shall endure his presence? . . . [Therefore] Christians are not distinguished from the rest of humanity either in locality or in speech or in customs. For they do not dwell off somewhere in cities of their own, neither do they use some

different language, nor do they practice an extraordinary style of life. . . .
But while they dwell in cities of Greeks and barbarians as the lot of each
is cast, . . . the constitution of their citizenship is nevertheless quite amazing
and admittedly paradoxical. They dwell in their own countries, but only
as sojourners. . . . *Every foreign country is a fatherland to them, and every fatherland is a foreign country.*[15]

That is one of the reasons behind the circumstance, which later students of Rome have sometimes found to be so puzzling, that it was
some of the "best" emperors, the best morally and the best politically,
like Marcus Aurelius and Diocletian, who also instituted some of the
fiercest persecutions of the Christians. Because Jesus was King, Christians could be provisionally loyal to Caesar; but because Jesus was
King, they could not give Caesar the measure of loyalty that the best
Caesars demanded, and perhaps even needed, for the Roman empire
to be, as Vergil had said it would be, *imperium sine fine*, "the empire
that will never end."[16]

One eventuality that these various Christian schematizations of
history and politics did not envisage was the possibility that Caesar
himself might acknowledge the sovereignty of Christ as King of kings.
"The Caesars too would have believed in Christ," Tertullian asserted,
"if Christians could have been Caesars"; but that was a contradiction
in terms.[17] Yet that moral contradiction became a political reality in
the fourth century, when the emperor Constantine I became a Christian, declaring his allegiance to Jesus Christ and adopting the cross
as his official military and personal emblem.

The question of the "sincerity" of Constantine's conversion to Christ
is a modern issue, both in the sense that it has been widely debated
in modern times and in the sense that it represents a modern—indeed,
an anachronistic—way of putting the matter. To his contemporaries
it was not a serious question: the contemporary *Life of Constantine* by
the court theologian and historian Eusebius of Caesarea is an encomium of the emperor cast in the form of a saint's life. But in the historiography of the nineteenth and twentieth centuries that account
has been fundamentally challenged, and Eusebius has even been
rejected as "the first thoroughly dishonest historian of antiquity"; for
in fact Constantine could be characterized, on the basis of the figure
of Napoleon, as "a great man of genius, who in his politics had no
sense of moral concern and who viewed the religious question completely and exclusively in the light of political utilitarianism."[18] On

the other hand, the "documents leave no doubt that . . . Constantine regarded himself as a Christian."[19] And so it is perhaps safest to suggest, with Ramsay MacMullen, that Constantine's spirit passed "not instantaneously from paganism to Christianity but more subtly and insensibly from the blurred edges of one, not truly itself, to the edges of the other," apparently without going through the center of either.[20]

Although Constantine himself may not have referred to the name of Jesus Christ very often until the 320s, at least in the surviving documents, that name did dominate the two most important Christian historical reconstructions of the events of the preceding decade, specifically of the so-called Battle of the Milvian Bridge of 28 October 312: that of Lactantius, tutor in Constantine's household, who died in 320; and that of Eusebius, who completed his *Life of Constantine* between the death of the emperor in 337 and his own death in 340. According to Lactantius, on the eve of the battle "Constantine was directed in a dream to cause a heavenly sign to be delineated on the shields of his soldiers, and so to proceed to battle. He did as he had been commanded" and marked on their shields the Chi-Rho.[21] It seems clear, then, that according to Lactantius's version of the events of 312, Constantine hitched his wagon to the star of Jesus Christ, was victorious through the victory of Christ, and from now on would exercise his own kingly authority through the eternal and indestructible kingship of Jesus.

At the hands of Eusebius, this historical and theological interpretation of Constantine's victory and kingship as an achievement of Christ the Victor and King through the sign of his cross became a full-blown theology of history and an apologia for the idea of a Christian Roman empire.[22] "Thus then the God of all, the Supreme Governor of the whole universe, by his own will appointed Constantine . . . to be prince and sovereign": this is how Eusebius begins his account. Eusebius reports Constantine's having narrated to him under oath many years later that on 27 October 312, as he was praying, he "saw with his own eyes the trophy of a cross of light in the heavens above the sun, and bearing this inscription, CONQUER BY THIS [*Toutō nika*]." The entire army of Constantine, moreover, also witnessed the heavenly apparition and "were struck with amazement." Only after that, according to Eusebius, did the dream come. "Then in his sleep the Christ of God appeared to him with the same sign which he had seen in the heavens, and commanded him to make a likeness of that sign which he had seen in the heavens, and to use it as a safeguard in all engagements with his enemies." And that was just what he did. "The emperor," Eusebius concludes, "constantly made use of this sign of salvation as a safeguard against every adverse and hostile power, and commanded that others similar to it should be carried at the head of all his armies."

In the version of Constantine's victory that Eusebius presents in his *History,* on the other hand, Eusebius reports that after the Battle of the Milvian Bridge Constantine ordered "a trophy of the Savior's passion, . . . the savior sign of the cross," to be placed in the hand of his own statue, which was to be erected in Rome to celebrate the victory, with the following inscription in Latin: "By this savior sign, the true test of bravery, I saved and freed your city from the yoke of the tyrant, and restored the senate and the Roman people, freed, to their ancient fame and splendor." Rome had passed into the protection of Christ. For Constantine, this successor of the Roman Caesars, Jesus the crucified King had become not only *Christus Victor,* but the very restorer of the traditional honor of the senate and the Roman people.[23]

Constantine returned the favor. "As a thank offering to his Savior for the victories he had obtained over every foe,"[24] he convoked the first ecumenical council of the church at a city named for *Nikē* (Victory), Nicea in Bithynia, for the purpose of restoring concord to church and empire. The fundamental question creating discord was the relation between the Godhead and Jesus as the Son of God: in the formulation of one modern scholar, "Is the divine that has appeared on earth and reunited man with God identical with the supreme divine, which rules heaven and earth, or is it a demigod?"[25] The answer of the Council of Nicea, and of all subsequent Christian orthodoxy, to that question was to declare that Jesus as the Son of God was "begotten not created, one in being [*homoousios*] with the Father."[26] That dogmatic formula was, according to Eusebius, the result of a direct personal intervention by Constantine himself in the deliberations of the council, when "our emperor, most beloved by God, began to reason [in Latin, with a Greek translation then supplied by an interpreter] concerning [Christ's] divine origin, and His existence before all ages: He was virtually in the Father without generation, even before He was actually begotten, the Father having always been the Father, just as [the Son] has always been a King and a Savior."[27]

Once the Council of Nicea had accepted these formulas, they became the law not only for the church but for the empire. To the church of Alexandria Constantine wrote that "the fearful enormity of the blasphemies which some were shamelessly uttering concerning the mighty Savior, our life and hope," had now been condemned and suppressed; "for that which has commended itself to the judgment of three hundred bishops cannot be other than the doctrine of God."[28] Therefore "whatever is determined in the holy assemblies of the bishops," Constantine wrote to all the churches in all his provinces, "is to be regarded as indicative of the divine will." He then issued an edict against heretics on that basis, forbidding them to gather and confiscating their church buildings and places of assembly.[29] That edict treated Christian dissenters far more harshly than it did pagans, to whom Constantine extended what was a remarkable measure of tolerance, forbidding anyone "to compel others" to accept Christianity.[30] It "served as the basis for all subsequent legislation on heresy by the Christian emperors."[31] The foundation of this legislation was the affirmation of the Nicene Creed that Jesus Christ as Lord and Son of God was one in being with the Father, and that "of his kingship there will be no end." Only those who conformed to that "apostolic discipline" of the Nicene Creed, as the *Theodosian Code* of the Roman law was to call it, would have the right to hold political office within the Christian empire. (Since this was still the law in the Holy Roman Empire of the sixteenth century, it was the political, though not the theological, reason why the Protestant Reformers made such a point of their loyalty to the orthodoxy of the trinitarian creeds.) As a result of the events of the fourth century, it was necessary, for the next thousand years and more, to accept Christ as the eternal King if one wanted to be a temporal king.

Yet that did not of itself settle the question of political sovereignty, for it was possible to draw the lines of connection between the eternal kingship of Christ and the temporal kingship of earthly rulers in several different patterns. Beginning already in the century of Constantine and in his two cities of Rome and Constantinople, the definition of Jesus Christ as King produced divergent political theories. One theory was the one with which Constantine himself seems to have been operating, or certainly it was the theory that evolved during the next two or three centuries in Byzantine Christendom, finding its climax in the career and thought of the emperor Justinian the Great. The remark of Eusebius that when Constantine the emperor entertained the bishops of the church at a banquet during the Council of Nicea, "one might have thought that this was a foreshadowing of the kingdom of Christ"[32] may tell even more than the author intended. Christ had promised his disciples that he would eat and drink with them anew in the kingdom of his Father (Matt. 26:29). The setting of this promise in the Gospel accounts of the institution of the Lord's Supper meant to most interpreters that, at each commemoration of the Lord's Supper, Christ through the celebrating priest was the host and the communicants were the guests, thus foreshadowing the eternal kingdom of Christ. But at Constantine's banquet the kingdom of Christ was foreshadowed when the divinely ordained emperor was the host and the bishops were the guests.

So it was also in the political order. Constantine's language in addressing bishops and clergy was properly deferential, but behind the deference was the firm hand of one who knew where the real power lay. As Eusebius put it at the conclusion of his *History*, the emperors— and not only Constantine—"had God, the universal King, and the Son of God, the Savior of all, as their Guide and Ally . . . against the haters of God."[33] God the Father as King of the universe had conferred authority on Jesus, to whom, as he said just before his ascension, "all authority in heaven and on earth has been given" (Matt. 28:18). That authority was transmitted to the emperor, beginning with Constantine; for Christ the King had elected to exercise his sovereignty over the world through the emperor, to whom he had appeared in visions. The emperor was "crowned by God [*theostephēs*]," a belief reflected in the Byzantine ceremony of coronation.[34] As early as 454, the patriarch of Constantinople performed the ritual of coronation for the emperor Leo I. But in Byzantium this did not come to mean, as it was taken to mean in the Latin West, that the authority of the emperor was derivative from that of the pope or even from that of the church. On the contrary, at the consecration of the patriarch the Byzantine emperor would declare: "By the grace of God and by our imperial power, which proceeds from the grace of God, this man is appointed patriarch of Constantinople." The emperor Justinian was Melchizedek, king and priest at the same time.[35] In a mosaic on the south gallery of Hagia Sophia in Constantinople there is a graphic presentation of this political theology. Christ the King is enthroned at the center, and his position makes it clear that he is Lord of all. On either side of him stand the emperor Constantine IX Monomachus and the empress Zoe, with no priestly intermediaries, for their sovereignty comes directly to them from his sovereignty. (The line was, however, sometimes less clearly drawn in political reality than it was in political theology; for Constantine was Zoe's third husband, and the mosaic is a palimpsest, on which his image has replaced that of his predecessor.) It was, moreover, to become evident in the iconoclastic controversy that even this authority had its limits: the emperor could rule in the name of Christ the King, but he had better not lay hands on the images of Christ the Image of God.

The dedication of the rebuilt city of Byzantium as Constantinople, often called New Rome, on 11 May 330 was the result, among other things, of Constantine's resolve to reunite his empire and of his wish to establish a truly Christian capital to replace the pagan capital of Old Rome. But when the capital left Rome for Constantinople, there was much of the aura of Rome that it could not export. That aura devolved, as it had already been doing, on the bishop of Rome. In 452 Pope Leo I confronted Attila, king of the Huns, at Mantua, and persuaded him not to lay siege to Rome; he also saved the city from other barbarian conquerors.[36] In that setting, the political implications of the authority of Christ the King came to mean something quite different in Old Rome from what they meant in New Rome. When Jesus Christ before his ascension declared, "All authority in heaven and on earth has been given to me," he went on to give his "great commission" to the apostles as the first bishops. To one of them, moreover, namely to Peter as the first pope, he had already entrusted the authority to "bind and loose"—to bind and loose sins, but also, so the interpretation eventually ran, to bind and loose political authority.[37]

The coronation of Charlemagne as emperor by Pope Leo III on Christmas Day in the year 800 at Saint Peter's in Rome became the model of how political sovereignty was believed in the West to have passed: from God to Christ, from Christ to the apostle Peter, from Peter to his successors on the "throne of Peter," and from them to emperors and kings. Therefore when Emperor Henry IV had defied the authority of Pope Gregory VII, it was not to the king but to the apostle Peter himself that the pope, at the Lenten Synod of 1076, addressed the bull excommunicating Henry and deposing him from the imperial throne. That theory of the political kingship of Christ was to be opposed, both in the name of the autonomy of the political order and in the name of the eternal kingship of Christ, by various thinkers of the later Middle Ages, including Dante Alighieri. Curiously, the act of legitimizing this papalist theory of political authority was eventually attributed to the emperor Constantine. The eighth-century forgery that came to be called *The Donation of Constantine* represented him as conferring on the pope imperial authority and jurisdiction in perpetuity, in gratitude for what Christ had done for him through Pope Sylvester I, who cured him of leprosy. Christ was King, the church was a monarchy, the pope was a monarch, and it was by his authority that earthly monarchs exercised their authority. Christ had said to his disciples that the two swords in their hands were "enough" (Luke 22:38), and so they proved to be: Peter and his successors had both the "spiritual sword" of ecclesiastical governance and the "temporal sword" of political governance, even though they might exercise the latter through the instrumentality of secular rulers.[38]

"So you are a king?" Pilate had asked Jesus, and in the inscription he placed on the cross he had called him one. But even when they celebrated the kingship of Jesus in the triumphalism of the Byzantine emperor or of the Roman bishop, those who professed obedience to him were obliged to consider the fuller implications of that encounter between Jesus the King and Pontius Pilate the king's procurator, as recorded in the eighteenth chapter of the Gospel of John, an encounter that provoked quite another question from Pilate as well:

> Pilate entered the praetorium again and called Jesus, and said to him, "Are you the King of the Jews?" . . . Jesus answered, "My kingship is not of this world. . . ." "So you are a king?" said Pilate. Jesus answered, "You say that I am a king. For this I was born, and for this I have come into the world, to bear witness to the truth. Every one who is of the truth hears my voice." Pilate said to him, "What is truth?" (John 18:33–38)

That latter question of Pilate has likewise called forth a great variety of answers through the centuries, all of them suggested by the figure of Jesus.

5
The Cosmic Christ

All things were created through him and for him. He is before all things, and in him all things hold together.

 In the first of a series of lectures called *Science and the Modern World*, one of the wisest men of the twentieth century, Alfred North Whitehead, came to speak about the scientific and philosophical belief that "every detailed occurrence can be correlated with its antecedents in a perfectly definite manner, exemplifying general principles." "Without this belief," he continued, "the incredible labours of scientists would be without hope. It is this instinctive conviction, vividly poised before the imagination, which is the motive power of research:—that there is a secret, a secret which can be unveiled." And then he put this fundamental question: "How has this conviction been so visibly implanted on the European mind?" His answer was:

When we compare this tone of thought with the attitude of other civilizations when left to themselves, there seems but one source for its origin. It must come from the medieval insistence on the rationality of God, conceived of as with the personal energy of Jehovah and with the rationality of a Greek philosopher.[1]

The epitome of that insistence and of that combination of beliefs— the "personal energy of Jehovah" plus the "rationality of a Greek philosopher"—was the medieval and Christian doctrine of Jesus Christ as the incarnate Logos.

By the fourth century it had become evident that of all the various "titles of majesty for Christ" adapted and adopted during the first generations after Jesus,[2] none was to have more momentous consequences than the title Logos, consequences as momentous for the history of thought as were those of the title King for the history of politics. Indeed, one Christian philosopher of that century could speak about "the titles of the Logos, which are so many, so sublime, and so great,"[3] thus attaching all the other titles as predicates to this one. To this day, people who have, as Ben Jonson said of Shakespeare, "small Latin, and less Greek" can often recite the opening words of the Gospel of John, *En archē ēn ho Logos;* and near the beginning of Goethe's *Faust* the aged philosopher Faust is sitting in his study pondering that very text and trying out several different translations for it: "Im Anfang war das Wort/der Sinn/die Kraft/die Tat": In the beginning was the word/the mind/the power/the deed.[4] The term Logos can have any and all of those meanings, and many other meanings besides, such as "reason" or "structure" or "purpose."

The chief monument of the fourth-century consideration of Jesus as the Logos was the dogma of the Holy Trinity, as enshrined in the Nicene Creed. Through most of Christian history, the doctrine of the Trinity has been the unquestioned—and unquestionable—touchstone of truly orthodox faith and teaching. It has given its outline to systematic theologies like the *Institutes* of John Calvin, to catechisms, and to sermons. Christian worship and hymnody, from the *Gloria Patri* of the Latin liturgy to the nineteenth-century hymn "Holy, Holy, Holy," by Bishop Reginald Heber, often gave better expression to faith in the Trinity than did theology; even Calvin thought that the Nicene Creed was better sung than said. The development of trinitarian dogma is an important chapter, one may safely say the most important single chapter, in the history of the development of Christian doctrine, and it must bulk large in any account of that history. But the identification of Jesus as Logos also made intellectual, philosophical, and scientific history. For by applying this title to Jesus, the Christian philosophers of the fourth and fifth centuries who were trying to give an account of who he was and what he had done were enabled to interpret him as the divine clue to the structure of reality (metaphysics) and, within metaphysics, to the riddle of being (ontology)—in a word, as the Cosmic Christ.

It is likewise from the fourth century that we have another kind of monument to the interpretation of Jesus as the Cosmic Christ. A Christian sarcophagus from that century, which belongs to the Lateran Museum in Rome, presents a striking depiction of his sovereignty over the universe. Between two elaborately carved scrolls at the center of the marble frieze along the side of the sarcophagus is the seated figure of Christ enthroned, raised higher than the figures on either side of him. His left hand holds a scroll, and his right hand is raised in the gesture of blessing and of authority. Beneath his feet is a personification of the cosmos. "He must reign," the apostle Paul declared, "until he has put all his enemies under his feet. The last enemy to be destroyed is death" (1 Cor. 15:25–26). And again, in words that sound like a hymn:

> He is the image of the invisible God, the first-born of all creation; for in him all things were created, in heaven and on earth, visible and invisible, whether thrones or dominions or principalities or authorities—all things were created through him and for him. He is before all things, and in him all things hold together. He is the head of the body, the church; he is the beginning, the first-born from the dead, that in everything he might be preeminent. For in him all the fulness of God was pleased to dwell. (Col. 1:15–19)

On a fourth-century sarcophagus intended to affirm victory over death as "the last enemy," through the one who was "the first-born from the dead," it was this cosmic dimension both of his victory and of his lordship that took visible shape, just as it was this same dimension that was taking conceptual shape at the very same time in the doctrine of the Trinity.

The opening words of the Gospel of John, "In the beginning was the Word," were evidently meant to be a paraphrase of the opening words of the Book of Genesis, "In the beginning God created the heavens and the earth. . . . And God said." That was, at any rate, how the early Christians were reading the two texts side by side.[5] Because the speaking of God (which is one way to translate Logos) made the world possible, it was also the speaking of God that made the world intelligible: Jesus Christ as Logos was the *Word of God* revealing the way and will of God to the world. As the medium of divine revelation, he was also the agent of divine revelation, specifically of revelation about the cosmos and its creation. His "credibility" was fundamental to all human understanding.[6] Therefore when, in the fourth century, Basil of Caesarea set about to interpret the meaning of the cosmos,

Christ Seated above a Personification of the Cosmos, **fourth-century Roman sarcophagus, Museo Laterano, Rome.**

he began with the story of creation in six days as recorded in the Book of Genesis and proceeded to expound it in his *Hexaemeron*—a curious mixture of theology, philosophy, science, and superstition—which was soon thereafter taken over and paraphrased in Latin by Ambrose of Milan.

As we have already seen, many early Christian thinkers brought to their interpretation of the biblical account of creation an understanding of the origins of the universe that had been profoundly shaped by the *Timaeus* of Plato, a use of Plato's cosmology that received significant reinforcement for Christians from their belief that Plato had read the Book of Genesis and that in the *Timaeus* he had perceived, however dimly, that the structure of the cosmos was cruciform.[7] From its very beginning, therefore, the Christian view of creation, even of creation through the Logos who was to become incarnate in Jesus, was what later generations were to call a "mixed doctrine," that is, one on which both divine revelation and human reason had something to say. The interaction between the two ways of knowing, whether it was seen as harmony or as contradiction, has helped to shape the history not only of theology but of philosophy and of science, well into the nineteenth and twentieth centuries.[8] For most of these fourth-century fathers, what bound together the religious-theological cosmogony of the Nicene Creed ("We believe in one God, Maker of heaven and earth and of all that is—visible and invisible") and the philosophical-scientific cosmology of Plato and of Platonism (as formulated by the *Timaeus* and its commentators, including its Christian commentators) was the further affirmation of the content of the Logos doctrine (though the term Logos itself did not appear in the Nicene Creed) when it declared that "through the one Lord Jesus Christ, the Son of God, all things were made." That affirmation, however, also drew the line where the two ways of perceiving cosmic reality diverged.

The test case for the relation between them was the definition of creation as "creation out of nothing [*creatio ex nihilo*]."[9] That definition was directed against the idea that matter was eternal, hence coeternal with the Creator.[10] Although "the philosophers of Greece have made much ado to explain nature," the best they could manage, in such works as the *Timaeus*, was "some imagination, but no clear comprehension" of that "hidden doctrine" of the Book of Genesis, which had been revealed by the Word of God to and through Moses.[11] To consider the universe in the light of divine wisdom rather than of worldly wisdom, therefore, meant to recognize that "the Word of God pervades the creation" from the very beginning and to the very present.[12] And the Word that God spoke, as well as the One to whom God spoke the words, "Let *us* make man in *our* image," was none other than "his Co-operator, the one through whom [God] created all orders of existence, the one who upholds the universe by his word of power," Jesus Christ the Logos seen as "the second person" of the Trinity and as the Cosmic Christ.[13]

To put this in the succinct formula of a fourth-century Latin interpreter of Greek Christian thought, "It is the Father to whom all existence owes its origin. In Christ and through Christ he is the source of all. In contrast to all else he is self-existent."[14] It was necessary in such a definition to clarify whether the Word that God spoke at creation, the Logos now present in Jesus, could say, in the words of the Book of Proverbs, "The Lord *created* me at the beginning of his work."[15] For then the Logos would be the first among creatures, but nevertheless still only a creature and part of the order of creation. There were, according to Christian orthodoxy, only these two possibilities: either creature or Creator. It was the conclusion of the bitter debates over the doctrine of the Trinity during the fourth century that the Logos as the Word of God spoken at the creation had been with God from before the creation, from eternity, and was therefore coeternal, "one in being [*homoousios*] with the Father." In the celebrated exposition of creation in book 11 of his *Confessions* Augustine, asking, "How, O God, didst thou make heaven and earth?" replied that it was in that Word which God spoke eternally and by which all creatures were spoken eternally: "In this Beginning, O God, hast thou made heaven and earth—in thy Word, in thy Son, in thy Power, in thy Wisdom, in thy Truth, wondrously speaking and wondrously making."[16]

But "Logos of God" when applied to Jesus Christ meant far more than "Word of God," more even than divine revelation; there were many other Greek vocables that would have sufficed to express that much and no more, and several of them were being used in the New Testament and in other early Christian literature. Employing the specific name Logos implied in addition to this that what had come in Jesus Christ was also the *Reason and Mind of the cosmos*. To be "without logos [*alogos*]" had meant, also in classical Greek, to be without reason or contrary to reason;[17] those second-century Christian heretics who were opposed to the use of the Logos doctrine—and to the Gospel of John because it contained that doctrine—had therefore been dubbed "the Alogoi," and those fourth-century thinkers who denied the eternity of the Logos were accused of teaching that God had once been *alogos*, insane.[18] "There never was a time when God was without the Logos," orthodox thought insisted, "or when he was not the Father."[19] As these Christian philosophers pondered the deeper connotations of this identification of Jesus as eternal Logos, the cosmological import of Logos as Reason in the framework of the doctrine of creation became apparent.

Asking the rhetorical question "In what then does the greatness of man consist?" one of them answered that it consisted "in his being in the image of the Creator." Then he analyzed the connotations of that doctrine for the relation of Christ to the creation:[20]

> If you examine the other points by which the divine beauty is expressed, you will find that in them too the likeness in the image [of God] which we present is perfectly preserved. The Godhead is mind and word; for "in the beginning was the Word," and the followers of Paul have "the mind of Christ" which "speaks" in them. Humanity too is not far removed from these; for you see in yourself word and understanding, which are an imitation of that authentic Mind and Word [namely, Christ as Logos].

There was, therefore, an analogy between the Logos of God, which had become incarnate in Jesus, and the logos of humanity, which was incarnate in each person and perceptible to each person from within. But since the Logos of God, related to the Father as word was to mind, was the divine Demiurge, through whom all of the cosmos had come into being, it followed that "this name [Logos] was given to him because he exists in all things that are."[21]

From this description of the relation between the cosmos as the creation of God and the Logos as the Reason of God there followed two implications for the theory of knowledge. On the one hand, the identification of the Logos as the Reason and Mind of the cosmos acted to countervail the tendency, which had seemed endemic to the Christian movement from the very beginning, to revel in the paradox of faith in Christ to the point of glorifying the irrational. Tertullian never said (or, to be accurate, never quite said) what is often attributed to him, *Credo quia absurdum*, "I believe it because it is absurd." But he did say, "The Son of God died; this is by all means to be believed, because it makes no sense [*quia ineptum est*]. And he was buried and rose again; this fact is certain, because it is impossible."[22] "After possessing Christ Jesus," he said elsewhere, "we want no curious disputation, no inquiries after enjoying the gospel! What does Athens have to do with Jerusalem?"[23]

Taken by themselves as literal and authoritative, as they have sometimes been in the history of Christian literalism and anti-intellectualism in all generations, such sentiments would have brought an end to philosophical thought and would have aborted scientific investigation, both of which depend on the assumption that there is a rational order in the cosmos. But by the latter half of the fourth century it had become possible for those who still accepted the paradox of faith in Christ to affirm nevertheless the validity of the rational process and to appeal to the evidence of "our very eyes and the law of nature."[24] For a creation that had been carried out by God the Father through his eternal Son the Logos could not be arbitrary or haphazard, nor could it be "conceived by chance and without reason"; but it had to have "a useful end."[25] A corollary of this affirmation of the rationality of the cosmos was a rejection of the special form of arbitrariness and chance represented in antiquity by the dominance of astrology.[26] It was a fundamental difference between humanity and other creatures that, having been created in the image of God and by a special action of the creating Logos, even the human body must be *logikos*, "capable of speech" or "suited to the use of reason" or in any case "mirroring forth the presence of the creating Logos."[27]

This confidence of fourth-century Christian philosophers that the divine Reason disclosed in Christ had endowed human reason with a capacity for penetrating the workings of created nature was, however, restrained from presumption by the other pole of the dialectic: a profound sense, also based on the revelation in Christ, of the limitations that had been placed upon human capacity for understanding ultimate reality. As happened so often, it was a Christian heretic who served as the catalyst for a fundamental insight: Eunomius, one of the ablest of fourth-century Christian philosophers, is quoted by more than one of his orthodox opponents as having claimed that he could know the essence of God as well as God himself did. We need not necessarily accept the historical accuracy of such quotations to recognize that, by contrast, his orthodox opponents made a point of declaring that there was much about God that they could not know.

For an investigation of creatures, it was enough to know their "names" in order to understand their "essences," but "the uncreated nature [of God] alone, which we acknowledge in the Father and in the Son and in the Holy Spirit, transcends all significance of names."[28] For "the Deity cannot be expressed in words"; "we sketch It by Its attributes" and so "obtain a certain faint and feeble and partial idea concerning It," so that "our best theologian" was one who spoke about God on the basis of these fragments of knowledge that were available.[29] The outcome was what can be called a "biblical positivism," as expressed in the motto of Hilary of Poitiers: "God is to be believed insofar as he speaks of himself [*Ipsi de Deo credendum est*]."[30] And God had spoken decisively in the Logos, incarnate in the historical flesh of Jesus Christ. Thus the cosmos was reliably knowable and at the same time it remained mysterious, both of these because the Logos was the Mind and Reason of God.

[handwritten margin note: God = Creation]

Because the Logos incarnate in Jesus was the Reason of God, it was also possible to see the Logos as the very *Structure of the universe*. Following the pattern, familiar by now, of combining the biblical account of creation in the Book of Genesis with the Platonic doctrine of the preexistence of the Forms, Basil of Caesarea provided a graphic description of that structure:

> Before all those things which now attract our notice existed, God, after casting about in his mind and determining to bring into being that which had no being, imagined the world such as it ought to be, and created matter in harmony with the form which he wished to give it. . . . He welded all the diverse parts of the cosmos by links of indissoluble attachment and established between them so perfect a fellowship and harmony that the most distant, in spite of their distance, appeared united in one universal sympathy.[31]

That harmony, binding together the atom and the galaxy, was expressed in a cosmic *systēma*, all of it brought about by the "magnificence of the Creator-Logos."[32] The concept of harmony in the universe expressed in the Greek word *systēma* also hovered over one of the most powerful of the New Testament statements we have quoted about the Cosmic Christ, as the one through whom, in Basil's phrase, "all things have their continuance and constitution," the one who had "primacy over all created things," in whom "everything in heaven and on earth was created," and in whom moreover "all things are held together [or: are made into a cosmic system, *synestēken*]."[33]

The identification of the Creator-Logos in Jesus as the foundation for the very structure of the universe and the belief that "the Logos of God is in the whole universe" had its basis in the even more fundamental identification of the Logos as the *Agent of creation out of nothing,* or, to use a term that was common to biblical and philosophical language, out of nonbeing.[34] The Creator could be described as "the one who is [*ho ōn*]," while creatures had their being by derivation from the Creator and participation in the Creator and they could not "be of themselves."[35] In the fullest sense, therefore, only the Creator could be said "to be." For the same reason, using the name Father for God was *not* a figure of speech. It was only because God was the Father of the Logos-Son that the term father could also be applied to human parents, and when it was used of them it *was* a figure of speech. As the Father of the Logos, God was, according to the New Testament, "the Father, from whom every family in heaven and on earth is named," and in human families both the parents and the children were an "imitation" of their divine prototypes.[36] That was also why the Logos could not be a creature, not even the primary creature; for all creatures had been brought out of nonbeing, and as the agent who had brought them out of nonbeing the Creator-Logos must "have being" in the full and nonmetaphorical sense of the word.[37]

Therefore it was the Logos as the Reason of the universe who "structures it into a cosmos of order."[38] Having been created out of nonbeing through this structuring Logos, the cosmos manifested in its "order and providence" the ordering presence of "the Logos of God who is over all and who governs all."[39] The universe was not "absurd" or "bereft of the Logos [*alogos*]," but it made sense because of the Logos. Conversely, however, its hold on reality was derived from its hold on the Logos, without whom it would slip back into the nonbeing out of which the Logos had originally brought it in creation. In sum,

> The one who is good cannot grudge anything. Therefore God does not grudge even being, but wants everything to be, so as to manifest steadfast love. God saw that all created nature, if left to its own principles, was in flux and subject to dissolution. To prevent this and to keep the universe from disintegrating back into nonbeing, God made all things by the eternal Logos of God itself and endowed the creation with being. . . . God guides [the universe] by the Logos, so that by the direction, providence, and ordering of the Logos, the creation may be illumined and enabled to abide always securely.[40]

Because sin was a turning of the eyes away from God and from the Logos, sinners were threatened with falling back into the abyss of nonbeing out of which the creating action of the Logos had called them.

To meet and to overcome this threat, the Logos, as the *Savior of the cosmos*, became incarnate in Jesus Christ, who suffered and died on the cross and rose from the dead victorious over sin, death, and hell. This was necessary because the world that the Logos had fashioned was now a fallen world. It was characteristic of the Greek Christian philosophers of the fourth and fifth centuries that, by contrast with the later Christian individualism manifest especially in Western thought, they always viewed humanity and the cosmos in close proximity. As this was the case, first of all, in the very understanding of creation through the Logos, so it had to be also in the diagnosis of the human predicament and in the prescription of the divine cure through the selfsame Logos, now incarnate in Christ. Not only, therefore, did "all things hold together" in Christ the Logos as the Structure of the cosmos, but it would also be in the Logos as Savior that "the universe itself is to be freed from the shackles of mortality and enter upon the liberty and splendor of the children of God."[41]

One reason for a greater emphasis on the Cosmic Christ in the thought of the Greek East than in that of the Latin West must be sought in the ideas about being and creation through the Logos that we have just been reviewing in the writings of Athanasius and other fourth-century Eastern thinkers. For it is possible to draw a distinction between those philosophical theologies that have interpreted death as the result of guilt and sin and those philosophical theologies that have tended to see death as the consequence of transiency and impermanence; neither emphasis exists utterly without echoes of the other, but the distinction is clear. If sin was defined as a relapse into the nothingness out of which the creating Logos had taken humanity, it was appropriate to describe the plight of the human soul as "imagining evil for itself" and therefore as supposing that "it is doing something" when, by committing the sin that is nonbeing, "it is in fact doing nothing."[42] Such a soul was deceived into believing that this nonbeing was the "only true reality" and that the reality of God was "nonbeing." This total reversal of the created metaphysical polarity between being and nonbeing was the meaning of the fall. For, in the formula of Athanasius, "humanity is by nature subject to transiency [*phthartos*], inasmuch as it is made out of what is not."[43] The adjective *transient* with its cognates was of decisive importance. For it put the understanding of sin and the fall into the context of the transiency and decay to which not only human nature but the cosmos itself was subject, by virtue of its having been created out of nothing. The fall both of humanity and of the world was a loss of the tenuous hold on true being and therefore a fall into the abyss. In the case of humanity, it was all the more tragic because only Adam and Eve, and not any of the other creatures on earth, had been created in the image of God, that is, in the image of the divine Logos.[44] Despite many statements to the contrary, this view of the human condition did concentrate on death as corruptibility and transiency rather than on death as guilt and the "wages of sin" (Rom. 6:23).

The corollary of this view of the human fall in the context of the cosmic fall was an understanding of the saving activity of Jesus the Logos that applied it not only to the expiation of the guilt caused by sin against the law and will of God, but to the repair of the fracture in being caused by alienation from the God who was defined as "the one who is"—thus not only to guilt but also to ontology.[45] By becoming incarnate in Jesus, the Logos had enabled human beings to transcend themselves and, in a pregnant phrase of the New Testament, "to become partakers in the divine nature" (2 Pet. 1:4). "The Logos of God has become human," one Greek father after another would say, "so that you might learn from a human being how a human being may become divine."[46] The original creation in the image of God, in which true human greatness consisted,[47] had been brought about through the Logos; that creation would now achieve not only restoration but consummation and perfection through the same Logos: his incarnation would achieve our deification. And the whole cosmos would have its proper share in that consummation; for "the establishment of the church is a re-creation of the world," in which "the Logos has created a multitude of stars," a new heaven and a new earth.[48]

From the ascription of the creation of the universe to Jesus the Logos it also followed, by a necessary inference, that the Logos was not only the beginning but the end, the *Goal of the cosmos*.[49] He was Omega as well as Alpha. When it was transposed into the key of Christian philosophy, this teaching was what had become of the primitive Christian expectation of the imminent end of the world and the immediate coming of Christ to judgment. The observation that time moved along in sequence should lead to the recognition that time would also have an end, just as it had had a beginning. Thus, "as we suppose the power of the divine will to be a sufficient cause to the things that are, for their coming into existence out of nothing, so too we shall not repose our belief on any improbability in referring the re-formation of the world to the same power."[50]

Underlying this vision of Logos as the telos of the universe was the outline of the drama of world history and of cosmic history quoted earlier from the fifteenth chapter of 1 Corinthians. Jesus had come as true man to be the Second Adam; "for as by a man came death, by a man has come also the resurrection of the dead." This he did as the "first fruits," and after him would come life for "those who belong to Christ." And "then comes the end, when he delivers the kingdom to God the Father. . . . For [Christ] must reign until he has put *all* his enemies under his feet. The last enemy to be destroyed is death. . . . that God may be all in all" (1 Cor. 15:20–28). But could the God who had come in Christ ever truly be "all in all" if there still were anywhere in the cosmos any illness beyond the reach of his healing love? If, according to the Gospel of John (John 1:9), the Logos was "the true light that enlightens every man," could there be any abyss so dark that the light which had now come into the world and had now shone in the Logos could not penetrate it? As the Word of God, the Logos had spoken in creation, and spoken in the prophets of Israel, and spoken again—and decisively—in the life and teachings of Jesus. As the Reason of God, the Logos made sense out of the madness of the world and the power of evil. As the Structure of the cosmos, the Logos held forth the promise that there could be a "system" and a connection between the disparate elements of the universe as it was experienced. As the Savior of the cosmos, the Logos had not snatched humanity out of the goodness of the created order, but had transformed the created order into a fit setting for a transformed humanity. And as the Goal of the cosmos, the Logos represented the hope that even the devil could finally be restored to wholeness in "the restitution of all things [*apokatastasis tōn pantōn*], and with the re-formation of the world humanity also shall be changed from the transient and the earthly to the incorruptible and the eternal."[51]

Yet lest we forget—and sometimes they do seem to have forgotten, though more often they remembered[52]—all of these metaphysical constructs of fourth-century Christian philosophers about the preexistent Word and Logos were supposed to find their religious and moral focus, and even their intellectual justification, in the historical figure of Jesus in the Gospels, in "the humble Word [*sermo humilis*]" and in "the glory of his passion" on the cross.[53] "In the beginning was the Word": this could have been said, and had been said, by many thinkers who had never heard of Jesus of Nazareth. But what made this portrait of the Logos as Cosmic Christ special was the declaration that the Word had become flesh in Jesus and that in Jesus the incarnate Word had suffered and died on the cross.[54] Yet if that declaration was true, there was ultimately no way to avoid declaring as well that nothing short of the cosmos was the object of the love that had come through him. For the Gospel of John, which opened with the Logos doctrine, went on to affirm, in its best-known verse: "God so loved the world that he gave his only Son, that whoever believes in him should not perish but have eternal life" (John 3:16). The "whoever" could indeed be taken to mean each individual, one at a time; but the Greek word for "world" in this passage was still *kosmos*.

6

The Son of Man

Behold the Man!

 It is evident from the Gospels that Jesus' favorite designation for himself was "the Son of Man," which occurs about seventy times in the Synoptic Gospels and eleven or twelve times in the Gospel of John.[1] In the Hebrew Bible the term was sometimes a way of referring to humanity, with the meaning "mortal man."[2] But by the first century C.E. its usage within Judaism had acquired apocalyptic connotations, which it also carries in many of the sayings of Jesus: "As the lightning comes from the east and shines as far as the west, so will be the coming of the Son of man. . . . All the tribes of the earth will mourn, and they will see the Son of man coming on the clouds of heaven with power and great glory" (Matt. 24:27, 30). In Christian usage after the New Testament the title almost immediately regained its original significance, particularly because it came to be used to refer to the human nature of Jesus, in parallel with the term "Son of God," which referred to his divine nature.[3]

Thus it was that although Jesus had from the very beginning been seen by his followers as the disclosure of the mystery of the nature of divinity, it was only as their reflection on him deepened that they came to recognize what it fully meant that he was at the same time the revelation of the mystery of the nature of humanity, and that, in the formula of the Second Vatican Council, "only in the mystery of the incarnate Word does the mystery of man take on light."[4] Logically it might seem that it should have been the other way around: diagnosis should have preceded prescription. If the logic of Christian catechisms and sermons or of books on doctrinal theology from every historical period is any guide, the doctrine of the creation and fall of man must come first, to be followed by the doctrine of the person and work of Christ as the divine answer to the human predicament. But historically that was not how it developed, for the position of Jesus as the Son of God, the Logos, and the Cosmic Christ had to be clarified first, before there could come a mature understanding of the human predicament. Rather than making the punishment fit the crime, Christian thought had to gauge the magnitude of the human crime by first taking the measure of the one on whom the divine punishment of the cross had been imposed and thus (shifting to the original metaphor of salvation as health) making the diagnosis fit the prescription. "Long before [Christianity] had achieved its final triumph by dint of an impressive philosophy of religion," Harnack has said, "its success was already assured by the fact that it promised and offered salvation."[5] But it became "an impressive philosophy of religion" when it drew from its gospel of salvation through Jesus Christ the necessary implications for a doctrine of man.

The grim painting *Light* by the powerful twentieth-century American artist Siegfried Reinhardt documents this thesis that the dimensions of the human predicament become fully clear only in the light of its redemption. The crucified Christ, the *Ecce Homo*, appears at the top of the painting, but the light from which the work takes its name is revealed in the figure of the risen Christ, standing out in third dimension from the dark figure on the cross. He shakes his crown of thorns, as though it were a tambourine, and demands attention. But he does not get it. Violating all the rules of unity in painting, the two other figures are both facing away—one of them lost in her ecstasy, the other blowing his saxophone in the opposite direction. It is not only that in their self-indulgence they choose to ignore Jesus the light of the world. Rather, it is his very appearing that, for the first time, reveals to them their true condition. Both the misery and the grandeur have now become visible through the coming of that light. For, in the words of the Gospel of John, "This is the judgment, that the light has come into the world, and men loved darkness rather than light, because their deeds were evil. For every one who does evil hates the light, and does not come to the light, lest his deeds should be exposed" (John 3:19–20).

The definition of how it was that the coming of the light should have proved to be the revelation of darkness,[6] the identification of the crime, and the clarification of the diagnosis—all of this was the historic achievement of Augustine of Hippo, who died a century after the basic statement of the orthodox doctrine of Christ as the Second Person of the Trinity, "God from God, Light from Light," at the Council of Nicea. First Nicea had to determine what Jesus the Light *was* before Augustine could determine why He *had to be* what He was. The historical reasons for this sequence are complex, not least among them the intellectual and religious development of Augustine himself. But within and behind those historical reasons is a reason that is to be found within the human predicament itself, a reason formulated with characteristic precision and verve by a faithful disciple of Augustine who was born almost twelve centuries after Augustine died, the French scientist and Christian philosopher Blaise Pascal: "The knowledge of God without that of man's misery causes pride. The knowledge of man's misery without that of God causes despair. The knowledge of Jesus Christ constitutes the middle course, because in him we find both God and our misery. . . . [both misery and] grandeur."[7] Pascal was saying that it is easy for any view of human nature to recognize either misery or grandeur, but that combining them in one view and drawing from that combination the necessary philosophical and psychological consequences has proved to be far more difficult. For Pascal, and for Augustine before him, the combination was made possible by "the knowledge of Jesus Christ." In seeking to understand this chapter in the history of the images of Jesus, it may be helpful as well to call upon a distinction formulated by the nineteenth-century thinker Friedrich Schleiermacher, who declared that "if men are to be redeemed [in Jesus Christ], they must both be in need of redemption and be capable of receiving it"; to assert either the need or the capability without asserting the other was "heresy."[8] It was the genius of Augustine's picture of Jesus Christ as the key to both the grandeur and the misery of humanity that he managed to hold together that which made Christ and redemption possible and that which made Christ and redemption necessary. Thus "the pride of man may be cured through the humility of God" in the person and life of Jesus Christ.[9]

While much of what Augustine said about the human predicament and human misery was his own special insight, he was, in the use of the figure of Jesus to define the *grandeur* of humanity, attaching himself to what had preceded him in the thought of the second, third, and fourth centuries, as this had been summarized for example by Gregory of Nyssa: "In what then does the greatness of humanity consist, according to the doctrine of the church? Not in its likeness to the created world, but in its being in the image of the nature of the Creator."[10] In the fullest sense of the word, the true image of God for Gregory of Nyssa and for his successors was the man Jesus. Yet when the Word was made flesh in the man Jesus, this was human flesh and not any other kind of flesh, because humanity had been created in the image of God and the incarnation in Christ renewed that very image.[11] Although Augustine had, in the course of his controversies over original sin, sometimes spoken as though the image of God had been altogether obliterated through the fall of Adam, he made it clear upon further reflection near the end of his life that the doctrine of the fall must not be interpreted "as though man had lost everything he had of the image of God."[12]

For if the image of God had been totally destroyed by sin and the fall, there would have been no point of contact between human nature as such and the incarnation of the Logos in the truly human nature of Jesus.[13] Jesus was, then, not only the image of divinity, but the image of humanity as it had originally been intended to be and as through him it could now become; he was in this sense the "ideal man." By sending him, God had proved how deeply he loved humanity; for "he who did not spare his own Son but gave him up for us all, will he not also give us all things with him?" (Rom. 8:32). "But," as Augustine explained those words of Paul, "God loves us, such as we shall be, not such as we [now] are."[14] The contours of this future condition were already visible now, not in our empirical humanity but in the humanity of Jesus, the Word made flesh; and as it viewed that prospect, empirical human nature was filled with yearning and with a desire to press forward toward that ideal. Thus "Christ Jesus is the Mediator between God and men, not insofar as he is divine but insofar as he is human," as not only the source but also the "goal of all perfection."[15] He was both Alpha and Omega.

The human Jesus had not always held this position of importance in the thought of Augustine, even in his thought as a Christian. Thus in his early treatise *The Teacher*, he had said that to gain wisdom "we do not listen to anyone speaking and making sounds outside ourselves. We listen to Truth which presides over our minds within us, though of course we may be bidden to listen by someone using words." That inner teacher was called "Christ," who thus did not have to be the truly human person in the Gospels to perform this function, but seemed to act in some Platonic fashion as the recollection of a truth hidden deep within the soul.[16] The same emphasis is evident elsewhere, in his familiar words, "What then do you wish to know? I desire to know God and the soul. Nothing more? Nothing whatever."[17] He eventually became far more critical of the Platonic doctrine of recollection, and he acknowledged that he had had difficulty making the transition from the "immutability of the Logos, which I knew as well as I could and about which I did not have any doubts at all" (and which one did not have to be a Christian to accept) to the full meaning of the words of the Gospel of John, "The Logos was made flesh," which, Augustine confessed, he had come to understand "only somewhat later."[18] But once he did understand these words, the Logos made flesh, whose humility was made known in the narratives of the Gospels, dominated his language about Christ, in his expositions of the Psalms, which were for him the voice of Christ,[19] and in his exposition of the Gospel of John, whose teaching about the Logos as preexistent and incarnate and yet "lowly" made it the most "sublime" of the four Gospels.[20]

It was likewise from the portrait of the preexistent and incarnate Logos in the Gospel of John that Augustine, in the same years in which he was expounding that Gospel, developed the most sublime of his own psychological insights into the content of the image of God: the definition of the image as an image of the Trinity. He investigated the various "footprints of the Trinity," the ways in which the human mind by its very structure as single and yet possessing relationship within itself, as one and yet three, could be interpreted as a reflection of the relation between Father, Son, and Holy Spirit.[21] This has inspired one twentieth-century writer and literary critic, Dorothy L. Sayers, to explore the "creative imagination" as reflected in writing and in the arts and to find its analogies with the trinitarian "creative image," the structure of the Trinity as reflected in the historic Christian creeds and in the thought of Augustine.[22]

One of these "footprints of the Trinity," according to Augustine, was the trinity of being, knowledge, and will, capacities that were distinct within the mind and yet were one mind: "for I am, and I know, and I will."[23] Again, "when I . . . love anything, there are three realities involved: myself, and the beloved, and the love itself."[24] Perhaps the most profound of the analogies was that of "memory, understanding [*intelligentia*], and will," which "are not three lives but one life, not three minds but one mind" and yet were not identical.[25] Augustine freely conceded the inadequacy, and obviously sensed the artificiality, of all such constructs, including the very language of the ecclesiastical doctrine of the Trinity itself (which was necessary if faith was not to remain altogether silent, but could not pretend to provide an accurate description of the mystery of the inner life of God).[26] But this much was certain: Jesus Christ was for the thought of the Catholic Augustine the key to the mystery of the Trinity, and through it the key to the mystery of the human mind.

Profound and provocative though this exploration of the psychological analogies to the Trinity in the human mind may have been, Augustine's most important contribution to the history of human psychology came in his doctrine of sin, his investigation, to use our earlier terminology, of what had made Christ necessary rather than of what had made Christ possible, of the *misery* rather than of the grandeur of humanity. Walter Lippmann was referring above all to Augustine's doctrine of sin when, in his column for 30 October 1941, four months after the German invasion of the Soviet Union and five weeks before Pearl Harbor, he was moved to reflect on the presence within human nature of what he called "ice-cold evil":

> The modern skeptical world has been taught for some 200 years a conception of human nature in which the reality of evil, so well known to the ages of faith, has been discounted. Almost all of us grew up in an environment of such easy optimism that we can scarcely know what is meant, though our ancestors knew it well, by the satanic will. We shall have to recover this forgotten but essential truth—along with so many others that we lost when, thinking we were enlightened and advanced, we were merely shallow and blind.[27]

In that thoughtful tribute to the Augustinian tradition of the "ages of faith" Lippmann was joined during those very years by Reinhold Niebuhr, whose Gifford Lectures, *The Nature and Destiny of Man* (delivered in 1939 and published in 1941–43), were an effort at a critical restatement of Augustinian anthropology.

What role did the figure of Jesus play in Augustinian anthropology? The most fundamental component in any answer to that question is to be sought in an assessment of his *Confessions* and of its form and tone.[28] For in its literary structure it is, from the first sentence to the last, one long prayer, which is of course why it is called a confession, defined as accusation of oneself and praise of God.[29] The principal literary inspiration for the prayer comes from the Latin Psalter, which Augustine seems to have known by heart and from which he could, as a kind of contrapuntal virtuoso, spin out rhapsodic cadenzas.[30] But because he read the Psalms as the voice of Christ, the principal religious inspiration for his *Confessions* was his awareness of the grace of God which he had come to know in Christ through the Catholic Church.

It was, then, "in the permissive atmosphere of God's felt presence" and grace that he wrote the prayer of the *Confessions*.[31] Even though there is inevitably a certain amount of self-deception in any such memoir, Augustine could speak with as much candor as he did in the *Confessions* because the sin he was confessing was the sin that God in Christ had forgiven.[32] He was expressing the "sacrifice of my confessions" in the presence of a God whose eye could penetrate into even the most closed of hearts and had penetrated even into his, and to whom therefore it was not possible to lie. But he was also expressing the "confession of a broken and contrite heart" in the presence of a God whose grace "through Jesus Christ our Lord" had granted him deliverance from the power of sin, and to whom therefore it was not necessary to lie. It was Christ, as "our very Life" who "bore our death," to whom, Augustine said, "my soul confesses, and he heals it, because it had sinned against him."[33] And in a series of apostrophes to Christ scattered throughout the *Confessions*, Augustine gave devotional expression to what he asserted and defended elsewhere as dogma: that Jesus Christ was the Son of God, the source of grace, the ground of hope, and the worthy object of prayer, adoration, and confession.[34]

Standing then in the presence of God in Christ and probing both his own soul and his own memory, Augustine in the *Confessions* focused his attention on various sins of his youth, at least two of which have achieved considerable psychological notoriety. One of these, described at the beginning of book 3, was being "in love with loving" but not knowing the true nature of love.[35] As T. S. Eliot paraphrases Augustine's words,[36]

To Carthage then I came
Burning burning burning burning

O Lord Thou pluckest me out
O Lord Thou pluckest
burning.

If lust is defined, in keeping with both the Hebrew Bible and the New Testament, not as natural sexual desire but as the tendency to regard another person as primarily a sex object, Augustine's probing of the hidden fires of sexuality begins to seem considerably less quaint than it may appear at first.[37] Alongside the undeniable extremes to which he often went in his language about sexual desire, even about sexual desire within the boundaries of matrimony, he was at the same time rejecting the heretical notion that "marriage and fornication are two evils, of which the second is worse," and substituting for it the orthodox Catholic principle that "marriage and continence are two goods, of which the second is better," which, whatever modern readers may think of it, did have warrant both in the teachings of Jesus himself and in those of the apostle Paul, as well as in those of noble pagans of late antiquity.[38] The clinching argument in favor of the holiness of marriage came for Augustine from some other words of the apostle Paul: "Husbands, love your wives, as Christ loved the church and gave himself up for it. . . . This is a great sacrament [*magnum sacramentum*], and I take it to mean Christ and the church."[39] Marriage was a sacrament of Christ and the church.

The other sin mentioned in the *Confessions* that has provoked great psychological interest is the famous anecdote of the pear tree, with which book 2 closes.[40] "Rum thing to see a man making a mountain out of robbing a peartree in his teens," commented Justice Holmes on this story.[41] But as a close reading of the entire passage will show, Augustine's recollection of the incident provided him with an opportunity to probe the mysterious depths of the motivation of evil acts. The pears were not particularly attractive to him, nor did he find them very good to eat; he did not need them. What he did need was to steal them, and having satisfied that need, he threw them to the pigs. Even though he might not have done it without the company of his peer group who egged him on, it was not their companionship but the theft itself that he loved. When, in summarizing the incident, he speaks of having "become to myself an unfruitful land," he is, in his characteristic allegorical fashion, echoing the story of the Garden of Eden and of what an English poet and theologian steeped in Augustine was to call

> the fruit
> Of that forbidden tree, whose mortal taste
> brought death into the world, and all our woe,
> With loss of Eden, till one greater Man
> Restore us, and regain the blissful seat.[42]

It was that "greater Man," Jesus Christ, in whose "fruits" the soul, liberated from the tyranny of irrational sin, could now "rejoice."[43] Therefore he was the Second Adam, through whom the grace of God had prevailed over the sin and death that had come upon humanity through the First Adam.[44]

While Augustine's theory about the misery of humanity was thus in one sense highly personal and downright autobiographical, he rejected indignantly any suggestion that he was only extrapolating from his personal views and experiences and generalizing these into a universal condition.[45] Rather, he was seeking to take account of what already was, empirically speaking, recognizable as a universal condition. For if, as some people seemed to think, every human being was exactly poised between good and evil and thus faced the very same choice that Adam and Eve had faced,[46] how was one to account for the statistical regularity with which every human being managed to make the same choice that Adam and Eve had made, in favor of sin and against the good?[47] This was not to deny that there could be "on earth righteous men, great men—brave, prudent, chaste, patient, pious, merciful"; yet even they could not be "without sin."[48] Who was more holy than the saints and apostles? "And yet the Lord [Jesus] prescribed to them to say in their prayer, 'Forgive us our debts.' "[49]

There was only one unqualified exception to the rule, Jesus Christ as the Mediator between a righteous God and a sinful humanity; and he was, to use a cliché that in this case is not a cliché at all, the exception that proves the rule.[50] For it was his status as the sinless Savior that proved the necessity of salvation, and anyone who denied the universality of sin was obliged, for the sake of consistency, to deny the universality of the salvation and mediation accomplished in him. This was for Augustine the decisive argument in his analysis of the human condition. For all "ordinary" people, death was not only universal but involuntary: there might be some choice about whether to die at this time or at that time, but no choice about whether to die or not to die. The exception was Jesus Christ, who was not mortal by nature but who "died for mortals" and therefore was the only one who could say of himself: "I lay down my life, that I may take it again. No one takes it from me; I lay it down of my own accord."[51] Augustine's most influential insight into human nature and psychology, the idea of original sin, was therefore not only a way of speaking about the misery of humanity, but a means of recognizing and praising the uniqueness of Jesus.

Despite the sensitivity and frankness of the introspection at work in the *Confessions*, it seems safe to say that he would not have come to this insight without the illumination of Christ, reasoning backward from the cure to the diagnosis. Further substantiation for that hypothesis comes from his use of the Virgin Birth.[52] The assertion that Jesus was born of the Virgin Mary without a human father appears in the Gospels of Matthew and Luke, though without any specific explanation of its significance; but it is absent from the other two Gospels, as well as from the epistles of Paul, whose statement that Christ was "born of woman" meant that Jesus was fully and truly human,[53] but did not imply anything one way or the other about human paternity. It remained for Augustine, together with his mentor Ambrose, to draw from the Virgin Birth the conclusion that since Jesus "alone could be born in such a way as not to need to be reborn," all those who were born in the normal way, as the result of the sexual union of their parents, were in need of being reborn in Christ through baptism.[54] The statement of the Psalmist, "Behold, I was brought forth in iniquity, and in sin did my mother conceive me," was spoken in the awareness of forgiveness through the "selfsame faith" in Christ that was now confessed by the Catholic Church.[55] That was why Augustine entitled the treatise just quoted *On the Grace of Christ and Original Sin*; for he found the knowledge of the grace of Christ unintelligible without the knowledge of original sin, but he also saw that the knowledge of original sin was unbearable without a knowledge of the grace of Christ.

Jesus was the only unqualified exception that Augustine would grant to the rule of the universality of original sin. There was, however, one other exception that he had to consider: Mary the Virgin Mother of Jesus. After rejecting the contention that various other saints, both male and female, had been totally sinless, Augustine continued: "We must except the Holy Virgin Mary, concerning whom I wish to raise no question when it touches the subject of sins, *out of honor to the Lord*; for from him we know what abundance of grace for overcoming sin in every particular was conferred upon her who had the merit to conceive and to bear him who undoubtedly had no sin."[56] The outcome of that additional exception was to have a profound effect not only on devotion and theology, but on art and literature for the next fifteen centuries. It took almost exactly a thousand years before a church council (the Council of Basel in 1439) would define the doctrine that among mortals Mary alone had been conceived without sin, and even that council was found not to have had the right to define it. Thus it was only in 1854 that Pope Pius IX made the doctrine binding that, "in view of the merits of Christ Jesus, the Savior of the [entire] human race," which included her, Mary had been permitted to become an exception to the universality of original sin.[57] But long before it became a dogma, the immaculate conception of Mary was the subject quite literally of thousands of paintings and poems, in which, with infinite variations on the theme, Augustine's phrase "out of honor to the Lord" found expression in the use of the figure of Mary as a means of celebrating the figure of Jesus: the familiar theme of late medieval painters, the coronation of the Virgin, for example, shows her receiving the crown from her divine Son. Conversely, whenever devotion or speculation glorified Christ as Lord and King in such a way as to lose touch with the Man of Nazareth, Mary would become a substitute for him—human, compassionate, accessible. And then the devotion to her and the speculation about her were no longer being carried on "out of honor to the Lord."

"Know thyself" was a motto carved on the temple of the oracle at Delphi. As the linking of the Delphic oracle and the prophet Isaiah suggests,[58] others before Augustine had applied that axiom, often attributing it to Socrates, to the need for a self-understanding in the light of Christ, and Etienne Gilson is certainly correct in speaking about what he calls "Christian Socratism"; but it is significant that he refers in that context above all to the "profound psychological speculations of Saint Augustine."[59] Those speculations had grown out of Augustine's existential needs, but they had led him to Jesus, "the humble Word," and to "the glory of his passion."[60] Here alone it was that he was able to confront, to understand, and to articulate those needs, for the Jesus of Augustine was the key to what humanity was and to what, through Jesus, it could become. As he said in the opening words of the *Confessions*:

> Great art thou, O Lord, and greatly to be praised. . . . And man desires to praise thee, for he is a part of thy creation—man, who bears about with him his mortality, the witness of his sin. . . . Thou hast made us for thyself,

and restless is our heart until it comes to rest in thee. . . . I call upon thee, O Lord, in my faith, which thou hast given me, which thou hast inspired in me through the humanity of thy Son.

7

The True Image

He is the image of the invisible
God.

The victory of Jesus Christ over the gods of Greece and Rome in the fourth century did not, as both friend and foe might have expected, bring about the demise of religious art;[1] on the contrary, it was responsible over the next fifteen centuries for a massive and magnificent outpouring of creativity that is probably without parallel in the entire history of art. How and why did that happen? How could Jesus have evolved from the very antithesis of all representations of the divine in images to become their most important concrete inspiration—and eventually their principal theoretical justification?

In the Ten Commandments of Moses, whose permanent validity Christians also accepted,[2] the prohibition of religious art as idolatrous was explicit and comprehensive: "You shall not make for yourself a graven image, or any likeness of anything that is in heaven above, or that is in the earth beneath, or that is in the water under the earth" (Ex. 20:4). Quoting such prohibitions from the Hebrew Bible as well as the opinions of such pagan thinkers as Cicero that "the deities which men worshiped were false," the followers of Jesus claimed to be joining themselves both to Judaism and to the best in classical paganism when they rejected images, but they chided enlightened pagans for their elitism and inconsistency in allowing the "vulgar and ignorant" to keep their images.[3] What was more, they went beyond

Judaism in denouncing as well the very notion of religious architecture: "The God who made the world and everything in it, being Lord of heaven and earth, does not live in shrines made by man."[4] They took the prohibition of images to apply not only to the idolaters who worshiped them but even to the artists who made them, who were practicing a "deceptive art," and they celebrated those "who refuse to look at any temples and altars."[5] Thus in contradistinction to paganism and in some ways even to Judaism, they claimed, in the name of the revelation of the divine that had come in Jesus, to be proclaiming a God who transcended all efforts of human hands to devise sacred images; for it was the rational soul that was the "image of God."[6] There were neither sacred images nor sacred places; not even the places where Jesus had been born and buried were possessed of any special holiness.[7]

Thanks to archaeological research at Dura Europos, carried on during the twentieth century, we know now, to an extent that previous generations of scholars did not, that the absolute prohibition of images in the law of Moses did not deter the Judaism contemporary with early Christianity from making holy pictures and exhibiting them in its places of worship. "The Dura Synagogue," according to Carl Kraeling, was "with its decorations one of the finest and most fitting monuments of ancient Judaism," and "the paintings of Dura can properly be called forerunners of Byzantine art."[8] Kraeling distinguished the work of two Jewish artists in the synagogue at Dura; one of them he characterized as a "Symbolist," which is not so surprising, but the other was a "Representationalist." It has even been suggested that "illustration archetypes [of the Dura frescoes] illuminated Greek copies of Biblical materials: translations like the Septuagint; Greek paraphrases of separate books or scripture sections; or other Greek literary types, such as epics or tragedies or histories, composed by Hellenistic Jews on Biblical themes."[9] Yet in the conclusion of his work Kraeling warns:

> A close study of the literary tradition indicates that the Christians, having adopted the Bible of the Jewish people, had to grapple with the selfsame prohibition of the use of images that had so much preoccupied the Jews of the post-Maccabean period, and found no easy solution. Even after Palestinian Judaism had found the way toward a more liberal interpretation of the Biblical commandment, Christian writers were still taking a conservative position in their discussion of it.[10]

Despite the intriguing and undeniable parallels between the artistic practice of early Christianity and that of Hellenistic Judaism, whether in Palestine or in the Diaspora, therefore, we may not explain the Christian development simply as an adaptation of the Jewish. Doing that would oversimplify the special qualities and the special problems of both. For early Christianity, those special qualities and special problems were clearly the ones associated with the life and person of Jesus. Although it had confronted these problems from the very beginning,[11] it was only with the challenge to the use of images in the eighth and ninth centuries that the orthodox Byzantine interpreters of the person and message of Jesus were compelled to articulate a comprehensive philosophical and theological aesthetic based on the person of Christ, an aesthetic within which the legitimacy of drawing images of the divine would take its proper place.[12]

Fundamental to any consideration of the issues in the aesthetics of Byzantine iconography was the unanimous affirmation of the New Testament and the fathers of the early church that, in a special and unique sense, "the image of God is his Logos, the genuine Son of Mind, the divine Logos, the archetypal light of light," as Clement of Alexandria had put it in an elaboration on the theme suggested by the Epistle to the Colossians;[13] for, in the formula of Vladimir Lossky, "it is in the context of the Incarnation (say rather: it is by the fact, by the event of the Incarnation) that the creation of man in the image of God receives all its theological value."[14] If, following Whitehead, as noted in the introduction to this book, we should look in any controversy of the past for the "fundamental assumptions which adherents of all the variant systems within the epoch unconsciously presuppose,"[15] the assumption that Jesus Christ was uniquely the image of God was shared by the proponents of both major alternatives in the controversies of the eighth and ninth centuries over images. But from this theological asssumption concerning Jesus Christ they drew conclusions about religious art that were diametrically opposed.

The earliest application of this assumption to the question of religious art came from the opponents of images.[16] Constantia, the sister of the emperor Constantine, wrote to Eusebius of Caesarea requesting an image of Christ. He replied: "I do not know what has impelled you to command that an image of our Savior be drawn. Which image of Christ do you want? Is it to be a true and unchangeable one, portraying his countenance truly, or is it to be the one which he assumed on our behalf when he took on the appearance of the 'form of a slave'?"[17] The alternatives as formulated by Eusebius bear careful consideration in their implications for iconography. In his bemusement at Constantia's interest in an image of Christ, Eusebius apparently could not imagine that anyone would be interested in an image of that countenance which Christ "assumed on our behalf when he took on the appearance of the 'form of a slave,' " for that was transitory and not permanently relevant—even though, presumably, an eyewitness in Jerusalem who saw Jesus in the flesh during the first century could have drawn such a picture of him or even, technology permitting, could have photographed him. But that would not have been "a true image" of the one who was himself the True Image. For Eusebius, a "true" image of that Image would have to be unchangeable, for only that would "portray his countenance truly." And such an image was, by definition, impossible. Thus the demands of the authentic doctrine of the person of Christ precluded, for Eusebius, any attempt at an image.

Eusebius became the "coryphaeus and acropolis"[18] for the iconoclasts of the eighth and especially of the ninth century, because he had put the issue of Christ as image at the center of the debate on the question of images. In applying the concept of Christ as Image to the issue, the iconoclasts invoked the authority of the councils of the fourth and fifth century, at which the status of Christ as the Image of the Father had been definitively formulated. The only way an image of Christ could be a true image was in the same way that Christ himself was the True Image of the Father. The Council of Nicea in 325 had formulated the meaning of the status of Christ as the true image of the Father within the Holy Trinity by declaring that he was "one in being" with the one whom he imaged.[19] Therefore, according to Emperor Constantine V, an icon of Christ could not be a true image of him unless it too was "one in being" with him, in the same way that Christ the Son of God was one in being with the Father.[20] Obviously, no work of art made by human hands—nor even, for that matter, the images supposedly made without hands, by angels[21]— could ever hope to meet such a qualification. The only image of Christ that could be said to be "one in being" with Christ in the same sense that Christ was one in being with the Father was the Eucharist, which contained the real presence of the body and blood of Christ. According to Constantine, the bread of the Eucharist was truly "an image of his body, taking the form of his flesh and having become a type of his body."[22] "It has been laid down for us," the iconoclasts taught, "that Christ *is* to be portrayed in an image, but only as the holy teaching transmitted by divine tradition says: 'Do this in remembrance of me.' Therefore it is evidently not permitted to portray him in an image or to carry out a remembrance of him in any other way, since this por- trayal [in the Eucharist] is true and this way of portraying is sacred."[23] Thus the Eucharist, as an image that everyone had to agree was one in being with its original, precluded every other so-called image of Christ.

After the Council of Nicea in 325, the most important church council was that held at Chalcedon in 451, at which the relation between the divine nature and the human nature in Christ was set down in a formula that has continued for fifteen centuries to be the definition of orthodox belief about the person of Jesus.[24] On the basis of the formulas of Chalcedon, the opponents of images insisted that Christ, as the True Image of God, was "beyond description, beyond com- prehension, beyond change, and beyond measure," since such tran- scendence was characteristic of God.[25] They seem to have held that this rule applied even to the miracles and to the sufferings of Christ in the days of his flesh, which it was "illegitimate to portray in im- ages."[26] Whatever the status of Christ "before the passion and the resurrection" may have been, however, latter-day artists in any case had no right to attempt to portray him now; for now "the body of Christ is incorruptible, having inherited immortality," and that was beyond the competence of any artistic representation.[27] Invoking the orthodox dogma of Christ, formulated by Chalcedon, as consisting of two natures, divine and human, in a single person, they put their opposition to images of Christ in the form of a disjunctive syllogism. Either those who painted images of Christ were portraying his deity by an icon, or they were not: if they were, they violated its essential nature as being beyond description and circumscription; if they were not, they were separating the two natures of Christ and thus dividing his single person. In either case they were guilty of blasphemy and heresy against the person of Christ as this had been defined by the orthodox church councils, particularly those of Nicea and Chalcedon. As the emperor Constantine V, perhaps the most profound theore- tician among the iconoclasts, put it, "if someone makes an image of Christ, . . . he has not really penetrated the depths of the dogma of the inseparable union of the two natures of Christ" as formulated by those two councils.[28]

Underlying these aspersions on the artistic portrayal of Jesus Christ appears to have been a deep-seated aversion to the material and physical aspects of his person: "It is degrading and demeaning to depict Christ with material representations. For one should confine oneself to the mental observation [of him] . . . through sanctification and righteousness."[29] By focusing the gaze of the viewer on these "degrading and demeaning" qualities of the man Jesus, the portrayal of him in an image inevitably diverted the attention from what was important about him, his transcendent rather than his immanent qualities. As the defenders of the gospel against the Greeks had long been able to quote the best of the Greeks in insisting, the requirement both of the Platonic tradition and of the Gospel of John, "God is spirit, and those who worship him must worship in spirit and truth," was being violated whenever the outward physical picture was substituted for the spirit and whenever the deception of the icon replaced the truth.[30] The Christian opponents of images in Byzantium during the eighth and ninth centuries, therefore, had behind them a distinguished history—Jewish, Greek, and Christian—of the struggle to extricate the divine from the unworthy physical representations of the divine. Jesus Christ himself was the True Image, every other image was false.[31]

"We join you in declaring that the Son is the Image of God the Father," the defenders of the icons said to the iconoclasts.[32] That was, in Whitehead's phrase, the fundamental assumption presupposed by all the adherents of all the variant systems of the epoch. But the Jesus Christ who was the True Image was the one who had been made human, and thus physical and material, by his incarnation and birth from the Virgin Mary, and therefore a Christian icon was not an idol but an image of the Image: such was in essence the case for a Christian art.[33] The logical implication of the view of Christ set forth in the orthodox tradition, as this was being cited by the iconoclasts, was a justification for the representation of Christ in pictures. This case for images in Christian art was set into the context of a total theory of images, which was yet another illustration of the artful combination of biblical and philosophical perspectives, of Hebrew and Greek language, to which we have pointed several times. All reality, both divine and human, participated one way or another in what might be called a great chain of images. For it was mistaken to charge that images were a novelty recently invented by those who were seeking to smuggle idolatry back into the churches. Who invented images? "God himself was the first" to do so, John of Damascus replied.[34] *God was the first and the original image-maker of the universe.*

In the most fundamental sense of the word *image*, the Son of God was uniquely the Image of God, "the living Image, who is his image in his very nature, who is the image of the invisible Father differing in no way from him" except by being the Son rather than the Father.[35] As the Epistle to the Colossians said, "He is the image of the invisible God" (Col. 1:15). The worship of the Son of God was therefore not idolatrous, because, in the oft-quoted formula of Basil of Caesarea, "the honor paid to the image [the Son] passes over to the prototype [the Father]."[36] All the other images in the chain of images had the right to be called "image" by some sort of participation in this primal and eternal image-making within the Holy Trinity. Even the Holy Spirit was, in turn, the image of the Son, since "no one can say 'Jesus is Lord' except by the Holy Spirit" (1 Cor. 12:3). Quite apart from human history, therefore, there was, in the very life of the Godhead, an image-making and an image-manifesting, which expressed the mystery of the eternal relation of Father, Son, and Holy Spirit. In this sense, the Son of God before the incarnation was not only "the image of the invisible God," but "the invisible image of the invisible God," unknown and unknowable except as he chose to make himself known and visible.

In a secondary and derivative sense, image could be taken to refer to the "images and paradigms in God of the things that are to be produced by him." Because God was absolute and unchangeable, with "no variation" (James 1:17), he did not, as the Artist-Maker of the cosmos, create the particulars of the empirical world directly. Instead, creation consisted in the designing of these images and paradigms, which could be called the "predeterminations [*proorismoi*]" of the empirical world.[37] Before any particular reality came into being as such, it had, as image, been predetermined within the "counsel [*boulē*]" of God, and in that sense it already possessed reality. That reality preceding the empirical was best exemplified in the work of a human architect, who, "before a house is constructed, already images in his mind the scheme and plan of what it is to be." For the tradition of Christian Neoplatonism expressed by the philosophers of the fourth century, these images of an empirical world yet to be were produced by and through the Logos, the cosmic Christ, since "all things were made through him, and without him was not anything made that was made" (John 1:3). God created the world we see through the Logos, his Image, who in turn called into being the Platonic forms, the images from which that world would come.

Although the entire created world was in this sense an image of God, or perhaps more precisely an image of the Image of God, the human creature had a special claim to that honorific title. For in the creation story of the Book of Genesis, the God of Israel was said to have created man in his own image. What is more, he had done so after taking counsel with himself: "Let us make man in our image, after our likeness" (Gen. 1:26). Whatever these Hebrew plurals in Genesis may have meant originally, Christian interpreters had, almost "in the beginning," taken them to refer to a counsel between the Father and the Son within the mystery of the Trinity;[38] and Augustine had even used them as the basis for his provocative hypothesis, discussed earlier, that the very image of God in man was itself trinitarian in structure.[39] For the image of God the Creator in man the creature was an example of an image "by imitation," mirroring forth in the structure of human life and thought the nature of God the image-maker. Thus the God who in the law on Sinai prohibited the making of images had himself made such an image in the very creature who was then forbidden to become an image-maker; and the polemic against images in early Christian thought had often been based on this very argument, that a living God could not have wood and stone as a fitting image, but only the rational soul of his supreme creature.[40] Hence the command not to make images was based not on a degraded view of images, but on an exalted one: because a proper image of God could only be something as noble as the human mind, it demeaned both God the image-maker and man the image to attempt to substitute for it some less worthy picture.

In addition to these usages of the word *image*, which we may call metaphysical, there were historical usages. Because of the way the human mind was constructed, it could not perceive spiritual reality except through the use of physical images. It could not describe even "creatures" that were nonphysical, such as angels, except by employing "physical" language.[41] The Bible itself had accommodated its ways of speaking to this characteristic of human thought and language, presenting its sublime content by means of simple and even homely analogies. For by no mental acrobatics was it possible to go around such analogies to a purely intellectual and spiritual vision of God; rather, "ever since the creation of the world his invisible nature, namely, his eternal power and deity, has been clearly perceived in the things that have been made" (Rom. 1:20). In these visible realities of the empirical and historical world, therefore, there were images of the transcendent being of God, and it was unavoidable to use these temporal realities as metaphors for the eternal reality, as the images and symbols for the Trinity itself showed.

As biblical usage likewise made clear, historical images of this kind could move in either direction within time, describing either "the things that are yet to be in the future" or "the things that have already happened in the past." According to the Christian way of reading it, the Hebrew Bible was filled with images and anticipations of what was to be fulfilled with the coming of Jesus. They were real in and of themselves: Israel did cross the Red Sea during the exodus from Egypt, on a date that historical research was, at least in principle, capable of fixing. But at the same time they were images of what was to come: the crossing of the Red Sea was a "type" of Christian baptism. On the other hand, there were likewise images that were intended to serve as "monuments of past events, of some wondrous achievement or of some virtue, for glory and honor and remembrance." A book of history written as a memorial of past events was such an image, whose purpose it was to inform later generations about what had happened and thus to instruct them about virtue and vice. Nonliterary images in memory of historical events and personages were intrinsically no different from books; they were, in fact, "books for the illiterate," differing from the Bible only in form but not in content.[42]

Between these two categories of images, the metaphysical and the historical, however, there was a great gulf fixed. So long as there was such a gulf, the only possible justification for religious art was the didactic one represented by the phrase "books for the illiterate." Idolatry was the vain attempt of the human worshiper to cross the gulf, by pretending that an artistic, historical image mounted on the wall or held in the hand was in fact a cosmic and metaphysical image with some genuine affinity to the First Principle of the universe. The prohibition of graven images in the Second Commandment was the divine assertion and restraint preserving the gulf. But that gulf—indeed, every gulf, including the very separation between the visible and the invisible, between time and eternity—had been bridged when the Logos became flesh. The incarnation of the cosmic and metaphysical Logos in the this-worldly and historical person of Jesus of Nazareth supplied what one can only call the missing link in the great chain of images. The fallacy of misplaced concreteness, by which idolatry had correctly intuited an identity of images in the abstract but had falsely executed it in the concrete, had now been replaced by the concrete events of the life of Jesus as described in the Gospels, as recounted by John of Damascus in what sounds like a catalogue raisonné of Byzantine icons:

> Because the one who by excellency of nature transcends all quantity and size and magnitude, who has his being in the form of God, has now, by taking upon himself the form of a slave, contracted himself into a quantity and size and has acquired a physical identity, do not hesitate any longer to draw pictures and to set forth, for all to see, him who has chosen to let himself be seen: his ineffable descent from heaven to earth; his birth from the Virgin; his baptism in the Jordan; his transfiguration on Mount Tabor; the sufferings that have achieved for us freedom from suffering; the miracles that symbolized his divine nature and activity when they were performed through the activity of his [human] flesh; the burial, resurrection, and ascension into heaven by which the Savior has accomplished our salvation—describe all of these events, both in words and in colors, both in books and in pictures.[43]

Thus the God who had prohibited religious art as the idolatrous effort to depict the divine in visible form had now taken the initiative of depicting himself in visible form, and had done so not in metaphor or in memorial but in person and, quite literally, "in the flesh." The metaphysical had become historical, and the cosmic Logos who was the true image of the Father from eternity had now become a part of time and could be portrayed in an image of his divine-human person as this had carried out the events of salvation history. The creation of Adam and Eve in the image of God had been an anticipation of the coming of Jesus the Second Adam and of Mary the Second Eve, so that the depiction of Christ and of his Mother could be at the same time the description of the true image of God in humanity. The image portrayed him in the individual specificity of his unique person, not as humanity in the abstract. Nevertheless, the humanity of Jesus depicted in the icons, and by derivation the humanity of his saints and of all who had been made alive in him, was a humanity suffused with the presence of divinity: it was, in this sense, the "deified" body of Christ that was being portrayed, and the most characteristic Eastern Orthodox way of speaking about the salvation granted in Christ has been to call it "deification" (*theōsis* in Greek, *obozhenie* in Russian).[44] The iconography of the icon (to resort deliberately to an almost unavoidable tautology) was well designed to carry out both of these themes simultaneously: specificity and deification, and therefore what one of the most profound twentieth-century interpreters of icons, Evgenii Nikolaevich Trubetskoi, has called "theory of colors" or "contemplation in images."[45]

An icon of Christ Pantocrator, Christ the All-Sovereign, which is probably to be dated to the sixth century and was probably produced at Constantinople, embodies that very combination of specificity and deification. It belongs to that small but important group preserved at the Monastery of Saint Catherine on Mount Sinai. One of the consequences of the thoroughness with which the iconoclasts carried out their task is the small number of preiconoclastic icons still in existence.[46] Among these Christ Pantocrator holds a special place, now that it has been found under the layers of later paint that had covered it. This is a specific human face, but in it, as André Grabar has said, "the artist achieves an effect of aloofness and timelessness, a pictorial expression of the divine nature." And yet, he continues, the artist has managed to use "abstracting features along with more naturalistic ones" so subtly that he "has been able to convey pictorially the dogma of the two natures of Christ, the divine and the human."[47] "The all-sovereign God, the Logos [*ho Pantokratōr Theos Logos*]" had long been one of the titles for Christ.[48] By depicting the indissoluble union between the timeless nature of the All-Sovereign and the historical nature of Jesus of Nazareth, this Byzantine icon of Christ Pantocrator succeeded in conceptualizing the one who was the embodiment not only of the True in his teaching and of the Good in his life, but of the Beautiful in his form as "the fairest of the sons of men" (Ps. 45:2).

Within that triad of the Beautiful, the True, and the Good, invoked in the introduction to this book as a way of expressing the many facets of the meaning of Jesus for human culture, it was the Beautiful that took by far the longest time to evolve. One of Augustine's early books, since lost except for his occasional references to it, was called *On the Beautiful and the Fitting*.[49] In one of the most memorable passages of his *Confessions* he exclaimed: "Too late have I loved Thee, Thou Beauty ever ancient, ever new, too late have I come to love Thee!"[50] Yet if Augustine may be said to have a theory of the Beautiful, it is worked out the most successfully in his analysis of language and its meaning, in connection with his aesthetic of signs,[51] and in his treatise *On Music*, both of which were to shape medieval aesthetic theory and practice in the Latin West for a thousand years.

But for the Christian justification of religious art, it was only with the ninth century and in the Greek East that an exploration and application of the deeper significance of the person of Jesus appeared. As the iconoclasts saw with great clarity, the Beautiful was (and is) the most subtle and the most dangerous of the triad: the dangers of identifying the Holy with the True (intellectualism) and with the Good (moralism) have manifested themselves repeatedly in the history of Judaism and of Christianity, but it is noteworthy that both the Second Commandment itself and the message of the Hebrew prophets singled out the identification of the Holy with the Beautiful as the special temptation to sin. The formulation of an aesthetic that came to terms with the reality of this temptation called for philosophical and theological sophistication. In addition, of course, there had to have been an inspiration for religious art, an inspiration of more than a flatly didactic sort, before there could be any such aesthetic justification; and a sophisticated philosophical-theological challenge to religious art was necessary before any sophisticated defense of it was possible. All of this—the inspiration and the challenge and the justification—was eventually provided by the person of Jesus, who came to be seen as both the ground of continuity in art and the source of innovation for art, and thus, in a sense that Augustine could not have intended, as a "beauty ever ancient, ever new."

8
Christ Crucified

*Far be it from me to glory except
in the cross of our Lord Jesus
Christ, by which the world has
been crucified to me, and I to the
world.*

The followers of Jesus came very early to the conclusion that he had lived in order to die, that his death was not the interruption of his life at all but its ultimate purpose.[1] Even by the most generous reading, the Gospels give us information about less than a hundred days in the life of Jesus; but for the last two or three days of his life, they provide a detailed, almost hour-by-hour scenario. And the climax of that scenario is the account of Good Friday and of his three hours on the cross. The Apostles' Creed and the Nicene Creed recognized this when they moved directly from his birth "from the Virgin Mary" to his crucifixion "under Pontius Pilate." What was said of the thane of Cawdor in *Macbeth* was true preeminently of Jesus: "Nothing in his life / Became him like the leaving it."[2]

It was above all the apostle Paul who formulated this distinctive place of the death on the cross. "Far be it from me," he said, "to glory except in the cross of our Lord Jesus Christ, by which the world has been crucified to me, and I to the world" (Gal. 6:14). But the gospel of the cross pervades the New Testament and early Christian literature. Christ was the "Lamb of God, who takes away the sin of the world" (John 1:29). The prophecy of the fifty-third chapter of the Book of Isaiah about the suffering servant who was "wounded for our transgressions, bruised for our iniquities" was taken to refer to Jesus on the cross.[3] The use of the sign of the cross, as a mark of identification and a means of warding off the power of demons, is not mentioned as such in the New Testament; but it appears very early in Christian history, and when it is mentioned it is already being taken for granted. Tertullian declares that "at every forward step and movement, at every going in and out . . . in all the ordinary actions of daily life, we mark upon our foreheads the sign," and the sign of the cross became the prime evidence for the existence of an unwritten tradition that everyone observed even though it was not commanded in the Bible.[4] Those who did not belong to the church could not help noticing the practice. The emperor Julian, whom Christians called "the Apostate" because he had forsaken the Christianity of his childhood, complained to the Christians in the fourth century: "You adore the wood of the cross and draw its likeness on your foreheads and engrave it on your housefronts";[5] when, in one of the most widely read novels to come out of World War II, a ship was torpedoed and was sinking, one of the crew noticed another "crossing himself, and remembered that he was a Roman Catholic";[6] and on 15 March 1897, Gustav Mahler, while visiting Moscow, observed that its people were "incredibly bigoted. Every two steps there's an icon or a church, and every passer-by stops, beats his breast, and makes the sign of the cross as is customary in Russia."[7] (The "customary" way of doing so in Russia is, of course, from the right shoulder to the left, rather than from the left to the right as in the West, and aficionados of spy stories will recall that many a Western operative whose Russian accent was impeccable blew his cover when, at table, he made the sign of the cross the wrong way.)

As Mahler observed in czarist Russia, the sign of the cross of Jesus Christ pervaded the culture and folklore of the nations of medieval Europe—their literature, music, art, and architecture—as no other symbol had. To lend at least some coherence to this welter of cruciform impressions in the culture of the Middle Ages, it may be useful to draw upon a distinction that comes from the apostle Paul. "We preach Christ crucified," he wrote, "the power of God and the wisdom of God" (1 Cor. 1:23–24). For although ultimately there is, as Augustine saw in explaining these words, no clear division in biblical usage between the power of God and the wisdom of God, the distinction does help.[8]

As the power of God, the sign of the cross was a talisman against evil. Medieval lives of the saints, both Eastern and Western, are replete with stories of its wondrous powers. In one of the apocryphal *Acts* of the apostles, for example, making the sign of the cross over a locked door causes it to open miraculously for the apostles to enter; and in one of the *Martyrdoms*, it is successful in silencing the barking of a dog.[9] Augustine reports that a woman in Carthage, suffering from cancer of the breast, "was instructed in a dream to wait for the first woman who would come out of the baptistery after being baptized, and to ask here to make the sign of Christ [the sign of the cross] upon her lesion. She did so and was cured immediately."[10] Remaclus, a Christian missionary in the seventh century, made the sign of the cross over a spring dedicated to pagan gods, driving out the gods and instantly purifying the water.[11] An "ordeal of the cross [*judicium crucis*]" became, in medieval legal practice, a way of settling disputes; thus an eighth-century code prescribes: "If a woman claims that her husband has never remained with her [i.e., that the marriage has never been consummated], let them go out to the cross; and if it be true, let them be separated."[12] Especially frequent in several folk literatures are accounts of how the cross provided a cure for diseases and wounds. The sight of a cross could break a fever or quiet hysteria. We have reports of hemorrhages on the battlefield or in knightly combat, which no tourniquet could stanch but which the cross succeeded in stopping. Sometimes it was even successful in raising the dead. And in the folklore of the Slavs and the Transylvanians the crucifix had special power against vampires, graphically described in *Dracula*, the novel and the film.

As that last example suggests, there was a close connection between these uses of the cross (many of which, to say the least, certainly bordered on the magical) and the ancient and medieval belief in the presence and power of demons. In a familiar epigram from Shirley Jackson Case, "the sky hung low in the ancient world."[13] The description continues:

> Traffic was heavy on the highway between heaven and earth. Gods and spirits thickly populated the upper air, where they stood in readiness to intervene at any moment in the affairs of mortals. And demonic powers, emerging from the lower world or resident in remote corners of the earth,

were a constant menace to human welfare. All nature was alive—alive with supernatural forces.

If anything, medieval Christianity reinforced that belief in demonic powers, but it also provided various charms to break their spell: holy water, relics, incantations, the consecrated host of the Eucharist, and, above all, the sign of the cross. These became vehicles for the power of God against the demons. Among them, the cross simultaneously could serve as a magical amulet and, because of its inseparable association with the crucifixion of Jesus, could act as a reminder, more or less effective as the case might be, that the power against demons and diseases was not resident in the amulet or the gesture, but was in fact the power of God, of that God who had come in the life and death of Jesus to break the power of evil.

A special case was the power available in the relics of the true cross. These were unknown in the first three centuries, but references to them begin to appear in the 350s.[14] Although Eusebius of Caesarea, our most important source of information about Constantine and his family, makes no mention of it at all, the discovery of the cross in Jerusalem was attributed to Saint Helena, mother of the emperor Constantine, in several different versions of the legend. In a chamber under the present Church of the Holy Sepulcher she was said to have found not one cross, but three. By divine inspiration she resolved to determine which cross was authentic by applying each one to a dead body: the one that raised the man from the dead would be the true cross.[15] After she had discovered the cross, the chronicler Socrates Scholasticus tells us,

> the emperor's mother erected over the place of the sepulcher a magnificent church.... There she left a portion of the cross, enclosed in a silver case, as a memorial for those who might wish to see it. The other part she sent to the emperor, who, *being persuaded that the city would be perfectly secure where that relic should be preserved,* privately enclosed it in his own statue ...at Constantinople....Moreover, the nails with which Christ's hands were fastened to the cross (for his mother, having found these also in the sepulcher, had sent them) Constantine took and had made into bridle-bits and a helmet, which he used in his military expeditions.[16]

But these two portions of the true cross, one in Jerusalem and one in Constantinople, were not to be the only ones. As early as 350 we find Cyril of Jerusalem asserting to those who would deny the crucifixion: "The whole world has since been filled with pieces of the wood of the cross."[17] We have references to such pieces of wood in Cappadocia and in Antioch during the second half of the fourth century, and by the beginning of the fifth century in Gaul; at the middle of that century the patriarch Juvenal of Jerusalem sent one to Pope Leo I in Rome. Pope Gregory I, who died in 604, presented one to the queen of the Lombards, Theodelinde, and to Recared I, king of the Visigoths, who became a Catholic. Helena's discovery (or, as it was called in Latin and then, with an unintentional irony in English, the "invention") of the cross became a day on the church calendar of the Middle Ages in the Carolingian era and was observed on 3 May (until it was abolished for the Latin rite during the Second Vatican Council, in 1960). The true cross itself was captured by the Persians in the seventh century and recovered by the emperor Heraclius, but in the twelfth century it was carried into battle by the bishop of Bethlehem and lost—except, of course, for all those fragments, with which, to use the words of Cyril of Jerusalem, the "whole world" was indeed filled in the Middle Ages, until, as the waggish saying had it, it would have been possible to rebuild the entire city of Jerusalem with the pieces of the true cross.

As the report in the *Ecclesiastical History* of Socrates makes clear, the cross was believed to be "the power of God" not only to ward off disease and other such perils, but above all in battle. Nor was this power restricted to the true cross: after his victory at the Milvian Bridge, Constantine had ordered a banner of the cross to be carried at the head of each of his armies when it went into battle. *Ho nikopoios stauros,* "the victory-granting cross," as Eusebius called it, became a military insignia on both land and sea.[18] With some help from the celebrated "Greek fire" (apparently a compound of sulphur, saltpeter, and naphtha, though the recipe is still a Byzantine secret) and with the tactical expertise of Byzantine military science, the cross did grant victory; and the strategic location of the city of Constantinople protected it against invaders for a millennium. In the West, too, the cross was thought to be a source of protection in war, and at the end of the eleventh century it became the central symbol of the expeditions to Palestine that acquired the name *crusades:* "to take the cross" meant to go off on a crusade.

The cross was believed to possess all of this victorious power because it had been the instrument for the greatest victory of them all, the cosmic victory of the power of God over the power of the devil in the death and resurrection of Jesus. "The word of the cross is called the power of God," John of Damascus said, "because the might of God, that is, his victory over death, has been revealed to us through it."[19] The earliest versions of the idea had described this victory as a trick that God had played on the devil, death, and sin, the alliance of enemies who had held humanity in thrall. In one of the most striking—and one of the most problematical—of images for the trick, the devil with his allies was depicted as a giant fish that had devoured every human being since Adam. When the humanity of Christ was cast into the pool, the fish took it to be yet another victim to be swallowed up. But hidden within this bait of the human nature of Christ was the hook of his divine nature, so that when the devil gobbled up the man Jesus in his death on the cross, he was impaled on the divinity. He had to regurgitate the humanity of Jesus, and with it all those whom Jesus had taken as his own; and death and the devil, who had taken the human race, were now themselves taken. Through the cross, therefore, liberation and victory had come.

In a more subtle and sophisticated form, this theory of the cross became the metaphor of *Christus Victor*, which Gustaf Aulén made the title of a controversial book on the meaning of the cross. Here, in what Aulén does not hesitate to call the "classic" theory of how the cross saves, the cross became the sign of God's invasion of enemy territory and of the "wondrous battle [*mirabile duellum*]" by which Jesus Christ had accomplished the salvation of the human race.[20] Shedding the cruder aspects of the earlier metaphor of deception, the theme of Christus Victor nevertheless retained the interpretation that the enemies of God and man were the ones with whom Christ on the cross had to contend. The death of Christ on the cross was therefore his capitulation to those enemies and to their power, before which he made himself weak. But he took those enemies into the grave with him. In the resurrection Christ was set free from their power, but they remained behind in the grave. Although this interpretation of the cross as the power of God was more prominent in the Greek East than in the Latin West, it was never lost even in the West; and, according to Aulén, the Reformation revived it. Thus the so-called Easter Cantata (Cantata 4), "Christ lag in Todesbanden," of Johann Sebastian Bach is a celebration of Christus Victor; and in Bach's *Saint John Passion*, the dying words on the cross, "It is finished!" become the occasion for an alto aria to exclaim:

Der Held aus Juda siegt mit Macht
Und schliesst den Kampf:
"Es ist vollbracht!"

Lo, Judah's Lion wins with might
And now victorious ends the fight:
"It is finished!"

As the act of divine power manifest in Christus Victor, the cross was interpreted as the enactment, in the arena of the cosmos and of world history, of the dramatic battle between God and the enemies of God over the future of humanity.[21] Whatever its theological advantages or disadvantages may have been, this theory of the atonement had the advantage, in relation to the art and music of the Middle Ages, of being able to connect the cross with the resurrection as two parts of a single action. In the liturgical music of the Middle Ages, that connection took the form of setting Good Friday and Easter into the greatest possible contrast: Good Friday was the only day in the church year when the sacrifice of the Mass was not celebrated, because on that day it was the original sacrifice of the cross on Calvary that was to be commemorated.[22] Following a tradition that went back at least to Origen in the first half of the third century,[23] medieval art depicted the crucifixion as having taken place on the very place where the skull of Adam was buried; and the processions and the liturgical drama of the Middle Ages kept the motif of Christus Victor alive even when Latin theology was no longer able to deal with it adequately because of its preoccupation with interpreting the death of Christ as an act of satisfaction.[24]

One of the greatest early poems in the English language, *The Dream of the Rood,* has the tree of the cross describe the "young Hero" who would ascend it for his combat with death and, succumbing in the combat, would nevertheless prevail. Already in the sixth century, the poet Venantius Fortunatus had put the dramatic interpretation of the cross into two Latin poems that were to become a standard part of medieval Lenten music and poetry.[25] One of them he was moved to write when, in 569, the Byzantine emperor Justin II sent a fragment of the true cross to Rhadegund, the Frankish queen. It served as the processional hymn for the arrival of that fragment:

Vexilla regis prodeunt,
Fulget crucis mysterium.

The royal banners forward go,
The cross shines forth with mystic glow.

The other poem made Christus Victor even more explicit:

Pange, lingua, gloriosi proelium certaminis
et super crucis tropaeo dic triumphum nobilem,
qualiter redemptor orbis immolatus vicerit.

Sing, my tongue, the glorious battle,
Sing the ending of the fray.
Now above the cross, the trophy,
Sound the loud triumphant lay;
Tell how Christ, the world's redeemer,
As a victim won the day.

Another ancient literary device that could likewise be adapted to the sign of the cross was the *carmen figuratum,* or figured poem. It combined poetic and visual forms by varying the length of the poetic lines to lay out a prescribed shape, which could then be supplemented with other figures. The cross lent itself very conveniently to such treatment. Of such poems on the cross, the best known was that of the ninth-century scholar and author Rabanus Maurus, *De laudibus sanctae crucis* (The Praises of the Holy Cross), in which the dominant theme celebrated by the "praises" was that of Christus Victor.[26] Most of its verses are cast in the form of square "grids," each formed by a number of letters equal to the number of lines in the text of that verse, a method that permitted crosses with arms of equal length to be superimposed on the text. A further elaboration could then be the arrangement of the traditional symbols for the four evangelists—a man for Matthew, a lion for Mark, an ox for Luke, and an eagle for John (Rev. 4:6–10)—in the form of a cross on the page.

Being the symbol of the power of God, the cross also served as the sign of the wisdom of God, which, as "the foolishness of God" in the Pauline formula, was wiser than any vaunted human wisdom (1 Cor. 1:25). "As the wisdom of the world is foolishness to God," Tertullian had said, "so also the wisdom of God is foolishness in the world's esteem."[27] In seeking to celebrate the cross as wisdom, the Christian writers and artists of the Middle Ages often took pains to revel first in its "foolishness." That was the valid point behind the formula quoted earlier and often misattributed to Tertullian, "I believe it because it is absurd," and especially behind the language of heightened paradox in such statements of Augustine as this:

Rabanus Maurus, *De laudibus sanctae crucis*, ninth century, Vienna Nationalbibliothek, Cod. Vindob. 652, fol. 20v.

The deformity of Christ forms you. If he had not willed to be deformed, you would not have recovered the form which you had lost. Therefore he was deformed when he hung on the cross. But his deformity is our comeliness. In this life, therefore, let us hold fast to the deformed Christ.[28]

From the legislation of Constantine forbidding the continuation of its use as the means of capital punishment, it is clear that the Christians never forgot, in their celebration of the cross as the "royal banner," that it was in the first instance an instrument of torture, a gallows, and therefore, in the language of the New Testament (1 Cor. 1:23), a stumbling block and an offense.[29] It was above all the mystery of the cry of dereliction on the cross, in the words from the psalm, "My God, my God, why hast thou forsaken me?" that evoked their awe and consternation.[30] The beginning of wisdom, therefore, was the acceptance of that mystery: the one whom they believed to be "one in being with the Father" had been—whatever sense anyone might, or might not, be able to make of it all—forsaken by his Father on the cross.

When they spoke of the cross as wisdom, it was often to cite Jesus on the cross as an example of patience and charity even in the midst of suffering: "For to this you have been called, because Christ also suffered for you, leaving you an example, that you should follow in his steps. He committed no sin; no guile was found on his lips. When he was reviled, he did not revile in return; when he suffered, he did not threaten; but he trusted to him who judges justly" (1 Pet. 2:21–23). One of the most widely read books in the Middle Ages was the *Moralia* of Pope Gregory I, composed at the end of the sixth century; it was a massive exposition of the Book of Job, which considered the sufferings of that "Gentile saint" of the Old Testament in such a way as to direct attention through them to the exemplary sufferings of Jesus. An eighth-century writer defined a Christian simply as "one who imitates and follows Christ in all things."[31] And in an epic of seven books about Paradise lost and Paradise regained (a work that poses no threat to the greatness of John Milton, but that embodies much of medieval piety and emotion), which abbot Odo of Cluny composed in the ninth century, Christ, who had come to save the world from pride, "teaches this especially by all the things that he does in utmost humility, saying, 'I am meek, all of you learn this from me.' "[32]

This continuing emphasis on the imitation of Christ's example as the foundation of true wisdom was never, however, the whole of the content of wisdom. Christ was not simply one of the saints to be followed; the wisdom of his cross was more than an example. Deeper reflection on the meaning of the cross led to a consideration of how it was possible to justify the ways of God to man. The very shape of the cross symbolized its comprehension of all the ways of God, the vertical and the horizontal bars representing the height and the breadth of the universe, and their point of convergence where the head of Christ was laid representing the unification and ultimate harmony of all in Christ crucified.[33] For the cross was, on the one hand, the most evident of all proofs for the power of evil in the world; as Pope Gregory the Great reminded a colleague in the midst of his suffering, Jesus had said to his captors in the Garden of Gethsemane, "This is your hour, and the power of darkness."[34] But the cross was at the same time the supreme proof that the will and way of God would eventually prevail, regardless of what human plans might conspire to do. As Joseph had said to his brothers in Egypt, so by the wisdom of God in the cross it could be said now for the whole world: "You meant evil against me; but God meant it for good, to bring it about that many people should be kept alive, as they are today."[35] True wisdom, the wisdom of the cross, consisted in the ability to hold both of these together, neither ignoring the presence and power of evil, as a superficial optimism was tempted to do, nor allowing the presence and power of evil to negate the sovereignty of the one God, as a fatalistic dualism tended to do.[36] Thus the providence of God, which the Christian philosopher Boethius had been able to define in relation to fate (without any reference to the Bible or to Christ) as "the divine type itself, seated in the Supreme Ruler, which disposes all things," became, in the hands of the Christian philosopher-theologian Thomas Aquinas, a part of his examination of the activity of God in relation to the world, an examination whose ultimate foundation was the unmerited love of God.[37]

The wisdom of the cross was, then, the disclosure not only of human morality but of divine love. Placing this at the center of his description of what Christ had done by his life and his death, Peter Abelard, in a sermonic essay entitled "The Cross," emphasized that the love of God in Christ lay beyond "our own power to share in the passion of Jesus by our suffering and to follow him by carrying our own cross."[38] Therefore he insisted that it was unfair to accuse him

of teaching that Christ had only provided an example for our imitation, as though such imitation were possible for the powers of an
unaided human nature to achieve. On the contrary, the fundamental
meaning of the wisdom of the cross was that contained in the words
of Jesus in the Gospel of John: "Greater love has no man than this,
that a man lay down his life for his friends" (John 15:13). Such love
had its ground and origin only in God; but from God it came to
humanity, and it did so through the cross. For "by the faith which
we have concerning Christ, love is increased in us, through the conviction that God in Christ has united our nature to himself and that
by suffering in that nature he has demonstrated to us the supreme
love of which he speaks." Nowhere else but in Jesus and in his cross
was the true nature of love visible. The purpose of the cross, therefore,
was to bring about a change in sinners, to thaw their frozen hearts
with the warmth of the sunshine of divine love. Christ did not die
on the cross to change the mind of God (which, like everything about
God, was unchangeable), as some pious language about the cross
that Abelard was criticizing seemed to imply, but "to reveal the love
[of God] to us or to convince us how much we ought to love him
'who did not spare even his own Son' for us."[39] True love was self-
sacrificing love, and God had demonstrated it uniquely by giving up
his own Son to the death of the cross. This exhibited the authentic
nature of love and the depth of divine love, thus making human love,
even self-sacrificing human love, possible.

Abelard's critics found such language about the wisdom of the cross
not so much incorrect as inadequate. Of course Christ crucified was
an example of patience, everyone would agree; and no one would
deny that the cross of Christ was the supreme revelation of the love
of God, and indeed of the very definition of love, whether divine or
human. The question was whether this language exhausted the wisdom of the cross or whether a more profound consideration of the
cross would lead to some other way of thinking and speaking about
it. That other way found its definitive formulation in one of the most
influential works of medieval thought, *Why God Became Man (Cur deus
homo)* by Anselm of Canterbury. More than any other treatise between
Augustine and the Reformation on any other doctrine of the Christian
faith, Anselm's essay has shaped the outlook not only of Roman
Catholics, but of most Protestants, many of whom have paid him the
ultimate compliment of not even recognizing that their version of the

wisdom of the cross comes from him, but attributing it to the Bible itself.[40]

Anselm's *Why God Became Man* belongs to a consideration of the theme of the "wisdom of the cross" for another reason as well. In it he develops his argument, as he says, "as though Christ did not exist [*remoto Christo*]," claiming to proceed by reason alone. The underlying presupposition of Anselm's thought was the consistency of God and the universe, which God did not violate by arbitrary acts, for such acts would undermine the moral order of the universe itself.[41] Anselm's term for that moral order was "rightness [*rectitudo*]." Rightness consisted in rendering to each a due measure of honor. Although created for participation in such rightness, the human race had refused to give God due honor and had fallen into sin. This God could not simply overlook or forgive by fiat, without thereby violating "rightness" and moral order; such was the demand of divine justice, which Anselm could have defined as "God taking himself seriously." Yet both human wisdom and divine revelation made it clear that God was a God not only of justice, but of mercy, who declared: "I have no pleasure in the death of the wicked, but that the wicked turn from his way and live" (Ezek. 33:11).

Such was the divine dilemma to which the wisdom of the cross provided a resolution, according to Anselm's reasoning. For the justice of God, having pronounced that violation of the moral will was worthy of death, clashed with the mercy of God, which desired life rather than death. The one who was guilty of the sin, man, could not pay the penalty except by being lost forever; the one who wanted to forgive, God, could not do so except by undercutting the moral order of the universe. Only a being able to pay the penalty (by being human) but capable of making a payment that was of infinite worth (by being divine) could simultaneously carry out the imperatives of divine mercy and satisfy the demands of divine justice. The payment, moreover, had to be voluntary, and could not be made by someone who owed it on his own behalf, for that would not avail for others. Therefore God had to become a man, and moreover had to die on the cross, so as to achieve the ends of divine mercy and yet to render satisfaction to divine justice and thus uphold "rightness." His death on the cross made it, one may say, morally possible for God to forgive.

As with the metaphor of Christus Victor, our interest here is not in the theological adequacy or inadequacy of Anselm's doctrine of satisfaction, but in its bearing on the cultural significance of the portrait of Jesus as "Christ crucified." If that metaphor gave expression to the dramatic accents of literature and art, this metaphor embodied themes that came from the structure and the practice of both church and society in the Western Middle Ages. The term *satisfaction* as a description of the act that had taken place on the cross came from the penitential practice and the canon law of the church: a sinner who was truly contrite for his sin, and who confessed that sin and was absolved, nevertheless had to make restitution of what the sin had taken away. So it was also on a cosmic scale with the sin of the entire human race, and the death of Christ on the cross was such an act of restitution and reparation, to which human acts of satisfaction then attached themselves. The ecclesiastical system of satisfaction, moreover, may have contained echoes of civil law as well, in which, according to the ancient Germanic requirement of *wergild*, one was obliged to make good for a crime in accordance with the standing of the injured party in society. Since in this case God was the injured party, only a *wergild* paid by one who was both God and man would have been adequate. By arriving at this definition *remoto Christo*, Anselm could set it forth as a "wisdom of the cross" that was pertinent to the total human situation and that could be perceived by human reason as well as through divine revelation. "Therefore," he said, "we have clearly come to Christ, whom we confess to be both God and man and to have died on our behalf."[42]

At every level of its culture, therefore, medieval society, whether Eastern or Western, was pervaded by the sign of the cross, both literally and figuratively. Thus regardless of the historical credence anyone may be prepared to give the statement of Cyril of Jerusalem quoted earlier, that "the whole world has been filled with pieces of the wood of the cross," we may see in the Middle Ages the fulfillment of another statement, which is apparently more modest but is actually more extravagant, in the first paragraph of the first book written by Cyril's older contemporary, Athanasius of Alexandria, when he was about twenty-two: "The power of the cross of Christ has filled the world."[43]

9

The Monk Who Rules the World

They left everything and followed him.

what does it mean to follow Jesus?

"If any man would come after me, let him deny himself and take up his cross and follow me" (Mark 8:34): these words of Jesus in the Gospels had been, from the very beginning, a summons to the discipline and self-denial of discipleship for all who strove to follow him.[1] But early in the sixth century they became the charter of Western Christian monasticism, which denied the world for the sake of Christ—and then went on to conquer the world in the name of Christ, the Monk who ruled the world.

This saying also shaped the image of Jesus as the perfect Monk, who had the right to issue such a summons because he himself obeyed it unconditionally. For he in a unique sense had denied himself and had taken up his cross. Neither enemy nor friend could succeed in deflecting him from this denial of himself and of the world. When the Tempter offered him "all the kingdoms of the world and the glory of them" (as though these were the Tempter's own to give), he indignantly refused (Matt. 4:8–10); when the spectators of his miracles "were about to come and take him by force to make him king, Jesus withdrew" summarily (John 6:15); and when the prince of the apostles sought to dissuade him from taking up his cross, Jesus rebuked him with some of the harshest words in the Gospels (Matt. 16:23), "Get behind me, Satan!" Although there are passages contrasting his way of life with that of the more ascetic John the Baptist (Luke 7:31–35), the fundamental imperatives of the monastic life were no less fundamental to the portrait of Jesus in all four Gospels. Yet by his denial of the world he had conquered the world and established his everlasting kingdom, in which he invited his followers to share by also denying the world, taking up their own cross, and following him.

Thus the monks began by patterning themselves after Christ. But by the time they were finished they were likewise patterning Christ after themselves. "Christ the Monk" is a motif carried out in many monastic manuscripts and altarpieces of the Middle Ages, as well as in modern adaptations of this monastic tradition. A twentieth-century example is the statue entitled *Pax Christi*, "the Peace of Christ." In it Christ is represented as dressed in the loosely hanging folds of the cowl now associated with the religious habit of a Benedictine monk (although originally there was no special habit for Benedictine monks),[2] and with sandals on his feet. His face is fully bearded, with bushy eyebrows, but otherwise is stylized. He is holding the book of the Gospel in his left hand, engraved with a cross at the center and with four circles for the four evangelists. With his right hand he is pronouncing the *Pax* or benediction. And yet both his garb and the book of the Gospel make it clear that he is at the same time pronouncing the summons to deny the world, take up the cross, and follow him, for only in obedience to that summons can there be the *Pax Christi*. Even for those who do not, or cannot, forsake society to enter the cloister, the summons stands as both a challenge and a promise.

Christian monasticism is, in a sense, older than Christianity, for there were both hermits and monastic communities in the Jewish as well as in the pagan environment where Christianity grew.[3] All three forms of monasticism—pagan, Jewish, and Christian—had their beginnings in the Egyptian desert. In the Egyptian desert dwelled the Therapeutae, a Jewish monastic community described by Philo, the Jewish theologian of Alexandria and contemporary of Jesus, in his treatise *On the Contemplative Life*.[4] So closely did the Therapeutae resemble the early Christian monastic communities that the fourth-century Christian historian Eusebius interpreted Philo's description as the account of a Christian group in the first century and used it to prove the apostolic antiquity of Christian monasticism.[5] And just a century ago some historians were still so struck by the resemblance that they sought to expose Philo's treatise as a Christian forgery from

Pax Christi, sculpture from Saint John's Abbey, Collegeville, Minnesota, author's collection.

the third century, a theory that was "adopted by a majority of scholars."[6] Nowadays everyone accepts the authenticity and the Philonic authorship of *On the Contemplative Life*, which has received further corroboration from the descriptions of Jewish monasticism in the Dead Sea Scrolls. Therefore the treatise stands today as evidence for the existence in Egypt of ascetic impulses that antedate Christian asceticism.

Christian asceticism in Egypt was to find its most abiding expression in the life and work of Saint Antony of Egypt, who lived from the middle of the third century to the middle of the fourth, and in the influential *Life of Antony* prepared after Antony's death by his friend, Athanasius, bishop of Alexandria. The biography, though composed by Athanasius in Greek, seems to have been written at least in part for Western readers, and soon after its appearance it was translated into Latin for them.[7] One of its Western readers, later in that same century, appears to have been Augustine.[8] He went on to establish a monastic community of his own and to write for it a letter that was eventually to become the basis of the so-called *Rule of St. Augustine* (although the *Rule* as such was apparently not written out by Augustine himself but by one of his pupils).[9] Yet by far the most influential document of Western asceticism, and one of the most influential documents of Western civilization, is the *Rule of Saint Benedict of Nursia*, written about a century later. It provides eloquent testimony for an interpretation of monasticism as a way of understanding the meaning of the life and person of Jesus, and therefore for identifying the image of Jesus as the Monk who ruled the world. For it was the central purpose of Benedict's *Rule* to teach novice monks how to "renounce themselves in order to follow Christ," how to "advance in the ways [of Christ] with the Gospel as our guide," and, by persevering in the monastic life, how to "share by patience in the passion of Christ and hereafter deserve to be united with him in his kingdom"—in a single formula, "not to value anything more highly than the love of Christ [*nihil amori Christi praeponere*]."[10] The love of Christ, moreover, modified one of the basic impulses that had originally led to the rise of monasticism. "Deep in the monastic consciousness is solitude," writes a historian of Western asceticism. But, he continues, "you discover to your vexation that deep in the Christian consciousness, ran the axiom that you must receive strangers as though they were Christ, and they really might be Christ." Therefore, quoting the

Gospel (Matt. 25:35), Benedict specified in his *Rule:* "All guests coming
to the monastery shall be received as Christ."[11]

Benedict was, in short, defining the life of the monk as a participation in the life of Christ. All three of the special monastic virtues
that constituted the vows of the monk—poverty, chastity, and obedience—were based on Christ as their model and their embodiment.
In a scene that was to become a commonplace in monastic biographies
throughout the Middle Ages, Antony just happened to be in church
when "the Gospel was being read, and he heard the Lord saying to
the rich man, 'If you would be perfect, go, sell what you possess and
give to the poor, and you will have treasure in heaven; and come,
follow me.' And Antony, as though . . . the passage had been read
on his account, went out immediately from the church and gave the
possessions of his ancestors to the villagers."[12] Similarly, Antony's
successful defense of his chastity was interpreted as his "struggle
against the devil, or rather this victory was the Savior's work in Antony."[13] And the virtue of obedience to the abbot, which was fundamental to Benedict's *Rule,* found its warrant in the position of the
abbot as one who is "esteemed to supply the place of Christ in the
monastery, being called by his name," and in the example of Christ,
who came not to do his own will, but the will of God, who had sent
him.[14] Even when the name of Jesus was not explicitly mentioned,
therefore, the way of life followed by the monk was seen as the *vita
evangelica,* the way of life prescribed by the Gospel, as this had been
first practiced and then enjoined by Christ. Everything the monk did
was, in one way or another, the practical application of the *vita
evangelica.*

Although the ascetic impulse had been present in the Christian
movement from the beginning, having been articulated for example
by the apostle Paul (1 Cor. 7:1–7), it is no coincidence that it should
have risen to prominence, in the life of monks such as Antony, precisely at the time when the church was making its peace with the
Roman empire and with the world. Part of the price the church paid
for that peace was the necessity of coming to terms with those who
could not, or at any rate did not, take its message with utmost seriousness, but who were willing to go along with being Christians much
as they had been willing to go along with being pagans, just as long
as it did not cost them too much. Now that it was easier to be a
nominal Christian than to be a nominal pagan, the multitudes who

began to crowd into the church were not looking to become "athletes" for Christ; but that was precisely the term that Athanasius used to describe Antony the ascetic, who underwent rigorous training in order to be able to compete and win in Christ's contest against the devil, the world, and the flesh.[15] These monastic athletes, as one scholar has put it, "were not only fleeing from the world in every sense of the word, they were fleeing from the worldly church."[16] Interpreted in this way, the monasticism of the fourth and fifth centuries was a protest, in the name of the authentic teaching of Jesus, against an almost inevitable by-product of the Constantinian settlement, the secularization of the church and the lowering of the standards of discipleship set in the Gospels.

Thus there was introduced into the life and teaching of the church a double standard of discipleship, based on a bifurcation of the ethical demands of Jesus into "commandments," which "imply necessity" and which were taken to be binding upon everyone, and "counsels of perfection," which were "left to choice" and which ultimately were binding only upon the monastic athletes.[17] "If you would be perfect," Jesus had said in the Gospel, "go, sell what you possess and give to the poor"; in the same chapter he had also spoken of those "who have made themselves eunuchs for the sake of the kingdom of heaven" (Matt. 19:21, 12). Neither of those was a commandment setting down what was necessary for salvation, but rather a counsel of perfection; and to make that clear, he had explicitly appended the proviso to the statement about renouncing marriage for the sake of the kingdom of heaven: "He who is able to receive this, let him receive it." To be sure, the medieval church defined matrimony as a sacrament, a sacred sign through which the grace of God was communicated, while it never made either celibacy or monastic vows such a sacrament—although holy orders or ordination to the priesthood, which in the West (though not in Byzantium) presupposed celibacy, was one of the seven sacraments. Nevertheless, the Sermon on the Mount demanded "perfection" of its hearers (Matt. 5:48); and the meaning of perfection was increasingly to be sought not in the family life and daily work of the Christian believer within society, but in the life of the monk and the nun, to whom the word *religious* applied in a strict sense as a technical term.

Yet this protest against a secularized church became a means of conquering that church, as well as of conquering the world with which the church had made its peace. The most striking mark of this monastic conquest in the Byzantine church was the requirement of celibacy for the bishop. At councils involving the entire church, including the first such council at Nicea in 325, representatives of the East consistently opposed the efforts of Western churchmen to make celibacy a requirement for all parish clergy: married men could be ordained, although ordained men could not enter into marriage.[18] As late as the fourth century, even some bishops in the East were married and remained married after assuming episcopal office; for example, Gregory of Nazianzus, who came to be known as "the Theologian" and who eventually became patriarch of Constantinople, was the son of Gregory the Elder, bishop of Nazianzus, who was already a priest when his son was born.[19] But beginning in that century, the legislation of the Eastern provinces of the church began to specify that while parish clergy could remain married, bishops had to be celibate. As incorporated into the civil law in the *Code of Justinian*, this legislation barred the father of a family from election to the episcopate, permitting it for a married man without children but only on the condition that he and his wife separate.[20] As the so-called Trullan Synod of the Eastern Church in 692 was to specify, this usually meant that she entered a convent.[21]

In effect, this combination of rules—celibacy required for bishops, but marriage permitted for parish clergy—granted the monks a virtual monopoly on the episcopate of the Eastern churches. A fifteenth-century Greek archbishop was to put it this way:

> [Monasticism] is endowed with such prestige and standing that practically the entire church seems to be governed by monks. Thus if you make diligent inquiry, you will hardly find anyone who has been promoted to the sacred hierarchy from the world [apparently including the secular clergy as part of the "world"]; for this has been allotted to the monks. And you know that if some are appointed to the holy offices [of bishop or patriarch], it is stipulated by the church that they should first put on the monastic habit.[22]

Ordinarily, therefore, a bishop or a patriarch came from the monastic life. If an unmarried parish priest or a widower was chosen for the office, he would, at least since the eighth century, take monastic vows before being consecrated. And when—as in the notorious case of the scholar Photius, who was selected as the patriarch of Constantinople in 858—the choice fell on a layman, the result was that "the monastic world all but unanimously refused allegiance to the new Patriarch."[23]

During the conflicts over the icons in the century preceding Photius's election, Byzantine monks had played an important, indeed eventually a decisive, role, as supporters of images and as agitators, stirring up the populace against the enemies of the images, including the most highly placed enemies, the emperor and the patriarch. Significantly, it was after the iconoclastic controversies that it became a rule for the patriarch-elect or bishop-elect to be a monk, or to become one. Those who had fled from the world that was in the church acquired dominion over the church that was in the world.

The dominant position of the monk in Eastern Orthodoxy continued to make itself visible in the two best-known literary descendants of Eastern Orthodoxy in the nineteenth century, Dostoevsky and Tolstoy. For the figure of Father Zossima in *The Brothers Karamazov* is the embodiment and the advocate of the monastic ideal of Byzantium and Russia, which had reached its climax in the *starets*, or elder:

> How surprised men would be if I were to say that from these meek monks, who yearn for solitary prayer, the salvation of Russia will perhaps come once more! For they are in truth made ready in peace and quiet "for the day and the hour, the month and the year." Meanwhile, in their solitude, *they keep the image of Christ fair and undefiled*, in the purity of God's truth, from the times of the fathers of old, the apostles and the martyrs. And when the time comes they will show it to the tottering creeds of the world. That is a great thought. That star will rise out of the East.[24]

Tolstoy, too, whose rejection of Russian Orthodoxy was far more radical than was Dostoevsky's, nevertheless emerges as the "authentic Greek monk."[25] Thus T. G. Masaryk, who regarded the discourses of Father Zossima in *The Brothers Karamazov* as "the essential portion of the book," went on to observe that Dostoevsky and Tolstoy, in spite of the drastic differences of belief and of ideology between them, had a "similarity of views" in their acceptance of the "ascetic ideal of the monk," which they shared with "their ecclesiastical environment."[26]

In the Latin West, the career of Jesus the Monk in the development of monasticism throughout the Middle Ages is the history of successive movements of reform. Each of them was intent on bringing rejuvenation to the monastic ideal; on achieving, through such a rejuvenation of the monastic ideal, the renewal of the church and the papacy; and on redeeming and purifying medieval society through such a renewal of church and papacy. The intellectual and institutional evolution of these reform movements during the almost exactly one thousand years between Benedict of Nursia (who founded the monastery of Monte Cassino in about 529) and Martin Luther (who entered the monastery of the Augustinian Hermits at Erfurt in 1505) is a story of inestimable importance for the history of Europe and of the world.[27] Over and over, it was the primitive model of Christ as Monk, and of the monk as the imitator of this model, that animated these reform movements. There is in some ways a depressing repetition of pattern, as each monastic reform in its turn protests against decline and stagnation in the monasteries, sets up new administrative and disciplinary structures to reverse the downward trend, prevails for a century or two, and then proves itself vulnerable to the same tendencies of stagnation and decline: Benedict of Aniane in the Carolingian period; Odo of Cluny and the Cluniac reform movement a century or so later; about a century after that the monastic reformation that began at Citeaux, which through the powerful life and Christocentric thought of Saint Bernard spread the Cistercian message throughout Europe; then the friars of the twelfth and thirteenth centuries in their new dedication to renewal; and, in reaction to the Protestant Reformation and under the inspiration of an intensified Christ-mysticism in sixteenth-century Spain, the Society of Jesus.

In each instance, however, it bears noting not only that reform once again became *necessary*, but that reform was once again *possible*, as the transforming power of the ideal represented by the figure of Jesus the Monk reasserted itself and as Jesus returned yet once more "and drove out all who sold and bought in the temple" (Matt. 21:12)—at least temporarily.

Through these reform movements within medieval monasticism, the monastic conquest of the church sought to make itself ever more complete. As early as the beginning of the fourth century, regional synods in Spain were requiring celibacy of parish clergy, and by the end of that century a series of popes and councils had made the requirement universal. It was, however, only several centuries later, when monasticism came into a dominant position within the organizational structure of the Western Church, that it was possible to begin enforcing the requirement with rigor and consistency. That enforcement is associated with the work of Hildebrand, the eleventh-century reformer and monk (although some scholars contend that he was not, technically, a monk) who was the gray eminence of the papacy for a quarter-century before finally becoming pope in his own right in 1073, when he took the name Gregory VII.[28] His training under the influence of the Order of Cluny, with its dedication to rooting out the corruptions that had infected Benedictine monasticism, inspired him in his program for the reform of the church. The Cluniac reform had convinced him that the way to bring the church and the papacy into conformity with the will of Christ was by restoring the monastic life to its original ideals, and then applying those ideals to the life of the church as a whole. A basic component of that program of reform was the strict enforcement of clerical celibacy, which may be defined, in a formula recently adopted by Pope John Paul II, as an imitation of Jesus Christ by which "a priest is a man who lives alone so that others should not be alone."[29] In the social and political setting of the eleventh century, it was a means of securing the economic independence of the priest and bishop from secular authorities—and therefore their dependence on the church and the papacy. Yet it is evident from the letters of Pope Gregory VII that he saw in this administrative reform of the priesthood and the episcopate something far more than this: nothing less than a spiritual renewal of the church's dedication to Christ.

And that new dedication and dependence was in turn a means for the reconquest of the world for Christ. The charter of Christian monasticism, the words of Jesus about denying oneself, taking up the cross, and following him, appear in the Gospel of Matthew just a few verses after the charter of the papacy, the words of Jesus to Peter: "I tell you, you are Peter [*Petros*], and on this rock [*petra*] I will build my church, and the powers of death shall not prevail against it. I will give you the keys of the kingdom of heaven, and whatever you bind on earth shall be bound in heaven, and whatever you loose on earth shall be loosed in heaven" (Matt. 16:18–19). Quoting those words, Gregory VII set the terms for Christ's reconquest of the world and of the empire:

> Now then tell me, are kings an exception to this rule? Do they not also belong to the sheep which the Son of God has entrusted to the blessed Peter? Who, I ask, can regard himself as excluded from the power of Peter in this universal grant of authority to forbid and to allow, except perhaps for someone who declines to bear the yoke of the Lord [Jesus], who subjects himself instead to the burden of the devil, and who refuses to be counted among the sheep of Christ?[30]

And in the famous confrontation with the emperor Henry IV at Canossa in 1077 (where the emperor's tactics may have won the battle, but the pope's strategy probably won the war), Gregory VII, having been addressed by the emperor as "Hildebrand, at present not pope but false monk," reaffirmed the authority of Christ to bind and loose sins by granting absolution to Henry. Hildebrand the monk had conquered not only the church and the papacy, but the empire and the world, in the name of Jesus the Monk.

Perhaps the most remarkable such conquest, however, was to come just over half a century later, when a Cistercian abbot was elected pope as Eugenius III in 1145. He was a disciple of Bernard, the abbot of Clairvaux, celebrated for his fervent mystical devotion to Christ as the Bridegroom of the Soul. To his son in Christ who had now become his father in Christ, Bernard addressed one of the most moving treatises in the history both of medieval monasticism and of the medieval papacy, *On Consideration*.[31] Drawing upon the monastic distinction between the contemplative life and the active life, Bernard admonished his former pupil not to allow the administrative details of the papacy to deflect him from what was primary in the church: the person of Jesus Christ. The pope should not, he urged, become the successor of Constantine, but of Peter. For the monastic ideals of contemplation and study were not irrelevant to the governance of the church, but central to it. The subsequent use of Bernard's treatise by church reformers of every stripe in the fifteenth and sixteenth centuries is a documentation of how the monastic ideal of denying the world for Christ did indeed conquer the world for Christ.[32]

One of the most lasting of monastic conquests for Christ was the work of medieval missions. The Christianization of the barbarian Germanic, Slavic, and Eurasian tribes who came into Europe was almost completely the achievement of monks. As Lowrie J. Daly has said,

> What is most evident in the history of the conversion of the barbaric peoples is the great missionary feat which the monks accomplished. Whether it was a mission sent from Byzantium or one setting out from Rome, whether it came from Celtic Ireland or from the recently converted English lands, the missionaries were monks. The tremendous achievement of winning the Teutonic and Slavic peoples to Christianity and then to civilization was brought about by the continual self-sacrifice and heroic labors of hundreds of monks in all parts of Europe.[33]

Protestant scholars have likewise acknowledged that the name of Jesus Christ would have remained largely unknown in Europe and in the Americas "but for the monks."[34] Thus the "apostles to the Slavs," Saints Cyril and Methodius in the ninth century, were Byzantine monks; and by designating them as "joint patron saints of Europe" together with Saint Benedict, Pope John Paul II has once again recognized the decisive contribution of monks, both Western and Eastern, in the mission and expansion of Christianity. Conversely, the abolition of the monastic orders by the sixteenth-century Reformers must certainly be reckoned as a major reason for the (almost, though not quite) total loss of the missionary imperative in most of Protestantism for more than two centuries.[35]

There is no indication that Benedict envisaged a missionary role for his monks when he founded Monte Cassino. There is likewise nothing in the *Rule*, not even the proviso that a portion of each day be given over to "sacred reading,"[36] that would have led inevitably to another of the great conquests of Benedictine monasticism, its dominance of European scholarship for centuries; for "no judgment either favorable or unfavorable as to the worth of learning or of the study of letters is to be found in the *Rule* of St. Benedict."[37] One may perhaps begin to comprehend how completely Christ the Monk conquered the scholarly world of the Middle Ages by checking, in the standard modern editions, how many works of antiquity even exist for us today only because they were copied by monks in some medieval scriptorium. And that applies to the works not only of the church fathers and Christian saints, but of classical and pagan authors. The almost idolatrous devotion of many medieval monks to scholarship, described in Umberto Eco's *Name of the Rose*, is summarized near the end of that book in the apocalyptic exclamation of the protagonist, William of Baskerville, after a holocaust has destroyed all the books of the abbey: "It was the greatest library in Christendom. Now the Antichrist is truly at hand, because no learning will hinder him any more."[38] Antichrist was restrained by that monastic library because the library represented the claims of Christian discipleship upon the mind, what an essay by Etienne Gilson once called "The Intelligence in the Service of Christ the King."[39]

Dedicated missionaries and scholars though they were, the monks never forgot—or, as we said of the fourth century, did sometimes forget, but were insistently reminded every time they did forget—that their service to this King was above all to be carried out in the worship of the mystery of Christ and in the imitation of the example of Jesus. *Opus Dei*, "the work of God," was and is the Benedictine term for the prayer and the liturgical service of the monastery, not for any of the other activities of the community or the individual monk. Although Benedict himself was a layman and did not found a monastic order consisting of men who were ordained to the priesthood, ordination of monks has become the pattern over and over, with the consequence that the "active life" in missions, parishes, and classrooms threatened to crowd out the "contemplative life." Then it was necessary to point out to monastic communities again what their primary "mission" was: in the formula of the *Rule of Saint Benedict* quoted earlier, "not to value anything more highly than the love of Christ."[40] It was in carrying out that mission that Benedictine monasticism became in the Middle Ages—and would become again in the twentieth century, at such abbeys as Saint John's in the United States, Solesmes in France, and Beuron and Maria Laach in Germany—the principal agent for the renewal and reform of the liturgy, of liturgical art, and of sacred music, with consequences that are evident, since the Second Vatican Council, in every Roman Catholic parish in the world.

Throughout this discussion of Jesus the Monk there has been no explicit reference to the one person in the Middle Ages, indeed in all of history, who most completely figured forth the ideal of the conquest of the world by Christ through the denial of the world for Christ: Saint Francis of Assisi, in whom, as Dante said, "a sunrise broke again upon the world [*nacque al mondo un sole*]."[41] The reason for that omission is that an entire chapter, "The Divine and Human Model," will be devoted to Francis as the *alter Christus*. It is nevertheless with Francis of Assisi as monk that this chapter, too, must close, because it is above all the picture of Saint Francis that everyone must irresistibly call to mind upon hearing the saying of Jesus, "If any man would come after me, let him deny himself and take up his cross and follow me" (Mark 8:34).

10

The Bridegroom of the Soul

My beloved is mine and I am his.

Jesu, Lover of my soul,
Let me to Thy bosom fly,
While the nearer waters roll,
While the tempest still is high.

Charles Wesley wrote this familiar English hymn soon after the conversion of his brother John in 1738, when his heart had been "strangely warmed" through a reading of Martin Luther's "Preface to the Epistle to the Romans." Since then, as the hymnologist John Julian has said, "its popularity increases with its age, and few collections are now found from which it is excluded."[1] Nevertheless, as Julian goes on to note, "the opening stanza of this hymn has given rise to questions which have resulted in more than twenty different readings of the first four lines. The first difficulty is the term *Lover* as applied to our Lord," which various revisions have bowdlerized to "Jesus, Refuge of my soul" or to "Jesus, Saviour of my soul." A few years earlier, Count Nikolaus von Zinzendorf, founder of the Moravian Church at Herrnhut (from which Wesley derived some of his inspiration, perhaps also for this poem), had written the no less popular hymn "Seelenbräutigam, O du Gottes Lamm!"[2]

The case for the legitimacy of calling Jesus "Lover of my soul" or "Bridegroom of the Soul" stands or falls with the legitimacy, both psychological and religious, of the total mystical enterprise, and then with the assessment of the particular subspecies of it usually labeled

"Christ-mysticism."[3] By a working definition, mysticism may be identified as "the immediate experience of oneness with Ultimate Reality."[4] It is, though not a universal phenomenon, at least one that is widely distributed across most of the races of the globe and most of the religions of humanity. In some religions, notably in Hinduism and then in Buddhism as it drew upon its Hindu sources, mysticism stands very close to the center of the normative understanding of the religious tradition that has come from its principal interpreters, so that the distinction between mysticism and religion becomes difficult to identify. In other religions, for example in certain strains of Confucianism, the mystical elements, if any, seem to be considerably more elusive.

In Christianity, Christ-mysticism is what emerged when the figure of Jesus of Nazareth became the object of mystical experience, mystical thought, and mystical language. Standing as he did in the line of succession of the prophets of Israel, Jesus in his own message has sometimes been interpreted as the very antithesis of much that would ordinarily be called mystical. For, in the epigrammatic distinction of Abraham Joshua Heschel, whose scholarship included research both into the prophets of Israel and into the great Jewish mystics, "what is important in mystical acts is that *something happens*, what is important in prophetic acts is that *something is said*."[5] Nevertheless, the prophetic literature of the Hebrew Bible, from the inaugural vision of Isaiah to the apocalyptic raptures of Ezekiel and Daniel, is replete with what sounds very much like mystical experience, mystical thought, and mystical language. In postbiblical Judaism, moreover, these elements have frequently assumed a dominant role.[6]

Although the mystical tradition within Judaism cannot be ignored, it is nonetheless appropriate to observe that the rise of Christ-mysticism was most closely associated not with this tradition, but with what, quoting Gregory Dix, we called earlier "the de-Judaization of Christianity." And it has not been in its Jewish gardens but in its Greek gardens that the church has cultivated the most delicate—and the most dangerous and problematical—flowers of Christ-mysticism. For much of the vocabulary of mysticism, even as employed in devotion to the person of Jesus, has come from Neoplatonic sources.[7] The understanding of the way to a relation with Ultimate Reality as an ascent (*anagōgē*), as well as the classic enumeration of the three steps of that mystical ascent as purification (*katharsis*), illumination (*ellampsis*), and union (*henōsis*), can all be traced to Proclus, the great systematizer of Neoplatonism in the fifth century C.E.; and through him much of it goes back to Plotinus, and ultimately even to Plato himself. Although both Plotinus and Proclus were critics of Christianity, they also owed much to it; and, in turn, their Christian opponents shared much of their Neoplatonism with them, especially these very elements of the mystical vision.

Therefore it did not come as a shock when, in the sixth century, there appeared a corpus of Greek writings that seemed to have blended Christian and Neoplatonic elements almost indiscriminately and that bore the name of Dionysius the Areopagite. This Dionysius was, in the report of the Acts of the Apostles, the only man named together with the women who "joined and believed" at Athens in response to the preaching of the apostle Paul; by the second century he seems to have been known as the first bishop of the Christian church at Athens; in the sixth century he suddenly produced this massive collection of Christian Neoplatonic speculations; and in the ninth century he came to be identified with Saint Denis, patron saint of France and third-century bishop of Paris.[8] Certified as it was with such impressive and all-but-apostolic credentials, the thought of Pseudo-Dionysius was accepted as authentic almost without dissent in the sixth century, and it retained its authoritative position, again almost without dissent, for an entire millennium, not being seriously challenged until the fifteenth and sixteenth centuries.

What place does the person of Jesus occupy in the mystical schema expounded by these pseudonymous writings of Dionysius the Areopagite? The answer is not easy. For while, in the words of a leading historian of Byzantine thought, "undoubtedly Dionysius . . . mentions the name of Jesus Christ and professes his belief in the incarnation," it must be acknowledged that "the structure of his system is perfectly independent of his profession of faith. 'Jesus' is for him . . . 'the principle, the essence . . . of all holiness and of all divine operation,' " but not in any central or decisive sense the son of Mary and the man of Nazareth.[9]

Whatever may have been the status of Jesus in the Christian Neoplatonic mysticism of Pseudo-Dionysius, however, the subsequent history of the Christ-mysticism inspired by it manifests a complex and subtle synthesis between Neoplatonic and biblical elements. The achievement of that synthesis was the historic accomplishment of

Maximus Confessor in the seventh century, who began his work in Constantinople but spent much of his life as an exile in the West.[10] By the time Western Europe had begun to come of age, that is, in the age of Charlemagne in the ninth century, mystical thought and imagery represented that synthesis; and it should be noted that both Maximus Confessor and Pseudo-Dionysius were translated from Greek into Latin during the Carolingian era and were thus made available to the West. From that ninth-century importation into the West of a literature that was Neoplatonic and Christian, Dionysian and Maximian—all at the same time—has come much of the Christ-mysticism of the Middle Ages and since.

Although Pseudo-Dionysius was undoubtedly the source for much of it, a major inspiration of Christ-mysticism was the interpretation of the Song of Songs (or Song of Solomon) as a Christian allegory. As most scholars would agree today, be they Jewish or Roman Catholic or Protestant, the Song was originally a poem celebrating the love between man and woman. But throughout its history it has in fact been read allegorically, and it may even be that it came into the Jewish canon that way. Defending its canonicity at the council of Jamnia in 90 C.E., which stabilized the canon of the Hebrew Bible, the celebrated Rabbi Aqiba declared: "The whole world is not worth the day on which the Song of Songs was given to Israel, for all the Scriptures are holy, but the Song of Songs is the Holy of Holies." From this interpretation comes the rule promulgated by the rabbis: "He who trills his voice in chanting the Song of Songs in the banquet house and treats it as a sort of song has no part in the world to come."[11]

Whether or not the allegorizing of the Song preceded its canonical status within Judaism is a matter of dispute among scholars; but by the time Christian interpreters took on the task of understanding it, it was definitely an allegory, and so it remained until modern times. As Jean Leclercq has noted, the Song of Solomon was "the book which was most read, and most frequently commented [upon] in the medieval cloister," more even than the four Gospels. And while, to use Leclercq's distinction, a scholastic commentary on the book "speaks mostly of God's relations with the entire Church, . . . the monastic commentary's object is rather God's relations with each soul, Christ's presence in it, the spiritual union realized through charity."[12] The earliest full-length Christian commentary on it we have comes from Origen in the third century, followed by that of Gregory of Nyssa in the fourth century; but the greatest commentary comes from Bernard of Clairvaux in the twelfth century, consisting of eighty-six sermons covering the first two chapters and the beginning of the third.[13]

As read through the eyes of Bernard's allegorization, the Song became an account of Jesus as the Bridegroom of the Soul. "By inspiration from above [Solomon] sang the praises of Christ and his church, the grace of holy love, and the sacraments of eternal marriage; and at the same time he gave expression to the deepest desires of the holy soul."[14] And therefore, he declared, *Ipsum saltem hominem homo hominibus loquor*: "As a human being, I speak of him as a human being to other human beings."[15] That declaration took him through all the successive stages of the life and humiliation of Jesus in the Gospels, "all the cares and bitter experiences of my Lord"—his infancy, labors, preaching, prayer, fasting, cross, and burial—as a commentary on the words of the Song (1:13), "My beloved is to me a bag of myrrh."[16] As the myrrh was an allegory for his suffering, so the lilies celebrated in the Song represented the glory and the blessings in "all the events in his life."[17] And so the "kiss" of which the Song speaks is "the man Christ Jesus," whose mouth gives the kiss; and through his human nature humanity receives the kiss.[18] "He it is," Bernard says, "whose speech, living and powerful, is to me a kiss . . . the imparting of joys, the revelation of secrets."[19] The soul responds to the summons of its Bridegroom and follows him into the chamber of his love. His love for the soul, as expressed in the cross, becomes the source and the object of the soul's love for him: "It is this which attracts my affection more sweetly, which requires it more justly, which retains it by closer ties and a more vehement force."[20] The end of this exchange of love between the soul and the Bridegroom of the Soul was the achievement of the union celebrated in the words of the soul-bride (Song of Solomon 2:16):

My beloved is mine and I am his,
he pastures his flock among the lilies.

As an earlier commentary on this verse had put it, "This done, the two are united: God comes to the soul, and the soul in turn unites itself with God. For she says, 'My beloved is mine and I am his, he pastures his flock among the lilies.' [I am] his who has transformed our human nature from the realm of shadowy appearances to that of ultimate truth."[21]

The mystical concept of ascent provided the framework for one of the masterpieces of medieval Christ-mysticism, *The Soul's Journey into God* (*Itinerarium mentis in Deum*) by Bonaventure.[22] The mind begins where it is, among the visible creatures of the sensible world. But as it ponders those creatures, it is filled with awe and reverence and aspires to rise higher. Its contemplation of itself, because of "the mirror of our mind," fills it with a longing for more and higher experience of God.[23] Held back as it is by its sins, it yearns for forgiveness and grace. Blinded as it is by the night of the world, a night both of its own making and of the evil that surrounds it, it strains for the eternal light. By successive stages, then, the mind moves from creature to Creator. To do this, the mystic must recognize not only the power of intellect, but also its limitations, and must acknowledge the primacy of will, of desire, of love. For each of these stages of the mystical ascent or *itinerarium*, according to Bonaventure, the "ladder" of the human nature of Jesus is decisive.[24] We rise from his feet to the wounds in his side to his head, once crowned with thorns and now crowned with glory. In the language of the Song of Songs, Jesus invites the soul to come to him and to abide with him. "If an image is an expressed likeness," Bonaventure argued, then "in Christ, the Son of God, who is the image of the invisible God by nature," humanity could "reach something perfect."[25]

Thus the three stages of mystical ascent—purification, illumination, and union—were easily adaptable to this imagery of Christ as Bridegroom of the Soul. Before the soul could even dare to hope for the object of its longing, it must be purged of its impurity and receive the forgiveness of sins. But it must be purified as well of its preoccupation with its own carnal self, with matter and the things of sense. Because of the inborn carnality of all human beings, "God the Word became flesh [*Verbum caro factum est*]," that is to say, became, quite literally, "carnal." For only thus could he "draw to the saving love of his sacred flesh all the affections of carnal men who were unable to love otherwise than in a carnal manner, and so by degrees to draw them to a pure and spiritual affection."[26] Jesus moved from infancy through to manhood, in order to grant this purification to every age of human life:[27] thus, in a perfect synthesis, Bernard blended the first step of the mystical ascent, purification, with the Gospel narrative of the human life of Jesus.

The second step of the mystical ascent was illumination, and this

too lent itself to the use of the familiar biblical metaphor of Jesus the
Light. This is well exemplified in the words of Julian of Norwich,
whom David Knowles called "in qualities of mind and heart, one of
the most remarkable—perhaps the most remarkable—Englishwoman
of her age."[28] For Julian, "the light is God, our Maker, Father, and
Holy Ghost in Christ Jesus our Saviour."[29] The suffering and cross of
Jesus become a way of overcoming what she called the "darkness of
sin" and the "blindness" of the soul.[30] For, she said, the darkness of
sin "hath no manner of substance nor particle of being" and is not a
reality in its own right but the absence of light, as evil is the absence
of good and does not exist as such. Because the soul does not know
this of itself, it lives in the darkness as though it were real. Only with
the coming of the light that is Jesus and with the revelation of his
suffering, does the power of this unreal darkness become evident and
thereby lose its hold.[31] The natural lights of the natural world lose
their hold as well when his light overwhelms them all. As another
English mystic, Robert Herrick,[32] put it,

> And these mine eyes shall see
> All times, how they
> Are lost i' th' Sea
> Of vast Eternitie.
>
> Where never Moone shall sway
> The Starres; but she,
> And Night, shall be
> Drown'd in one endlesse Day.

And after purification and illumination will come union. Here it
was especially the language of the Gospel of John that lent itself to
the uses of Christ-mysticism. "Abide in me, and I in you," Jesus says
to the disciples in that Gospel (John 15:4); and in his high-priestly
prayer on the night of his betrayal he implored his Father for his
followers, "that they may all be one; even as thou, Father, art in me,
and I in thee, that they also may be in us" (John 17:21). When such
sayings of Jesus were combined with the words of the Song of Songs
quoted earlier, "My Beloved is mine and I am his," the eternal union
between Jesus and the Father in the mystery of the holy and indivisible
Trinity became the ground for what Protestant devotion came to call
the *unio mystica*, "the mystical union" between Bridegroom and bride,
between Christ and the soul.

Without imposing an artificial rigidity upon it, it is even possible to read the *Divine Comedy* of Dante Alighieri as a celebration of these three stages—not, of course, as though its three *cantiche* of *Inferno, Purgatorio, Paradiso* corresponded to purification, illumination, and union, for they do not (since none of the three is possible in hell); but the three themes mark the steps of the soul's ascent, and thus of the poet's ascent. The *Purgatorio*'s recitation, one by one, of the means by which each of the seven mortal sins is purged away through penance and the grace of Christ is an almost clinical analysis of what the mystics meant by the *via purgationis*. Thus in canto 17, with many echoes from Augustine, sin is traced to a disordering, "through excess or through deficiency," of the love with which and for which the human heart was created.[33] Purgation, then, consists in the reordering of love in accordance with the will of God. The illumination sought by Christ-mysticism is proclaimed in the very opening lines of the *Paradiso*:

> La gloria di colui che tutto move
> per l'universo penetra e risplende
> in una parte più e meno altrove.
> Nel ciel che più della sua luce prende
> fu' io.

As John Sinclair translates these words, "The glory of Him who moves all things penetrates the universe and shines in one part more and another less. I was in the heaven that most receives His light." And in the closing canto of the *Paradiso* this "luce etterna che sola in te sidi" overpowers the poet's mind. Leaving behind the claims of intellect, he turns instead, as mystics like Bonaventure had said one must, to the will and to its desire, which bring him to harmony and union with divine Love:

> ma già volgeva il mio disio e 'l velle,
> sì come rota ch' igualmente e mossa,
> l'amor che move il sole e l'altre stelle,

which Sinclair renders: "But now my desire and will, like a wheel that spins with even motion, were revolved by the Love that moves the sun and the other stars."

The themes of purification, illumination, and mystical union with Christ the Bridegroom of the Soul also shaped the depictions of the lives of the saints in both literature and art. Many of these appeared in the *Lives* of female saints, both during the Middle Ages and in the age of Counter-Reformation and Baroque.[34] The thirteenth-century Franciscan saint Margaret of Cortona, "the new Magdalene," is an especially striking example, for her revelations and mystical experiences resulted from a conversion to Christ that followed the tragic death of a young nobleman with whom she had been living for nine years outside the sacrament of matrimony. Her official biography in the *Acts of the Saints* tells us that "she heard Jesus Christ calling her in a sweet manner," and that, "lifted up to the extremes of ecstasy, she lost all consciousness and motion."[35] That experience has been vividly portrayed in Giovanni Lanfranco's *Ecstasy of Saint Margaret of Cortona* from about 1620, in which "the saint, lost in the utter transport of ecstasy and held up by the angels," has her gaze fixed on "Christ upon a throne of clouds, borne by angels."[36] On the basis of the iconography as well as of the hagiography, it does not seem exaggerated to see "more than a suggestion of a sublimated erotic experience" in "the excited movement of the rumpled draperies and the swift, flickering play of light and dark" in Lanfranco's depiction of her "vehement emotions."[37]

The attitude of medieval mystics and thinkers toward these tendencies in Christ-mysticism was by no means naive or uncritical, and many of them sought to curb the potential dangers. The most obvious of these dangers, as evidenced both by Christian art and by Christian mystical commentaries on the Song of Songs, was eroticism. The Song is, after all, still a love poem, and a very explicit love poem at that, even if one reads it as an allegory; and the allegory can easily revert to the very eroticism it is intended to transcend.[38] In many of the poems of the troubadours, as their editor has put, "the worship of the lady suggests a kind of literary mariolatry; but the love celebrated, for all its refinement, was adulterous."[39] Thus lyrics addressed to the Blessed Virgin Mary and lyrics addressed to a sweetheart often became interchangeable, with the devotional lines being used to conceal—or, rather, to conceal and thus to reveal—the poet's true desire for his lady love. The word "soul" is feminine in most of the languages of Europe: *psychē* in Greek, *anima* in Latin and its descendants, *Seele* in German, *dusha* in the Slavic tongues. That made it all the easier to transpose the metaphors about the Bridegroom of the Soul into highly charged sexual images. Nor does the insistence upon the identity of Jesus the Crucified as the Bridegroom protect against such images. Julian was careful, when she declared that "our sensuality is only in the second Person, Christ Jesus," to put such statements into the context of a fully developed doctrine of the Trinity.[40] But in some hymns and prayers addressed to Christ Crucified (for example, those of the Moravian Church at Herrnhut), the wound in his side became the object of a veneration and yearning for union that acquired strikingly sexual overtones. The line from emotion to sentimentality was easy to cross, and so was the line from love as the *agapē* of Christ to love as *erōs* for Christ; it was just as easy to cross both lines at once.

Also easy to cross, especially in the later Middle Ages, was the line separating Christ-mysticism from pantheism.[41] The yearning for union with the divine frequently seemed to become a yearning for the obliteration of the distinction between Creator and creature. Jewish mysticism had frequently addressed this problem, but for Christ-mysticism the temptation would appear to have been even more insidious. For the very orthodoxy invoked against such tendencies has at its center the dogma that in the person of Jesus, as Bonaventure put it, "there is joined the First Principle with the last, . . . the eternal with temporal man."[42] This could be taken to mean that in him the distinction between Creator and creator had been transcended, perhaps even obliterated. The goal and the achievement of Christ-mysticism had been formulated in the words of the New Testament: "We are God's children now; it does not yet appear what we shall be, but we know that when he appears we shall be like him, for we shall see him as he is" (1 John 3:2). That could be interpreted as a promise that the creaturely state of the soul, now captive in the prison of the body, would be sloughed off when the soul would fly "from the alone to the Alone." Various mystics of the fifteenth century were accused, especially by more orthodox mystics, of harboring an eschatology in which everything, having come from God, would be reabsorbed into God.[43]

Likewise implicit in many strains of Christ-mysticism, already in the Middle Ages and even more in Pietist Protestantism, was individualism; in the words of one extreme critic, "in the midst of its struggle for unselfish love, mysticism proves to be the most refined form, the acme of egocentric piety."[44] As we noted earlier, the scholastic tradition of mystical commentaries on the Song of Songs read it as an exposition of the relation between Christ and the church, just as one rabbinical tradition saw it as an allegory of the relation between God and the people of Israel. But in the monastic tradition, it often became instead an allegory of Christ and the individual soul. "My beloved is mine and I am his" became a way of describing my very own private relation to Jesus, and his relation to me, to the exclusion, or at least the diminution, of others. A well-known sentimental religious song has expressed this individualism quite unabashedly:

> I come to the garden alone,
> While the dew is still on the roses.
> And the voice I hear,
> Falling on my ear,
> The Son of God discloses.
> And He walks with me and He talks with me,
> And He tells me I am His own.
> And the joys we share, as we tarry there,
> *None other has ever known.*

Whether sentimental or sublime, Christ-mysticism has repeatedly been the supreme instance of how, within the classic triad of the Good, the True, and the Beautiful, it has been the Beautiful that has been able to portray him the most effectively—and the most seductively. Responding to the deepest yearnings of the human spirit for transcendent meaning and authentic fulfillment, the experience of purification, illumination, and union with the "Beautiful Savior" has succeeded in ennobling every natural sensibility and elevating it into a means of grace: nothing need be profane, everything can be sacramental. But in the process, it sometimes proved all too tempting to lose sight of the Good and the True in the blinding light of the Beautiful, or "to dissolve historical events into religious experience," with the real danger of "not an abandonment of the dogma of the Incarnation of the Son of God, but an underestimation of it," producing "a morass of spiritualizing exposition which has no legitimate ground in historical reality."[45] Cutting itself loose as it does from the strict grammatical sense of the biblical text, a mystical exegesis is especially vulnerable on this count. But as this issue arose in the Christ-mysticism of the High Middle Ages, so it was in the same era that there appeared a new subjectivity that stood the whole issue on its head. For the figure who was the apex of the development of Christ-mysticism was at the same time the fountainhead for a new appreciation of the Historical Jesus of Nazareth as the Divine and Human Model.

11

The Divine and Human Model

*Take my yoke upon you, and learn
from me.*

If a public opinion poll were to ask a representative group of informed and thoughtful people "Which historical figure of the past two thousand years has most fully embodied the life and teachings of Jesus Christ?" the person mentioned most often would certainly be Francis of Assisi.[1] That answer might, if anything, be even more frequent if the people polled were not affiliated with any church. And it is probably also the answer that many of his own contemporaries would have given to such a question—or, at any rate, those who lived within a century or so after him. For in Francis of Assisi the imitation of the life of Jesus and the obedience to his teachings (which were, at least in principle, binding on every believer) attained such a level of fidelity as to earn for him the designation, eventually made official by Pope Pius XI, of "the second Christ [*alter Christus*]."[2]

There was little in his early life to suggest that Giovanni di Bernardone would ever assume any such place in history. Born in 1181 or 1182 to a merchant family in Assisi, he aspired to the rank of knight, and to a chivalric career. Instead, he was converted to be a chevalier of the cross of Christ and the "herald of the great King."[3] The reasons for any conversion are generally more complicated than the later explanations provided by the convert or the convert's followers. So it had been been with Paul and Augustine, and so it was with Francis.

From the documents of the life of Francis, which have been subjected to meticulous study, it is evident that his transformation was not one single moment of blinding incandescence, but a gradual movement away from his old manner of life to a new understanding of himself and of his mission in the world. It is no less evident that at the center of this transformation was the person of the historical Jesus as the Divine and Human Model. At prayer one day, Francis beheld the figure of the crucified Christ, and the vision stayed with him all his life. He understood the vision to mean that Christ was summoning him personally in the words of the Gospel, so familiar through the centuries of monastic history, "If any man would come after me, let him deny himself and take up his cross and follow me" (Matt. 16:24).[4]

That was what Francis did. "From that time on," his official biography reports, he "developed a spirit of poverty, with a deep sense of humility, and an attitude of profound compassion."[5] The summons of Christ to take up the cross and follow him included the specific instruction to "go and repair my house [the church], which is in total disrepair." At first Francis interpreted this command in a literal sense, undertaking to repair several church buildings in the vicinity that needed restoring. But gradually it dawned on him that the church to whose rebuilding Christ had called him was not merely this sanctuary or that parish church, but nothing less than the very church of Christ on earth. The central content of that mission was disclosed to Francis on 24 February 1209—a date marked by his followers every year, along with other anniversaries of his life. On that day Francis perceived the words of Jesus, at the first sending of the twelve apostles during his earthly ministry (as distinct from the sending after the resurrection reported in Matt. 28:19–20), to have been spoken also to him: "Preach as you go, saying, 'The kingdom of heaven is at hand.' Take no gold, nor silver, nor copper in your belts" (Matt. 10:7, 9).[6] Despite the austerity of that requirement—or, to be utterly precise, because of its austerity—Francis almost immediately began to attract followers, who wanted to share this radically evangelical way of life: first there were five, then there were twelve; but by 1221 there were at least three thousand. The small Church of Saint Mary of the Angels (Santa Maria degli Angeli), popularly called Portiuncula, near Assisi, was one of the buildings that Francis restored. It then became, in the words of Bonaventure, "the place where St. Francis founded the Order of Friars

Minor by divine inspiration."[7] (It would also be the place where Francis died on 3 October 1226.)

Like Benedict and other monastic founders throughout the Middle Ages, Francis prepared a monastic rule for his small band of followers. It was approved by Pope Innocent III soon after its composition, thus in 1209 or 1210. The pope's approval was not, however, written down anywhere. Moreover, the first *Rule* itself has not survived in a written form, and we are dependent on various (and sometimes conflicting) accounts of what it contained. It does appear from all accounts that in it Francis avoided lengthy prescriptions of structure or conduct for the order, preferring to "use for the most part the words of the holy Gospel."[8] But that explanation omits the decisive factor in the way the order was organized and governed: the personality of Francis himself. The sources that survive compel us to the conclusion that his must have been an almost magical presence. It was this that drew followers from various regions and from many different walks of life. They came because of the magnetic pull of Francis, and they came because of the authority of the Gospel of Jesus—and these two reasons were one in their eyes. For Francis was devoted to what his first biographer, Thomas of Celano, would call "the humility of the incarnation" of Christ.[9]

That devotion to Christ took the form of a deliberate conformity to the details of his life "in all things." So literal and total was the conformity that followers of Francis in subsequent generations evolved a special literary form, the double biography. The widely read *Parallel Lives* of Plutarch had treated the great men of Greece and of Rome side by side, for example Alexander the Great and Julius Caesar, comparing and contrasting them and drawing a moral lesson. The double biography of Jesus and Francis carried this method several steps further. In both instances, the existing sources—the four Gospels and the original *Lives of Francis*—were quite fragmentary and, as biographies, less than satisfying to a disciple who wanted to know everything possible about the Master. The way to satisfy this yearning was to fill in the gaps from the parallel life; for because Francis had been the most perfect among all the imitators of Christ, it was possible to know more about either one by studying the life of the other.

By far the most dramatic evidence of the parallel between the lives of Jesus and of Francis came near the end of the life of Francis, in

September 1224. As was his wont, he had gone on retreat to Alvernia (La Verna in Italian), a mountain between Arezzo and Florence, where a chapel to Saint Mary of the Angels had been built for the Franciscans a few years earlier. Following the example of Christ in the desert before his temptation (Matt. 4:2), who had in turn followed the example of Moses (Ex. 34:28), Francis spent forty days on the mountain. On or about the feast of the Exaltation of the Cross, 14 September, he had a vision. He beheld an angel, a seraph with six wings (Isa. 6:1–13), and between the wings of the seraph Francis suddenly descried the figure of the crucified Christ. He was overwhelmed by the vision, and then, in the words of his biographer Bonaventure,

> as the vision disappeared, it left his heart ablaze with eagerness and impressed upon his body a miraculous likeness. There and then the marks of nails began to appear in his hands and feet, just as he had seen them in the vision of the Man nailed to the Cross. His hands and feet appeared pierced through the center with nails. . . . His right side seemed as if it had been pierced with a lance and was marked with a livid scar which often bled.[10]

From the statement of the apostle Paul, which the disciples of Francis were to recall, "I bear on my body the marks [Greek, *stigmata*] of Jesus" (Gal. 6:17), these markings were called "stigmata."[11] In the *Paradiso* Dante has Thomas Aquinas—who was a Dominican, not a Franciscan—call them "the final seal [*l'ultimo sigillo*]."[12]

Francis appears to have been the first person in history to have undergone a stigmatization, but there have been other instances of it since, perhaps as many as three hundred having been fairly well authenticated according to one census.[13] Nowadays only the most incurably skeptical would question the historical accuracy of the reports that Francis actually did bear the marks in his limbs and side. At least some of the more recent cases have also been verified fully, sometimes even by physicians who were not themselves believers. Whether such cases are attributable to a miracle or to autosuggestion is, however, quite another question. There are, after all, cases on record of devout Muslims on whose bodies have appeared the marks of the wounds incurred by the prophet Mohammed in battle. It does seem arbitrary to attribute these to autosuggestion and then to claim a miracle in the case of all the Christians who have had a similar experience. Whatever the right answer to this dilemma may be, almost everyone would agree that the stigmatization of Francis represents a special case, in many ways one of a kind. The reason for its uniqueness is, basically, the uniqueness of Francis himself as "the second Christ": if it was fitting for anyone ever to bear in his body the stigmata of the sufferings of Christ, Francis was the one to whom it ought to have happened. He himself, it is clear, did not take the stigmata as an occasion for self-esteem; indeed, he even imitated Christ (Matt. 16:20) in keeping his special identity a secret.[14] Nor did he, for that matter, regard them as the primary form of his imitation of Christ. That place of honor, or of lack of honor, belonged rather to poverty.

Poverty had always been a prominent feature of the kingdom of God as Jesus had perceived it, lived it, and proclaimed it.[15] "Foxes have holes, and birds of the air have nests," the Gospel of Matthew has Jesus say, "but the Son of man has nowhere to lay his head" (Matt. 8:20). With the development of Christian monasticism, as we have noted earlier, poverty became the mark of those athletes of Christ who strove to carry out more fully the counsels of perfection that exceeded the competence of workaday believers out in the world. Together with lifelong chastity and obedience, the vow of poverty was required by the *Rule* of every monastic order—required of the individual, that is, but not necessarily of the order itself. Throughout the Middle Ages that distinction had been a source of difficulty and of corruption. Monasteries acquired vast holdings of land, their libraries expanded, and their treasures of gold and jewels made them rivals of the great noble houses of Europe. Satirists and moralists enjoyed contrasting this with the saying of the disciples in the Gospel, "Lo, we have left everything and followed you" (Mark 10:28).

Francis made a radical break with the ambiguities of this monastic tradition. The second written version of his *Rule* described his followers, in the words of the New Testament, as "strangers and pilgrims in this world," who were detached from the tyrannical hold that material possessions exerted over those who owned them.[16] The ground of this detachment was the literal imitation of the example of Christ and the strict observance of his teaching. Poverty was not merely the absence of property, but was a positive good, "the Queen of the Virtues," because of its identification with Christ and with Mary.[17] One of the early legends of Francis, popularized in several paintings, described him as searching for poverty in the woods, when he met a woman who asked him what he was doing there. Upon his explanation, "I have gone forth to look for poverty, for I have cast away riches, and I will go on seeking and calling her until I meet her," the woman let it be known to him that her name was *Paupertas*, Lady Poverty. He resolved to make her his bride, and the marriage was performed by Christ himself.

It would, however, be a grave error to interpret the Franciscan detachment from material wealth as the expression of a hatred for the material and natural world. Quite the opposite: Francis of Assisi was responsible for the rediscovery of nature, and he introduced into medieval Christianity a positive enjoyment of the natural realm for which there were few precedents. It was, Chesterton has said, as if Europe had first been obliged to pass through a tunnel of purgation, in which it was cleansed of the degrading nature-worship it had inherited from both its classical and its barbarian origins, so that then, in Francis, "man has stripped from his soul the last rag of nature-worship, and can return to nature."[18] In his familiar *Canticle of Brother Sun*, the first significant work in the history of Italian vernacular literature, Francis sang,

> All praise be yours, my Lord, through all that you have made,
> And first my lord Brother Sun,
> Who brings the day.

The moon was his sister, the wind his brother; and, in a stanza said to have been added at his last hour, "Sister Death," too, was a gift from God.[19] Many of the most familiar hymns of praise to God for nature, including the well-known "All Things Bright and Beautiful" by Cecil Frances Alexander, are reworkings of this Franciscan material.

In a paradoxical form, that attitude of regard for the created world is evident also in the way Francis thought and spoke about the human body. At one level, his aspersions on the physical side of human nature went to lengths that almost anyone would find excessive. He mingled ashes with his food to keep it from being too palatable, and he "would hurl himself into a ditch full of ice" when he felt sexually tempted.[20] Yet even these extremes of ascetic self-denial were part of a total view of the world and of life. All of them belonged to his commitment as a follower of Christ and a bearer of the cross, for he reminded himself of the words of the apostle Paul: "Those who belong to Christ Jesus have crucified the flesh with its passions and desires. If we live by the Spirit, let us also walk by the Spirit" (Gal. 5:24–25). The purpose of all these acts of self-mortification was to discipline the body for the sake of a higher goal. There are more than superficial similarities between ascetics like Francis and present-day athletes, who set their faces grimly, strain every muscle, bend every nerve, and punish their bodies—all to win. "They do it to receive a perishable wreath," Francis could have said with the apostle, "but we an imperishable. I pommel my body and subdue it" (1 Cor. 9:25, 27).

A direct corollary of discovering nature and of identifying the sufferings of his body with the sufferings of Christ was a new and deeper awareness of the humanity of Christ, as disclosed in his nativity and in his sufferings. It was, so the followers of Francis believed, as if "the Child Jesus had been forgotten in the hearts of many," but "was brought to life again through his servant St. Francis."[21] If Jesus were now finally to be taken with utmost seriousness, he had to have an authentic image here within human history. Therefore both the beginning of the human life of Jesus Christ and its end found new forms of expression through the life and work of Francis. The celebration of Christmas had come rather late in the development of the Christian calendar, after the other festivals had already been established.[22] Its growing importance was probably related to the increasing emphasis of the fifth and sixth centuries on the true and complete humanity of Jesus. Francis, according to Thomas of Celano, "observed the birthday of the Child Jesus with inexpressible eagerness over all other feasts, saying that it was the feast of feasts."[23] As his principal contribution to the observance of this festival, Francis in 1223 set up a *presepio* or crèche at the Umbrian village of Greccio, where midnight Mass was celebrated on Christmas Eve in that year, with Francis, as the deacon of the Mass, preaching "about the birth of the poor King, whom he called the Baby of Bethlehem in his tender love."[24]

Important though this theme of Franciscan faith in Christ was for the history of art and the history of devotion, the most lasting impression he left in both areas came through his concentration on the Jesus of the cross. He made his own the New Testament determination "to know nothing except Jesus Christ and him crucified" (1 Cor. 2:2). Throughout his life Francis identified himself with the events of the suffering of Christ—so much so that it would probably be possible to reconstruct almost the entire Gospel history of the Passion from the individual scenes in which Francis has been depicted as a participant. "Christ hung upon his Cross, poor and naked and in great pain," Bonaventure writes, "and Francis wanted to be like him in everything."[25] Francis strove to conform himself to Christ and to imitate him perfectly in life and in death. So reciprocal was the relation between the contemporary perception of Francis and the image of Christ that the story of the friar with the stigmata led to a deeper awareness of his Divine and Human Model. The Christ of Francis was not one in whom the presence and power of the divine had anesthetized his human nature so that the pain of the cross left him unaffected. Rather, as the New Testament had said, "we have not a high priest who is unable to sympathize with our weaknesses, but one who in every respect has been tempted as we are, yet without sinning" (Heb. 4:15). The experience of Francis as the second Christ, and specifically of his conformity to the cross, served to endow painting and poetry with a new realism, as they struggled to give form to the fundamental conviction that in the suffering and death of Jesus on the cross both the mystery of divine life and the mystery of human life had become manifest.

Yet it was not conformity to Christ in his crucifixion, but conformity to Christ in his poverty, that proved to be the most controversial item on the Franciscan agenda. Both by his own actions in relation to Lady Poverty and by the language of his instructions to his followers, Francis had made clear his own strict construction of the vow of poverty.[26] Christ, the Virgin Mary, and the apostles had abstained from all ownership of money and property; therefore absolute poverty was essential to the perfection of the Gospel. Following the death of Francis, one party among his followers, which came to be called the Spirituals, insisted that this strict construction was the only acceptable one, since the *Rule* and the *Testament* of Francis were divinely inspired. Combining this insistence with a denunciation of the church and its institutions for its compromises with secularism, some of them came to see themselves as the forerunners of a new "spiritual church," in which the purity of the Gospel, as announced by Francis the "angel with an eternal Gospel" (Rev. 14:6), would be restored and absolute poverty would prevail. The more moderate party among the followers of Francis, sometimes called Conventuals, refrained from posing such a radical antithesis between the institutional church and the "spiritual church." They found their most balanced interpreter in Bonaventure—theologian, philosopher, mystical writer, and Franciscan saint— whose normative reinterpretation of the *Rule* and authorized *Life* of Francis, intended to supplant all the preceding *Lives*, made Franciscanism acceptable to the church and made Bonaventure, as he is often called, the "second founder of the Friars Minor."

This controversy over poverty had some unlooked-for political consequences. Nothing would seem to be more otherworldly and apolitical—indeed, downright idealistic—than the doctrine that because Christ, Mary, and the apostles had practiced total poverty, it was incumbent on the church to obey their example and to abstain from owning anything. Yet by one of those curious ironies with which history, and perhaps especially the history of the church, is fraught, this otherworldly position formed an alliance with various radical secularists of the fourteenth century, who were asserting the authority of the state over against that of the church. The eminent Franciscan philosopher and theologian William of Ockham attacked Pope John XXII for modifying the requirements of the *Rule* and *Testament* of Francis on poverty. During the ensuing conflict, Ockham found political asylum at the court of the Holy Roman Emperor, Louis of Bavaria, who was engaged in a struggle with the papacy over the relative prerogatives of church and state. Taking over some of Ockham's arguments and adapting them in a manner that was in fact quite un-Franciscan and that Ockham, as a devoted churchman and (so he insisted) an orthodox Catholic, had not intended, the emperor and his supporters cast themselves in the role of liberators of the true church from the burdens of property and power. In the process, then, this image of Jesus made a contribution to the formulation of the founding principles and "secular values" of modern political philosophy.[27] This was a long distance indeed from the Francis of the stigmata and his quest for the simplicity of the life set forth in the Gospels.

Even amid the political turbulence of the later Middle Ages, that quest for the authenticity of the Gospels continued to exercise its hold upon human hearts and lives. Although historians have sometimes tended to emphasize the political battles of the time to the exclusion of everything else, the Franciscan dedication to Christ as the Divine and Human Model was in many ways a more universal, as well as a more abiding, theme. Early in the fifteenth century there appeared a book entitled *The Imitation of Christ*, which is said to have achieved a greater circulation than any book in history save the Bible itself. The book, which was anonymous, is generally attributed to the Rhenish mystic Thomas à Kempis, who died in 1471. Whoever the author of the book may have been, the central figure of the book is unquestionably Jesus Christ. "Ever put before thee," it admonished (in a sixteenth-century English translation), "the image of the crucifix"; and it exclaimed, quite in the spirit of Francis: "Would God we had naught else to do, but only to praise our Lord Jesus Christ with all our heart."[28] In its very first chapter it announced, "Let our sovereign study be—in the life of Jesu Christ." That study was the foundation both of an accurate self-knowledge and of a true recognition of the reality of God. Nor was it enough to know the church's doctrines or the sayings of the Bible, "for whoever will understand the words of Christ plainly and in their full savour must study to conform all his life to his life." Once again, the Franciscan glorification of Jesus as the Divine and Human Model was asserting itself as an alternative to the smugness of conventional religion.

And it goes on doing so. During 1926, the seven-hundredth anniversary of the death of Francis, two million pilgrims came to Assisi. Most of them were, of course, devout members of the church, who believed, as had Bonaventure and Francis himself, that loyalty to the institutional church and the imitation of Christ were not at all incompatible, but mutually supportive and ultimately identical. On the other hand, Francis has also become the patron saint, whatever his own original intention may have been, of that growing number in the modern world who become more devoted to Jesus as they become more alienated from the church, who find an irreconcilable conflict betweeen ecclesiastical Christianity and the permanently relevant teaching of the Gospels—or, as they have often phrased it, between the religion *of* Jesus and the religion *about* Jesus. Homes in which no religious pictures or icons appear, where there is not even so much as a cross, will nevertheless often have a plaque, sometimes rather sentimentalized, with the familiar *Prayer of Saint Francis:* "Lord, make me an instrument of your peace." And the interpretation of Francis that has had the widest influence in modern times has not been the official one of the church, based on Bonaventure's, but that of Paul Sabatier, who believed that the original message of Francis had been expurgated by his later disciples, notably Bonaventure, in order to make him acceptable to church authorities.[29] Present-day scholars may be less skeptical than Sabatier was about the orthodox version of Francis, but even they have had to rely on his researches and editions to argue against him.

That ambiguity runs through the entire history of Francis and of

Christ Militant ("Ego sum via, veritas, et vita"), sixth-century mosaic,
The Archiepiscopal Chapel, Ravenna. See p. 7.

Marc Chagall, *The White Crucifixion*, 1938, The Art Institute of Chicago. See p. 20.

Michelangelo, Sistine Chapel ceiling: *Delphica*, 1509–10. See p. 38.

Michelangelo, Sistine Chapel ceiling: *Isaiah*, 1509–10. See p. 38.

Christ Enthroned between the Emperor Constantine IX Monomachus and the Empress Zoe, eleventh-century mosaic, south gallery, Hagia Sophia, Constantinople. See pp. 54–55.

Siegfried Reinhardt, *Light*, 1959, author's collection. See p. 72.

Bust of Christ Pantocrator, sixth-century encaustic icon, The Monastery of Saint Catherine, Sinai. See p. 93.

Giovanni Lanfranco, *The Ecstasy of Saint Margaret of Cortona*, 1618–20, Galleria Pitti, Florence. See p. 130.

Giotto, *The Dream of Pope Innocent III*, 1297, upper basilica of Saint Francis, Assisi. See p. 143.

El Greco, *The Savior*, c. 1610–14, Museo del Greco, Toledo. See p. 148.

Lucas Cranach the Younger, *The Last Supper* (Memorial to Joachim of Anhalt), 1565, Dessau-Mildensee. See p. 162.

William Blake, *Christ Appearing to the Apostles after the Resurrection*, c. 1795, Yale Center for British Art. See p. 198.

the Franciscan spirit. It is the theme of one of the oldest of the innumerable legends about Saint Francis, enshrined in a painting attributed to Giotto. After receiving the revelation of Christ that called him from his former way of life to the life of the Gospel, Francis came to Rome to obtain the pope's sanction, required for founding a new religious order. As has been noted, Francis received this sanction, albeit only orally, in 1209 or 1210. But, at least according to the legend and Giotto's picture, it happened in a remarkable way. Although Pope Innocent III was deeply touched by the sanctity of Francis and by the power of his evangelical commitment, he withheld any response to the application for approval until he could consult the princes of the church, the cardinals. Various members of this body expressed misgivings about Francis, particularly about the evident parallels between the preachments of various heretical movements abroad in the land and his message of radical poverty in obedience to Christ the Divine and Human Model. Others were more positive in their reactions.

Ultimately, of course, the decision was up to the pope himself. The following night Pope Innocent III had a dream (which is why one of the names for Giotto's mural was *The Dream of Pope Innocent III*). Two figures dominate the fresco—Francis on the left and Pope Innocent on the right. The pope, attended by two watchmen, is asleep on a sumptuous canopied bed. He is, even in his sleep, wearing a miter, the symbol of his episcopal office, as well as an elegant cape. Francis, the subject of the pope's dream, is, by contrast, attired in the coarse habit that became his trademark, with a cord about his waist and with bare feet. His left arm is akimbo, but with his right he is holding up a building, the venerable Basilica of Saint John Lateran, which had been donated to the church by Emperor Constantine I and was the seat of authority for the pope as bishop of Rome. The church was tilted at a dangerous angle, and was, in Innocent's dream, in danger of falling over until this young man came to its rescue. On the basis of the vision in the dream, the pope granted the request and confirmed the first *Rule*.

The contrast could not have been more striking. Here was the most powerful man ever to occupy the Throne of Saint Peter, whom the earliest *Life of Francis* called "a famous man, greatly learned, renowned in discourse, burning with zeal for justice in the things that the cause of the Christian faith demanded."[30] He had just turned thirty-seven when he became pope in 1198, and for almost two decades he piloted the Bark of Peter with a sound instinct for just what it needed. A man of blameless character and great eloquence, he had believed before his election that the pope, as the successor of Peter, was the one to whom Christ had addressed his words: "On this rock I will build my church" (Matt. 16:18). After his election, he strove to live up to what he had believed about the papacy, and he succeeded. The pope, he believed, was "less than God but more than man," mediating between them. At the greatest church council of the Middle Ages, held in 1215 at the Lateran, he was hailed as "lord of the world [*dominus mundi*]." The continuity of the church, without which, historically speaking, there would be no Gospel—and no Francis of Assisi—and the presence and power of Christ became visible, almost tangible, in the pontificate of Pope Innocent III. And on the other side of Giotto's picture is the simple figure of the young man from Assisi, in his late twenties at the time. His eyes are lifted to heaven, and seemingly without any strain he has taken on one shoulder the entire weight of the Lateran—and of the world. Giotto's painting and subsequent history join to compel the question, though not to answer it:

Now which of the two was truly the "Vicar of Christ"?

12

The Universal Man

As the truth is in Jesus, be re-
newed in the spirit of your minds,
and put on the new nature.

"The Discovery of the World and of Man" and "The Development of the Individual" were two major themes of
the Renaissance of the fourteenth, fifteenth, and sixteenth
centuries, as formulated by its most celebrated modern
interpreter, Jacob Burckhardt:

In the Middle Ages both sides of human consciousness—that which was
turned within as that which was turned without—lay dreaming or half awake
beneath a common veil. The veil was woven of faith, illusion, and childish
prepossession, through which the world and history were seen clad in strange
hues. . . . [But in the Italian Renaissance] the *subjective* side . . . asserted itself
. . . : man became a spiritual *individual,* and recognized himself as such. Observe the expressions *uomo singolare* and *uomo unico* for the higher and highest
stages of individual development.[1]

Burckhardt does not say that this change was due to a rejection of
the authority of the figure of Jesus; interestingly, he just does not
refer in this context to the figure of Jesus at all.

Ironically, however, the very concept and name Renaissance (*ri-
nascimento*), whatever the ultimate origins of the idea may have been,
had come into the vocabulary of European civilization principally
through the teachings of Jesus.[2] "Truly, truly, I say to you," the
Gospel of John has him declare to Nicodemus, "unless one is born

anew [*renatus* in the Vulgate], he cannot see the kingdom of God" (John 3:3). And near the end of the Book of Revelation attributed to the same apostle John, Jesus, "who sat upon the throne, said, 'Behold, I make all things new' " (Rev. 21:5). Although they often set the "new birth" of the Renaissance into contrast with the supposed "Gothic" or barbarian decadence of the Middle Ages, the humanists of the Renaissance yielded to no exponent of medieval theology in their admiration for Jesus and their devotion to him. In fact, Erasmus of Rotterdam, citing the passage from the Gospel of John just quoted, made the identification of the Renaissance with the person of Jesus altogether explicit. "What else is the philosophy of Christ," he asked in the preface to his edition of the Greek New Testament in 1516, "which He Himself calls a 'rebirth [*renascentia*],' than the restoration of [human] nature to the original goodness of its creation?"[3] Dante's *Vita Nuova* may be seen as sounding the same theme of renewal and "new life." Therefore, in the apt formula of Konrad Burdach, "the Renaissance, which establishes a new concept of humanity, of art, and of literary and scholarly life," arises "not in opposition to the Christian religion," as so much of modern historiography since Burckhardt has imagined, "but out of the full vitality of a religious revival."[4] Hence the very title Universal Man, which has come to be known, even in popular magazines, as the slogan of the Renaissance,[5] and which the humanists not only employed but strove to embody, may well serve as a summary of the place that Renaissance thought and art accorded to Jesus, as the only one who could be called *uomo singolare* and *uomo unico* in the strict and total sense. For "the Universal Man" had been his title in the Christian tradition all along,[6] and in the Renaissance it came into its own.

The effort to see the Renaissance as a naturalistic revolt against such traditional and medieval ideas of Christ as the doctrine of the incarnation and the concept of the two natures, divine and human, seems to have become almost canonical among certain nineteenth-century historians of Renaissance art. For the origins of this interpretation, as for so much of the origins of both the history of ideas and the history of aesthetics in the nineteenth century, we must look to Goethe. His essay on Leonardo da Vinci's *Last Supper*, written in German in 1817 and published in English translation only four years later, characterized Leonardo's portrayal of Jesus as "the boldest attempt to adhere to nature, while, at the same time, the object is supernatural," with the result that "the majesty, the uncontrolled will, the power and might of the Deity" were not expressed.[7] In his widely influential book *The Renaissance. Studies in Art and Poetry*, Walter Pater, acknowledging his debt to Goethe, set forth his own conclusion that "though [Leonardo da Vinci] handles sacred subjects continually, he is the most profane of painters." Therefore Pater sought to interpret Leonardo's *Last Supper*, dealing though it did with one of the most sacred of subjects, as a painting in which the institution of the Lord's Supper by Jesus on the night in which he was betrayed provided "merely the pretext for a kind of work which carries one altogether beyond the range of its conventional associations." The inspiration of the work was an aestheticist naturalism far removed from the themes conventionally associated with the image of Jesus:

> Here was another effort to lift a given subject out of the range of its traditional associations. Strange, after all the mystic developments of the middle age, was the effort to see the Eucharist, not as the pale Host of the altar, but as one taking leave of his friends. . . . Vasari pretends that the central head was never finished. But finished or unfinished, or owing part of its effect to a mellowing decay, the head of Jesus does but consummate the sentiment of the whole company—ghosts through which you see the wall, faint as the shadows of the leaves upon the wall on autumn afternoons. This figure is but the faintest, the most spectral of them all.[8]

More recently, however, historians of Renaissance art have come to interpret this supposed naturalism more subtly and more profoundly. Thus a monograph by the art historian Leo Steinberg on how Renaissance painters portrayed the sexuality of Jesus has taken a subject that could have lent itself to sensationalism, but has instead related this theme to the central motifs in the doctrine of the incarnation as "the centrum of Christian orthodoxy." It argues that unlike many of its predecessors in Christian history, "Renaissance culture not only advanced an incarnational theology (as the Greek Church had also done), but evolved representational modes adequate to its expression." Therefore, it concludes, "we may take Renaissance art to be the first and last phase of Christian art that can claim full Christian orthodoxy."[9] Although it would be possible to take issue with this interpretation of the theological implications of the Byzantine icons, the case is far stronger for this interpretation of the Renaissance Christil, an interpretation in which art history and intellectual history come together.

One of the many Renaissance portraits of Jesus as Universal Man to combine magnificently several of the motifs and "images" that we have been discussing throughout this book is *The Savior* by Kyriakos Theotokopoulos, whom posterity calls El Greco. The model for the portrait was a Jewish young man in Toledo, for El Greco wanted to take seriously the Jewishness of Jesus. It is clear that he had learned the style of the portrait from the masters of the Italian Renaissance, specifically from his teacher Titian. But what sets this portrait apart from many others of the period is another quality: "The light of his paintings almost has nothing in common with daylight. It represents a type of 'supernatural explosion of color,' as René Huyghe describes it. . . . It has been described as 'a kind of spiritual experience emanating from the eye of the faith-filled soul of El Greco.' "[10] This Jesus is indeed a historical figure, and he is indeed Jewish; but he has been pictured in a way that also stands in the tradition of the Byzantine icon, as the Jesus of the Transfiguration. And all of this has been suffused with the spirit of the Spanish Christ-mysticism of the sixteenth century, in whose atmosphere El Greco worked. The result is a remarkable synthesis of several artistic, mystical, and theological traditions—a synthesis that makes its presence felt throughout the Renaissance perspective on Jesus as the Universal Man.

A representative spokesman for this Renaissance view of the Universal Man was Donato Acciaiuoli, a humanist and statesman who belonged to one of the most eminent families of Florence. In a sermon preached on 13 April 1468, dealing with the same subject as da Vinci's painting, he set his exposition of the Eucharist apart from the "many subtle investigations which the [scholastic] doctors have made concerning its matter, its form, its efficient cause and its final cause, and how the substance of the bread and the wine is transformed into the most true body of Christ." But it would be a serious anachronism to read such a polemic against the philosophical theology of scholasticism as a rejection of the orthodox doctrine of the incarnation of the Son of God in the man Jesus. On the contrary, Acciaiuoli reaffirmed that doctrine with sincerity and vigor even as he broke with the scholastic version (or, as he would have it, distortion and unnecessary complication) of it:

> Our Savior Jesus Christ, my beloved fathers, having so greatly benefited human nature by first assuming this flesh of ours and then through all the course of his life in teaching the people and spreading his doctrines among

readers, in freeing the weak and raising the dead, in taking away sins and in most holy works, gave himself as a most singular example of every kind of virtue.

Therefore the Eucharist was for Donato, as Trinkaus has put it, "the most important mode by which Christ reinforces faith in his doctrine, as it is a commemoration of the divine Incarnation by which and through which Christ became the great teacher of mankind." In his reverence for Jesus as "the teacher and exemplar," Donato Acciaiuoli joined himself to the Franciscan revival (or, perhaps better, "renaissance") of the Gospel portrait and to the Jesus who had been celebrated earlier in the same century by the *Imitation of Christ*. It is, then, "difficult and essentially arbitrary either to separate the humanists' views of human nature from their peculiar approaches to religion [above all, their picture of Jesus], or on the other hand to do the reverse."[11]

Dante Alighieri, whose place in the history of Christ-mysticism has been examined earlier, occupies an important place also in the history of the Renaissance image of Jesus. Champions of the Middle Ages and of the Renaissance may dispute over which of them has a more proper claim upon Dante; but for our present purposes it is necessary only to point out, as Jacob Burckhardt himself acknowledged, that "in all essential points" of his systematic interpretation of the Italian Renaissance "the first witness to be called is Dante," perhaps most eloquently in Burckhardt's exposition of the very ideal of *l'uomo universale*, the Universal Man.[12] Yet to a degree that Burckhardt did not adequately appreciate, Dante's inspiration for that ideal, as well as for both his poetry and his politics, was inseparable from the person of Jesus.

That inspiration makes its presence felt in the very title of Dante's first book, the *Vita Nuova*. The "new life" of which it speaks refers in the first instance to Dante's own youth, as the poet's use of the very same phrase in the *Divine Comedy* to describe his early years indicates.[13] But reducing its meaning to that alone does much less than complete justice to the phrase itself and to the argument of the work, with its subtle images and its multilayered plays on words. Thus in the *Vita Nuova* Dante introduces a young woman named Giovanna (Joan), the sweetheart of his "first friend," Guido Cavalcanti; her nickname was Primavera (Spring). But Dante is told here that Giovanna is called Primavera because, as the forerunner of Be-

atrice, "prima verrà [she will come first]." In a sense, then, her name
is derived from her nickname, and she is called Giovanna in honor
of John the Baptist, who likewise came first as the one sent to announce the coming of Christ.[14] Beatrice herself, therefore, as the very
incarnation of love, is, in Singleton's phrase, "an analogy and a metaphor of Christ."[15]

If that is what Beatrice is "already in the *Vita Nuova*," then she
becomes "in the *Commedia*, a symbol of theology, learning illuminated
by grace, even the Christian faith."[16] Near the end of the *Purgatorio*
she promises Dante that he will be "with me forever a citizen of that
Rome where Christ is a 'Roman,' " that is, of Paradise.[17] The *Paradiso*
is throughout a panorama of how that promise is to be fulfilled. As
the poet's "sweet and dear guide,"[18] Beatrice has the function of
leading him—and the reader—to Christ and to the Mother of Christ,
who are always inseparable and sometimes well-nigh indistinguish-
able. In the words of Beatrice to Dante that follow, Mary is "the rose
in which the divine Word was made flesh," but like all the other
flowers in the divine "garden," she, too, "blossoms under the rays
of Christ," not finally of her own powers.[19] She is "the fair flower
which I always invoke morning and evening," to whom angelic love
itself sings that it will continue to "circle around you, Lady of Heaven,
until you follow your Son and make even the highest sphere more
divine by entering it."[20] It is amid the strains of a hymn to the Queen
of Heaven, the *Regina coeli*, that Peter and the church triumphant
receive their "treasure" of "victory, under the exalted Son of God and
of Mary."[21] On the basis of such scenes as the final three cantos,
describing the Empyrean with Bernard of Clairvaux and the Virgin,
some eminent Dante scholars have suggested that the focus of the
Paradiso is on Mary rather than on Christ, who seems by the end of
the poem to have become so transcendent as to be inaccessible. After
having given "Beatrice a place in the objective process of salvation
. . ., an element which disrupts the doctrine of the church," Dante
appears to have fused Beatrice and Mary into a prototype of Goethe's
"eternal Feminine" and a substitute for Jesus Christ.[22] But if that is
the impression of some scholars, it was not the intention of the poet.[23]
For even while he is transported by the rhapsody to Mary, he describes her countenance as "the face that most resembles Christ."[24]
With her eyes she directs the poet's attention to "the eternal Light,"
by which she too is illumined, and to eternal Love, by which she too

has been saved and sustained, the Light and the Love that have come solely through Jesus, the Universal Man, the Son of God and the Son of Mary.[25]

Dante also drew on the figure of Jesus for his political theory. He was, as a Ghibelline, a supporter of the rights of the empire against the temporal claims of the papacy. The theological justification for those claims was the commission of Christ to Peter, granting him the keys of the kingdom of heaven, so that "whatever [*quodcunque*]" he would bind and loose here on earth, be it in church or state, would also be bound and loosed in heaven (Matt. 16:18–19). But Dante insisted that Christ had not intended this "whatever" to be taken "absolutely" and indiscriminately, but had meant that it "must be related to a particular class of things," namely, the authority to grant absolution and forgiveness.[26] Although the biblical doctrine of the creation of a single humanity in the image of God implied that a single world government would be best, this did not mean that the papacy should have both spiritual and temporal authority or that it should function as such a world government.[27] For man was created for a twofold goal: "the bliss of this life . . . and the bliss of eternal life."[28] The bliss of eternal life was the gift and achievement of Christ and of his suffering; but in the very midst of the suffering the same Christ had declared to Pontius Pilate: "My kingship is not of this world" (John 18:36).

According to Dante, this was not to be taken, as a later secularism would contend, "as if Christ, who is God, were not lord of this world"; rather, it meant that "as an example for the Church," he would not exercise dominion over the kingdoms of this world.[29] It would, then, be fair to Dante's position in the *De Monarchia* to say that what was at issue for him was the relation between two sets of sayings of Jesus, both of them authoritative, and the familiar hermeneutical problem of deciding which sayings were to be interpreted in the light of which. It was, he was arguing, most faithful to the will of God as articulated in the life and teachings of Jesus to let the church be the church and the empire be the empire, and not to subordinate the essential character of either one to the other. Moreover, as Kantorowicz has tellingly observed,

> A duality of goals does not necessarily imply a conflict of loyalties or even an antithesis. There is no antithesis of "human" versus "Christian" in the work of Dante, who wrote as a Christian and addressed himself to a Chris-

tian society, and who, in the last passage of the *Monarchy*, said clearly that "after a certain fashion [*quodammodo*] this mortal blessedness is ordained toward an immortal blessedness."[30]

For that, too, his highest authority was the revelation that had come in Jesus Christ.

Nevertheless, most Renaissance scholars would probably concur in the judgment that "if we try to assess the positive contributions of humanist scholarship to Renaissance theology, we must emphasize above all their achievements in what might be called sacred philology."[31] "Sacred philology" in this sense participated in the more general "revival of antiquity," as Burckhardt calls it, in which the humanists of the Renaissance were caught up. "Had it not been for the enthusiasm of a few collectors of that age," Burckhardt suggests, "who shrank from no effort or privation in their researches, we should certainly possess only a small part of the literature, especially of the Greeks, which is now in our hands."[32] The zeal for the literature of classical antiquity was more than nostalgia or acquisitiveness, though both of these were undoubtedly present. It was grounded in the conviction that a major source for the superficiality and the superstition of the present was an ignorance of the classical past and that therefore a recovery of that past would serve as an antidote. "Ad fontes!" was the watchword: "Back to the sources!"

Although these classical "sources" were in both Latin and Greek, with Cicero being perhaps the most important single author, the great innovation introduced by Renaissance humanism was the new interest in the study of Greek. Petrarch received a manuscript of Homer from Nicholas Sygeros of Constantinople and cherished it, but never learned to read it, so that it was, he said in a letter to the donor, "certainly a pleasure, though no advantage, to regard the Greeks in their own dress."[33] This touching story may serve as a reminder that the *Iliad* and the *Odyssey* had been largely unknown in the Middle Ages, except as background for the *Aeneid*. But when refugee Greek scholars came to the West from Constantinople, clutching manuscripts of their classics, they helped to stimulate a knowledge of Greek authors.[34] The list of such authors, however, included not only the classical Greek philosophers, poets, and dramatists, but the Greek church fathers and hymnographers.[35] Above all, the one Greek text that everyone was eager to learn to read was the Greek New Testament. For just as the Greek of Homer and Plato had been largely unknown through much of the Middle Ages, so also most of the leading medieval theologians and preachers had not been able to handle the original text of the New Testament with any authority. Even Augustine's knowledge of biblical and patristic Greek was shaky. Exegetical genius though he was, he could not draw independent philological judgments of his own or make use of the Greek Christian scholars for whom the original language of the New Testament had been their mother tongue. This circumstance was to result in "a 'splendid isolation' that would have momentous consequences for the culture of the Latin church."[36] Thomas Aquinas, too, was dependent on the Latin translation of the Bible, and sometimes on its mistranslations, for his interpretations. For example, he followed his predecessors in applying the words of Ephesians 5:32 about marriage, "This is a great mystery," translated in the Vulgate as "Sacramentum hoc magnum est," as a biblical proof text that matrimony was one of the seven sacraments of the church.[37]

The reappropriation of the Greek New Testament by Western scholars in the fifteenth and sixteenth centuries brought on a systematic philological review of all such proof texts. The pioneer in this campaign was the Italian scholar Lorenzo Valla, who was "among the most original and influential Italian Humanists."[38] In a satirical *Encomium of Saint Thomas Aquinas*, he called for a return from scholasticism to an authentic Christian antiquity represented by Augustine and other church fathers, but above all by the New Testament.[39] Valla's *Annotations on the New Testament* was not a comprehensive and systematic commentary on the Gospels and epistles, but consisted of intermittent grammatical and philological notes on various texts. He attacked the simplistic equation of the original Greek word *mystērion* with the Latin *sacramentum*, for the term did not refer to the ritual actions of the church instituted by Christ, but to the truth that God had previously hidden and had now revealed in Christ. Similarly, the summons with which the preaching of Jesus began did not say, as medieval misreading had supposed, "Do penance [*Poenitentiam agite*]," but "Repent," that is, "Turn your mind around"; and the salutation of the angel to the Virgin Mary, *kecharitōmenē* in Greek, did not mean "full of grace [*gratia plena*]," as the Ave Maria had it, but "highly favored."[40]

Although Valla's application of sacred philology to the Greek texts of the Gospels evoked controversy in his own time and, together with the Reformers' use of such philology, helped to provoke the Council of Trent into making the Latin Vulgate the official version of the Bible, it was not Valla, but his even more celebrated colleague Erasmus of Rotterdam, who elevated the recovery of the original message of Jesus, on the basis of the Greek sources, into a comprehensive program of church reform and theological renaissance. He did so in 1505, when he published Valla's *Annotations on the New Testament*, with a preface of his own that has been called "Erasmus' Inaugural Lecture as Professor-at-large to Christendom."[41] Theology, he insisted, had to be founded on grammar. "Ad fontes!" indeed: a knowledge of the New Testament in the original Greek was essential for an interpreter of the message of the Gospels. The original Greek New Testament had to be freed of the mistranslations in the Vulgate, the misinterpretations imposed upon it by later theologians, and the corruptions of the text introduced by copyists. To that end Erasmus in 1516 published his most important book, *Novum instrumentum*, the first printed edition of the Greek New Testament to be issued, which revolutionized forever the image of Jesus in Western culture. Its most obvious impact may have come through the Protestant Reformation, but the study of the Greek New Testament was by no means confined to Protestants. For not only Roman Catholic humanists like Valla and Erasmus, but the dominant Roman Catholic churchman of Spain, Cardinal Ximénez, archbishop of Toledo and founder of the University of Alcalá, fostered such study, producing a sumptuous edition of the Bible in several languages, the *Complutensian Polyglot* in six volumes; its New Testament was printed already in 1514, two years before the *Novum instrumentum*, but it did not circulate until after that of Erasmus.

Although Erasmus is best remembered for his Greek New Testament and for his works of satire, particularly *The Praise of Folly* of 1509, he was, also in these works, engaged in his lifelong vocation: to use sacred philology as a means of discovering, and of recovering, *philosophia Christi*, "the philosophy of Christ." In *The Praise of Folly* he called upon the popes to take seriously their title as "vicars of Christ" and "to imitate His poverty, tasks, teachings, crosses, and indifference to comfort"; for it was obvious from a reading of the Gospels that "the entire teaching of Christ inculcates nothing but meekness, tolerance, and disregard for one's own life."[42] Most eloquently of all, he expounded this *philosophia Christi* in his *Enchiridion militis Christiani*

(Handbook of the Christian Knight), published in 1503. Its central theme was: "Make Christ the only goal of your life. Dedicate to Him all your enthusiasm, all your effort, your leisure as well as your business. And don't look upon Christ as a mere word, as an empty expression, but rather as charity, simplicity, patience and purity—in short, in terms of everything he has taught us." For Jesus was "the sole archetype of godliness."[43]

The authentic Jesus, then, was the Jesus of the Gospels, whose life and teachings were to be studied on the basis of the original sources in the Greek New Testament. In the conclusion of the *Enchiridion* Erasmus defended the combination of *philosophia Christi* and Christian humanism against "certain detractors who think that true religion has nothing to do with the humanities [*bonae literae*]" or with "a knowledge of Greek and Latin."[44] But it was precisely through the humanistic study of the Gospels, using the same literary methods and philological scholarship that Erasmus's fellow humanists were applying to other texts of classical antiquity, that the reader could discover the meaning of the Gospels and thus learn the "words of life" spoken by Jesus, which "flowed from a soul that was never for a moment separated from the divinity and that alone restores us to everlasting life."[45] The Gospels were the key to knowing Jesus. At the same time, however, the converse also applied: Jesus was the key to knowing the meaning of the Gospels and of the Bible as a whole. Instead of "remaining content with the bare letter," even if this was textually sound and grammatically correct, the reader should "pass on to the more profound mysteries," which were available only through the person of Jesus. For "no one knows the Son except the Father and any one to whom the Son chooses to reveal him."[46]

In his effort to disentangle the person and message of Jesus from the complications that the scholastic theologians had imposed upon them, Erasmus harked back to the "Christian Socratism" of various early Christian writers. The maxim "Know thyself" was one that ancient classical writers had "believed to have been sent from heaven," but a Christian was to accept it because it agreed with the message of the Bible and the teaching of Jesus. As "the author of wisdom and Himself Wisdom in person, the true Light, who alone shatters the night of earthly folly," Jesus Christ had taught that "the crown of wisdom is that you know yourself."[47] His message, therefore, was a revelation from God himself, without which there would be "folly" and darkness. And yet Erasmus could also make the appeal: "The way of Christ is the most sensible and logical one to follow. . . . When you abandon the world for Christ, you do not give up anything. Rather, you exchange it for something far better. You change silver into gold, and rocks into precious gems."[48] And, in keeping with this Christian Socratism, he could "recommend the Platonists most highly" among all the classics, because "not only their ideas but their very mode of expression approaches that of the Gospels."[49] For that harmony with the best that had been thought and known everywhere was what made Jesus the Universal Man.

This apparent equation of the *philosophia Christi* with pagan philosophy persuaded Martin Luther that Erasmus was not serious in his espousal of the biblical message, but was essentially a skeptic, "an Epicurus," and a moralist. Because so many historians of the Reformation and historians of Christian doctrine have been the products of the Lutheran heritage, they have tended to follow Luther in this judgment. But in doing so they have not only misread Erasmus but borne false witness against him. As one interpreter of Erasmus has well said, "the fool's part, mistaken for pagan frivolity in serious times, has betrayed Erasmus."[50] For when he died on 12 July 1536, Erasmus, faithful to the end to the *philosophia Christi* and to the church founded by Jesus the Universal Man—not as the church was, but as Jesus had intended it to be—received the sacraments of that church, the chrism of anointing and the food for his final journey in the *viaticum,* and died with a prayer to Jesus on his lips, which he repeated over and over: "*O Jesu misericordia,* O Jesus, have mercy; *Domine libera me,* Lord deliver me."[51]

13

The Mirror of the Eternal

He who has seen me has seen the Father.

 The Reformation broke out as an appeal from the authority of the institutional church to the authority of the historical Jesus. On 31 October 1517 Martin Luther, Augustinian friar and doctor of theology at the University of Wittenberg, posted ninety-five theses, challenging all comers to debate. The first of those theses read: "In the Name of Our Lord Jesus Christ. Amen. When our Lord and Master Jesus Christ said, 'Repent [*Poenitentiam agite*]' (Matt. 4:17), he willed the entire life of believers to be one of repentance."[1] This appeal to the message of Jesus in the Gospels was a direct application of the sacred philology and New Testament scholarship of Christian humanists like Valla and Erasmus to the sacramental life of the church. Before his life had ended, Martin Luther in his work as a theologian and interpreter of the Bible had ranged over not only the Gospels but most of the books of Old and New Testament alike. In particular, it was the epistles of the apostle Paul that became his focus, especially in the debates over the doctrine of justification by faith. Luther became the Reformer when, as he described in the *apologia pro vita sua* written just a year before his death, he was pondering the meaning of Paul's words in Romans 1:17: "In [the gospel] the righteousness of God is revealed through faith for faith; as it is written, 'The righteous shall live by faith.' "[2] He was deeply puzzled over the question of how it could be the

content of the gospel of Christ, as "good news," that God was a
righteous judge, rewarding the good and punishing the evil: Did Jesus
really have to come to reveal that terrifying message? Then he suddenly broke through to the insight that the "righteousness of God"
of which Paul spoke in this text was not the righteousness by which
God *was* righteous in himself (passive righteousness), but the righteousness by which, for the sake of Jesus Christ, God *made* sinners
righteous (active righteousness) through the forgiveness of sins in
justification. When he discovered that, Luther said, it was as though
the very gates of Paradise had been opened for him.

For the understanding of Luther and the Reformation as a chapter
in the history of the church and the history of theology, therefore, it
is certainly appropriate to concentrate on his work as an interpreter
of the apostle Paul—though not perhaps with as much neglect of his
work on other parts of the Bible as characterizes many discussions of
him. But what Luther and the other Reformers learned from the
apostle Paul was above all "to know nothing except Jesus Christ and
him crucified" (1 Cor. 2:2). Justification by grace through faith was
the restoration of the right relation with God accomplished by God
through the life, death, and resurrection of Jesus: that was the central
affirmation of the Reformation. In a characteristic phrase of Luther,
Jesus was the "Mirror of the fatherly heart [of God], apart from whom
we see nothing but a wrathful and terrible judge."[3] For John Calvin
likewise, "Christ is the Mirror wherein we must, and without self-
deception may, contemplate our own election."[4] "Let Christ," said
Calvin's Zurich colleague Heinrich Bullinger in an official confession
of the Reformed Church, "be the Mirror in which we contemplate
our predestination."[5]

"Mirror" was, then, "a key metaphor" in Reformation thought.[6]
And therefore the way the Reformers interpreted the figure of Jesus
as the Mirror of the Eternal was central both to the religious achievements of the Reformation and to its cultural contributions. At the
same time, it is obvious that the Reformers all found different reflections in that Mirror. They would all have agreed in principle with
what we have seen to be the universal Christian consensus that Jesus,
as the Mirror of the Eternal, was the revelation of the True, the Beautiful, and the Good (though they might not always have regarded
such abstract philosophical terminology as very congenial). Yet it was
only on his significance as Mirror of the True that they would have

found substantial agreement: <u>Christ was the true revelation of what
Luther called "the hidden God [*Deus absconditus*]," and the source of</u>
divine Truth as this had been set down in the Scriptures. Calvin was
no less persuaded than Luther that for the true knowledge of God it
was necessary to look to the revelation that had come in Jesus, the
Mirror of the True. Quoting the words of the New Testament, "the
light of the knowledge of the glory of God in the face of Jesus Christ"
(2 Cor. 4:6), he explained that "when [God] appeared in this, his
image, he, as it were, made himself visible; whereas his appearance
had before been indistinct and shadowed."[7]

As Karl Holl has said, referring not only to Luther but to the entire
Reformation movement of the sixteenth century, "the Reformation,
in fact, enriched all areas of culture."[8] Principal among these were,
on the one hand, literature, art, and music, inspired by Jesus as Mirror
of the Beautiful, and, on the other hand, the political order, illumined
by Jesus as Mirror of the Good. All of these areas experienced revival
and renewal throughout Reformation Europe, and no one of the Reformation churches had a monopoly on any of them. Nevertheless, a
sharp difference appears between the two main Reformers, Luther
and Calvin, and between the two principal Reformation traditions,
Lutheran and Reformed, on the definitions of Jesus as Mirror of the
Beautiful and as Mirror of the Good; for Calvin and his followers were
suspicious of the idolatrous possibilities in the former, while Luther
and his followers proved to be extremely hesitant about the political
implications of the latter. The cultural and social relevance of these
differences over the precise meaning of Jesus as Mirror, which is
certainly not unrelated to the theological differences over doctrine,
has had an even more far-reaching importance in the history of the
past four centuries.

Although Luther's principal theological contribution was certainly
his doctrine of justification, his most important literary achievement
was no less certainly his translation of the New Testament into German, which he accomplished in a period of eleven weeks from the
middle of December 1521 to the beginning of March 1522. Eventually,
of course, he would translate the entire Bible, but it was his first
rendition of the New Testament that made history; with various revisions, it was to go through about one hundred separate editions in
his own lifetime, and innumerable ones since. Even those who regarded his theology with indifference or with alarm had to concede

that he was a linguistic genius; indeed, several of his theological enemies during the next two decades were to pay him the ultimate linguistic compliment of borrowing from him extensively for their own translations of the Bible into German.[9] Heinrich Bornkamm is not exaggerating when, in commenting on the 1521 translation of the New Testament, he speaks of "the difference between the eaglelike flight of Luther's language and the diction of his medieval predecessors," and therefore concludes that Luther was "entirely dependent on himself for the task of pouring the New Testament into a true mold of the German language." He adds that "a wonderful providence had placed Luther, the greatest sculptor of the German language," into just the right time and place to make his historic contribution to the creation of modern German.[10] Latin had truly achieved the status of a world language only when Jerome's Vulgate translation of the Bible had opened a new chapter in the history of the language.[11] So also the various Reformation translations of the Bible into the vernacular, with Luther's in the vanguard, became turning points for their languages in turn—a process that has continued, with additional languages, ever since.

In Luther's translation of the Gospels, as well as in his sermons on the Gospels that have been preserved (they number one thousand or more), both the teachings and the life of Jesus were set forth in vivid detail.[12] Spurning the traditional methods of allegorical interpretation, even for the Old Testament but especially for the New, because they made the Bible into a "nose of wax" that anyone could distort in any direction, he applied himself instead to reconstructing the history of the Jesus of the Gospels and making him live for his hearers.[13] The comment of Heinrich Heine that Luther, "who could scold like a fishwife, could also be as gentle as a sensitive maiden"[14] is nowhere more apt than in Luther's translation and paraphrases of the Gospels and in the narratives he based on those texts for his preaching. Far from transposing the language of the Gospels into the key of the Pauline epistles—as he might have been expected to do and as some scholars claim he did—he endeavored to allow each evangelist, or rather Jesus according to each evangelist, to speak in a distinctive accent. For even though he insisted that "the notion must be given up that there are four Gospels and only four evangelists," since there was in reality a single Gospel,[15] he constantly drew comparisons and contrasts between the way the several Gospels handled particular subjects.[16]

The outcome was a depiction of Jesus marked by such freshness of language that Jesus became a sixteenth-century contemporary. To hearers who cooed sentimentally over the Infant Jesus and clucked over his poverty, "If only I had been there! How quick I would have been to help the Baby!" Luther retorted: "Why don't you do it now? You have Christ in your neighbor."[17] The familiar admonition of the Sermon on the Mount to consider the lilies of the field and the birds of the air (Matt. 6:26–27) became at Luther's hands a discourse about how Jesus

> is making the birds our schoolmasters and teachers. It is a great and abiding disgrace to us that in the Gospel a helpless sparrow should become a theologian and a preacher to the wisest of men . . . , as if he were saying to us: "Look, you miserable man! You have house and home, money and property. . . . Yet you cannot find peace."[18]

The enemies of Jesus sound very much like the enemies of Martin Luther, and the reader sometimes needs to be reminded that the original language of the Gospels was not German but Greek. In Calvin's exegesis, too, as in Luther's, the scenes of the Gospel story acquired directness and challenging force, as becomes visible for example in his vivid exposition of the encounter between Jesus and the woman at the well.[19]

The literary power with which Luther was able to make Jesus a contemporary was an expression of his conception of Jesus as Mirror of the Beautiful. In painting, Luther strove to infuse into the religious art of the later Middle Ages his understanding of what the authentic message of the Gospels was: it was specifically the humanity of Jesus that was the Mirror of the Eternal. Therefore when he criticized medieval painters of the Virgin Mary, it was not for doing violence to the literal meaning of the Gospels by picturing her in modern dress and in a contemporary setting, but for depicting her in such a way "that there is found in her nothing [lowly] to be despised, but only great and lofty things"; what they should have done was, as she herself had said in the Magnificat, to show "how the exceeding riches of God joined in her with her utter poverty."[20] Albrecht Dürer shared Luther's ideas and reflected them in his art; his biographer speaks of "a conversion—both in subject matter and in style" brought about in

Dürer's faith and life through his acceptance of Luther's teachings, as a consequence of which "the man who had done more than any other to familiarize the Northern world with the true spirit of pagan Antiquity now practically abandoned secular subject matter except for scientific illustrations, traveler's records and portraiture."[21]

In keeping with this willingness of Luther to use painting as a means of achieving contemporaneity with the Christ of the Gospels as Mirror of the Eternal, Lucas Cranach the Younger several times portrayed the events of the Gospels as though Martin Luther had been present personally when they happened. The most successful of Cranach's paintings in this genre was probably *The Last Supper*, executed for the Church of Saint Mary in Dessau-Mildensee and dedicated in 1565. As in countless paintings before, Jesus is shown instituting the Lord's Supper, and the twelve disciples seated around the table are dressed as sixteenth-century German burghers, including Judas with his thirty pieces of silver. But suddenly, there in the midst of the group at table are the unmistakable faces of Martin Luther, of his colleague at Wittenberg, Philip Melanchthon, and of the prince of Anhalt. Quite unabashedly, then, the events of the first century have been transported into the sixteenth.

Perhaps nowhere has the contemporaneity of Luther's renditions of the Gospels come through more dramatically and convincingly than in the settings of the Gospel accounts of the suffering and death of Jesus in the *Saint Matthew Passion* and *Saint John Passion* of Johann Sebastian Bach. As one of the most profound historians of the modern spirit has observed, the true significance of Luther and the Reformation "cannot be fully appreciated merely on the basis of works of dogmatics. Its documents are the writings of Luther, the church chorale, the sacred music of Bach and Handel, and the structure of community life in the church."[22] One of the planks in the Reformation platform for the renewal of church life was, along with the translation of the Bible into the vernacular and the revitalization of preaching on the basis of such translations, the composition of vernacular hymns for congregational singing. Some Reformation groups objected to the creation of new songs, preferring to rely on paraphrases of "God's hymnbook," the Psalter, and producing such masterworks as the *Geneva Psalter* and the *Bay Psalm Book*. But Luther was "not of the opinion that the gospel should destroy and blight all the arts, as some of the pseudo-religious claim." He would, he added, "like to see all the arts, especially music, used in the service of Him who gave and made them."[23] Taking up and developing the style of hymns and chorales that had arisen during the later Middle Ages, he gave them new life, and the Lutheran chorale, as it reached its pinnacle in the work of such poets and composers as Paul Gerhardt, became one of the Reformation's principal cultural monuments.

It was the genius of Bach that he brought together, already in the cantatas and then on a larger scale in the *Passions*, these two Reformation elements: the text of the Gospel in Luther's translation and the Lutheran chorale. As a result, hearers could experience the meaning of the life and death of Jesus as Mirror of the Eternal with unmatched freshness and power. In the words of Nathan Söderblom,

> The Passion music, which was created within the church and which experienced a new depth, a new richness, and a new intensity in the sixteenth century, constitutes in its way the most important addition that has ever been made to the sources of revelation in the Old and New Testament. If you ask about a fifth Gospel, I do not hesitate to name the interpretation of salvation history as it reached its acme in Johann Sebastian Bach. The *Saint Matthew Passion* and *Mass in B Minor* give deep insight into the mystery of the passion and salvation.[24]

Bach was the fifth evangelist.

It would, however, violate both historical honesty and ecumenical integrity to concentrate on Jesus as the Mirror of the Eternal in these Protestant cultures while ignoring the transforming presence of his person in the religious and cultural revival fostered during the sixteenth century by the Catholic Reformation. The presence of Christ was the central theme of one of the masterpieces of the Catholic Reformation in Spain, *The Names of Christ* by Luis de León. As is evident from its very title, the book presents itself as a continuation and expansion of the treatise *On the Divine Names* of Pseudo-Dionysius the Areopagite, which had played such an influential role in the history of medieval Christ-mysticism. Luis de León seems to have concluded that now it was time to become explicit about the "Christ" in Christ-mysticism, and to specify the meaning of his names. "The names which Scriptures give to Christ," he says in book 1, "are numerous, like his virtues and attributes."[25] Throughout the remainder of this treatise, the author exploits his knowledge of Hebrew to analyze various names mentioned in various texts of the Hebrew Bible, basically ten in number, that can appropriately be used for Jesus.

"Jesus' spirit," he writes, "penetrates and changes" the human soul and the human personality; for "in Jesus Christ, as in a deep well, as in a vast ocean, we find a treasure of Being."[26] That treasure had brought "beauty" and "virtue" through "the new laws given to us by Jesus."[27] It was the purpose and the fulfillment of human life to find the treasure and to live in obedience to the "new laws."

The Christ-mysticism voiced by Luis de León achieved even greater heights both of spirituality and of literary power in the poems of Saint John of the Cross, whom many historians and literary critics regard as the finest poet in the Spanish language. Like Dante, he was both a poet and a philosopher, one who had been schooled in the thought of Thomas Aquinas, striving to resolve the tensions between intellect and will, between the knowledge of God and the love of God. The resolution came for him in the person of Jesus as Mirror of the Eternal, who was simultaneously the ground for the knowledge of God and the revelation of the love of God. In his *Songs of the Soul* (*Canciones de el alma*) he explored "the path of spiritual negation,"[28] which, as we have seen, had been the philosophical foundation for the Greek-speaking Christian Neoplatonists of the fourth century as they explored the meaning of the Cosmic Christ. But knowledge of Christ, even this profound knowledge through negation, was not sufficient of itself: love of Christ had to follow. Therefore in the madrigal "Of Christ and the Soul," he used the predicament of a young lover, "with love in his heart like a ruinous wound," as a metaphor for the mystical love between the soul and Christ.[29] The two themes of knowledge and love converged in his ballad "On the Incarnation,"[30] where Saint John of the Cross rehearsed a conversation between Jesus and his heavenly Father about the mystical earthly bride whom the Father had found for him. "Perfect love" would be fulfilled in the union between Jesus and this bride. But at the same time Jesus says to God the Father:

> How better blazon your might,
> sweet reason and deep mind?
> I'll carry word to the world,
> news of a novel kind:
> news of beauty and peace,
> of sovereignty unconfined.

Thus the mind and reason of God, the divine Logos, and the love and will of God, the divine Bridegroom, were present together in Jesus, the Mirror of the Eternal.

With the fundamental ideas in this image of Jesus as the Mirror of the Beautiful (if not always with its language) Luther might have had little difficulty, for he often used similar metaphors himself. But when it came to defining Jesus as the Mirror of the Good for the political order, Luther drew the line against seeking to make the person and message of Jesus contemporary or relevant in any direct way. Some of the radical Reformers of the sixteenth century, in their redefinition of the demands of "discipleship," called for the transformation of the entire social, economic, and political system. Nothing less than that was necessary, they believed, to bring society into conformity with the will of God announced in the law of the Bible, as that law had been fundamentally recast in the teachings of Jesus, which were summarized in the Sermon on the Mount. In his sermons of 1530–32 expounding the entire Sermon on the Mount, Luther attacked those "who have failed to distinguish properly between the secular and the spiritual, between the kingdom of Christ and the kingdom of the world." They had not recognized that in the Sermon on the Mount Jesus "is not tampering with the responsibility and authority of the government, but he is teaching his individual Christians how to live personally, apart from their official position and authority." For "there is no getting around it, a Christian has to be a secular person of some sort."[31] As such, the Christian was not to attempt to use the teachings of Jesus or the laws of the Bible to govern the state. That was best done on the basis not of revelation but of reason, by the legislation of "the mirror of the Saxons [Sachsenspiegel]," not by the decrees of Jesus, the Mirror of the Eternal. Jesus forbade taking oaths, the government required it; and both were right, each in the proper sphere. One did not have to be a Christian to rule justly, and the interpreter of the message of the Gospels did not, as such, have any special insight into the specifics of what it meant to rule justly. Therefore, politically involved though he and his Reformation undoubtedly were—when he died in 1546, he was engaged in mediating a conflict between princes—Luther did not, as an expositor of the Gospels, evolve a "Christian politics," for that was not why Jesus Christ had come to earth.

For the articulation of a Christian politics in the age of the Reformation, and one that would, especially in the English-speaking world, fundamentally redefine the nature of government, we must look not to Wittenberg but to Geneva. For, apart from such doctrinal issues as double predestination and the nature of the presence of the body and blood of Christ in the Lord's Supper, the principal difference between Luther's Reformation and Calvin's Reformation should be sought here in the definition of the political and social significance of the image of Jesus as the Mirror of the Good. Calvin was not as content as was Luther to trust secular rulers to find their own guidance in reason and legal tradition, important though these were as components of sound rule. He acknowledged in the concluding chapter of his *Institutes* "that Christ's spiritual Kingdom and the civil jurisdiction are things completely distinct."[32] But he went on in the very next paragraph to assert:

> Civil government has as its appointed end, so long as we live among men, to cherish and protect the outward worship of God, to defend sound doctrine of piety and the position of the church, to adjust our life to the society of men, to form our social behavior to civil righteousness, to reconcile us with one another, and to promote general peace and tranquillity.[33]

Magistrates, therefore, were to "submit to Christ the power with which they have been invested, *that He [Jesus Christ] alone may tower over all.*"[34] "The president and judge of our elections," he urged in keeping with this, was to be God. God had laid down in his law how the state and society were to function, and how magistrates were to govern in achieving those ends. It was, therefore, at his insistence that the ruling magistracy of Geneva, the Council of Two Hundred, pledged on 2 February 1554 "to live according to the Reformation, forget all hatreds, and cultivate concord." "To live according to the Reformation" implied, moreover, that they would seek to bring the laws of Geneva into harmony with the word and will of God, as mirrored in the law of the Scriptures and above all in the person and message of Jesus, so that, as Calvin said in the *Institutes*, Jesus Christ "alone may tower over all."

But if the government was to achieve such a faithfulness to Christ as the Mirror of the Good, it was essential that the word of God be preached and taught in all its truth and purity and be applied concretely to the total life of the individual and of society. In principle, to be sure, the Reformation idea of the universal priesthood of all believers meant that not only the clergy but also the laity, not only the theologian but also the magistrate, had the capacity to read, understand, and apply the teachings of the Bible. Yet one of the contributions of the sacred philology of the biblical humanists to the Reformation was an insistence that, in practice, often contradicted the notion of the universal priesthood: the Bible had to be understood on the basis of the authentic original text, written in Hebrew and Greek, which, most of the time, only clergy and theologians could comprehend properly. Thus the scholarly authority of the Reformation clergy replaced the priestly authority of the medieval clergy. Functionally, therefore, the quest for a form of government that would embody the will that God had revealed for society in Jesus Christ the Mirror led to a system that has often been called "theocracy." John T. McNeill has sought to clarify in what sense it was, and in what sense it was not, theocratic:

> The word "theocracy" is often applied to the Geneva of Calvin's time, but the word is now ambiguous to most minds. Many [including, one could add, many clergy] confuse "theocracy," the rule of God, with "hierocracy," the rule of the clergy. . . . Calvin wished the magistrates, as agents of God, to have their own due sphere of action. But so intense was his consciousness of vocation, and so far did his mental energy outstrip that of his political associates, that he ultimately gained ascendancy to the point of mastery.[35]

It was, moreover, thanks to Calvin's understanding of civil government and of its duty to shape society on the basis of the law of Christ that when his followers finally established a society in which it was possible to carry out that duty, the underlying assumption of that society was that the law of Christ did have a message, and often a very specific and concrete message, for both rulers and ruled. The election sermons of Puritan divines in colonial New England were based on that assumption.[36] "It is better," John Cotton declared, "that the commonwealth be fashioned to the setting forth of God's house, which is his church, than to accommodate the church to the civil state."[37] And, as one scholar has commented on Cotton's statement, "every Puritan would have agreed."[38] One of the few not to agree with this assumption was Roger Williams, who denied the continuity between biblical "government," either in the kingdom of Israel or in the kingdom of God proclaimed by Jesus, and the "rule of the saints" claimed by Puritanism.[39] In many ways, as a later chapter on Jesus the Liberator will suggest, it was Abraham Lincoln who, during the conflict over slavery, found the fallacy in the traditional assumption.[40] And the decisive authority for this was, also according to Lincoln, the person of Jesus as the Mirror of the Eternal, who thus provided, in two of the traditions that could be traced to the Reformation, both the justification of "theocracy" and its most telling refutation.

14

The Prince of Peace

To us a Child is born, to us a Son
is given; and his name will be
called Prince of Peace.

One of the *Names of Christ* to which Luis de León, in the spirit of the Catholic Reformation, devoted his treatise under that title was "Prince of Peace," derived from the words of the prophet Isaiah (Isa. 9:6): "To us a Child is born, to us a Son is given; . . . and his name will be called . . . Prince of Peace."[1] There was reason enough in the age of the Reformation, which was also the age of the Wars of Religion, to emphasize once again that Jesus, as Prince of Peace, called upon his followers in every age to seek the ways of peace and not of war. One of the last of the Reformation leaders, John Amos Comenius (Jan Amos Komenský), who with his Moravian church and nation had suffered the consequence of the Wars of Religion, insisted that Jesus Christ was

the only real deliverer from all slavery of soul and body (John 8:32–36). For *the way of peace they knew not* at all, who about the kings of the earth, instead of a sceptre, have gathered spears, swords, wheels, halters, crosses, flames, and headsmen, so making them rather to be feared than loved. Is this what was taught by the best of Teachers? Does this proceed from the teachings of Him who commended to His followers nought but love, and affection, and mutual help?[2]

That was a very good question to put to all the descendants of the Reformation, regardless of their denomination, in 1667, exactly one hundred fifty years after Luther's Ninety-five Theses. For because the Reformation was raising anew so many of the questions that had seemed to be settled forever, it compelled reconsideration also of the question of war: "Is this," as Comenius asked, "what was taught by the best of Teachers?"

The Reformation answered the question of what the person and teaching of Jesus meant for the problem of war, as it answered most other questions, with a spectrum of theories, some of them reflecting historic views of war and some presenting new variations and new alternatives. The standard threefold typology of theories about "Jesus and war" across that spectrum may conveniently serve to organize the variety: the doctrine of "just war," the theory of a "crusade," and the ideology of Christian pacifism.[3] For each of these Jesus provided fundamental justification.

Perhaps the most widely circulated sixteenth-century defense of the doctrine of just war as what "the best of Teachers" had taught about war was a treatise by Luther on the subject. It was addressed to the question, in Luther's words,

> Whether the Christian faith, by which we are accounted righteous before God, is compatible with being a soldier, going to war, stabbing and killing, robbing and burning, as military law requires us to do to our enemies in wartime? Is this work sinful or unjust? Should it give us a bad conscience before God? Must a Christian only do good and love, and kill no one, nor do anyone any harm?[4]

Luther's answer was consistent both with his theology and with his political theory. The distinction described earlier between the two kingdoms, the spiritual kingdom of Christ and the earthly kingdom of this world, together with the corresponding distinction between the public office and the private person, gave him the framework within which to resolve the contradiction between the absolute ethic of love as announced by Jesus and the concrete duties of political life and even of military service. Absolute love was incumbent on the follower of Jesus as a person; but it was not to be the norm by which to regulate the duties of the public office that the same follower of Jesus might occupy, and such duties were therefore not subject to the same imperatives. Hence the coming of Jesus and of his new ethic of the kingdom of God did not, according to Luther, overthrow the structures of political authority in human society, not even such structures as the office of the soldier to wage war.

The nature of both kingdoms was, according to Luther, set forth in the words of Jesus to Pontius Pilate (which Dante had also used in *De Monarchia*): "My kingship is not of this world; if my kingship were of this world, my servants would fight" (John 18:36). These words implied, on the one hand, that Christ did not want to interfere with the kingdoms of this world and with their structures, since his kingship belonged to another order, and that therefore military action was not an appropriate means of defending the kingdom of Christ. But they meant as well, according to Luther's reading of them, "that war was not wrong" in and of itself, since Jesus was saying, on the other hand, that in the kingdoms that did belong to this world it was appropriate for his "servants" as citizens to fight. Similarly, as both Calvin and Luther argued,[5] John the Baptist did not tell the soldiers who came to him with the question "And we, what shall we do?" that it was their duty, in the name of love, to renounce their sinful office of fighting and killing; he only "said to them, 'Rob no one by violence or by false accusation, and be content with your wages' " (Luke 3:14). In short, according to Luther, "he praised the military profession, but at the same time he forbade its abuse. Now the abuse does not affect the office." The coming of Christ meant, therefore, the introduction of a radically new imperative, the imperative of suffering love; but that imperative was not addressed to Pilate and the other officers of the Roman empire of his day, nor to soldiers, be they pagan or Christian, whose task it was to go on obeying the imperatives of their public office.[6]

An even more adroit and skillful exegesis enabled Luther to cope with another saying of Jesus that appeared to be applying the radical love ethic to prohibit the use of force by his disciples. When Peter, in the garden of Gethsemane, sought to protect Jesus against his captors by striking one of them with a sword, Jesus reproved him, saying, "Put your sword back into its place; for all who take the sword will perish by the sword" (Matt. 26:52). On the face of it, those words of Jesus did seem to forbid the use of the sword, also adding the threat that such use would ultimately bring a similar violence upon the perpetrators of any such violence. Thus the commandment of Jesus would appear to be an extension and further application of the words addressed by the Lord to the people of Israel in Deuteronomy (Deut. 32:35), as quoted by the apostle Paul (Rom. 12:19): "Beloved, never avenge yourselves, but leave it to the wrath of God; for it is written, 'Vengeance is mine, I will repay, says the Lord.' " But in the light of Luther's doctrine of the two kingdoms, the warning in the words of Jesus really meant that "the sword" was "a godly estate," through which that vengeance which was God's sole prerogative would be carried out: "All who take the sword [as private persons rather than in the faithful execution of a public office] will perish by the sword," a sword to be wielded by the incumbents of a public office— be they executioners or soldiers, pagans or Christians. "Hence," Luther concluded, "it is certain and clear enough that it is God's will that the temporal sword and law be used for the punishment of the wicked and the protection of the upright"; it could, moreover, be used also by Christians.[7]

As for the prohibition of Jesus in the Sermon on the Mount, "Judge not" (Matt. 7:1), it, too, was to be taken in the light of the declaration "Vengeance is mine" (Rom. 12:19).[8] Rather than prohibiting war and the use of force, the imperative of Jesus made it incumbent upon his followers to respect established political order. They were to do so, moreover, even when rulers were unjust and oppressive. For "if this king keeps neither God's law nor the law of the land, ought you to attack him, judge him, and take vengeance on him?" That was precisely what Jesus was forbidding in the Sermon on the Mount. Luther read the ethic of Jesus, therefore, as a condemnation of revolution, but not as a condemnation of war. For revolution was by definition an act of injustice, but war could be an instrument of justice. Thus the mainstream of the Reformation, whether Lutheran or Calvinist or Anglican, in its understanding of the implication of the love ethic of Jesus for the problem of war, attached itself to the medieval "just war" tradition of Augustine and Thomas Aquinas.[9]

Augustine had denounced Roman militarism, with its glorification of armed violence, and had used war as evidence that human beings could be far more cruel and bloodthirsty than wild animals.[10] Nevertheless, he had, somewhat reluctantly, conceded that there could be "just wars," made necessary by human wrongdoing; but he added that one must, even in these cases, "lament the necessity of just wars" rather than glory in them.[11] He elaborated his views in a letter to the Christian governor of the province of Africa, who had sought his counsel about various of his political duties, including the waging of war. "Peace should be the object of your desire," Augustine warned, and therefore "war should be waged only as a necessity, and waged only that God may by it deliver men from the emergency and preserve them in peace." The priority of peace over war was fundamental for Augustine: "Peace is not sought in order to kindle war, but war is waged in order to obtain peace." A "just war" was one whose purpose and intent it was to achieve peace. From this it followed that "even in waging war" a follower of Christ was to "cherish the spirit of a peacemaker." And the clinching argument for this interpretation of war and peace came from Jesus, who had said in the Beatitudes of the Sermon on the Mount (Matt. 5:9): "Blessed are the peacemakers."[12] In his consideration of war, Thomas Aquinas quoted many of these same sayings of Jesus and other New Testament passages, and he also proceeded from the distinction between private person and public office. Thus he systematized Augustine's definition of just war by specifying three conditions necessary to make a war just: the one who wages the war must have the authority to do so; there must be a "just cause"; and the war must be carried on with the "right intention" of advancing the good and achieving the peace. The sayings of Jesus such as the word of the Sermon on the Mount, "Do not resist evil" (Matt. 5:39), were indeed the ultimate authority for the follower of Jesus as a private person; "nevertheless, it is sometimes necessary for the common good for a man to act otherwise" in the execution of a public office.[13] Later followers of Thomas would add a fourth condition (and one that has become important in recent discussion of nuclear war): that the war be carried on "*debito modo*, with appropriate [and thus appropriately limited] means."[14]

In their explanation of how there could be a just war in the light of the unqualified way Jesus had condemned violence and the unequivocal way he had exalted peace, Reformers such as Luther repeated much of the medieval doctrine of Augustine and Aquinas, while adding their own perspectives on the ethical and political meaning of the Gospels. There was, however, one aspect of the treatment of war in medieval theology on which Luther broke radically with his predecessors: the idea of a crusade. As a solution for the moral ambiguity of war that went beyond the tragic necessity implied in the Augustinian idea of just war, the crusade imprinted the sacred sign of the cross of Jesus on the cause of "Holy Peace and Holy War."[15] "To take the cross" meant to go off to war against the Turk in Palestine, wearing a cross of red cloth on the shoulder of one's outer garment. While there is serious inconsistency between the accounts given by our several sources on the sermon preached by Pope Urban II at the Council of Clermont on 27 November 1095, it does seem clear that he promised remission of sins and indulgences to those who took the cross. He seems, moreover, to have described the death of those who, after taking the cross, fell in battle against the Turkish infidels as a kind of participation in the sufferings and death of Christ. In the event, as Runciman has put it, this "Crusading fervour" in the name of Jesus "always provided an excuse for killing God's enemies" and led to pogroms against Jews; it even led to what he calls "the great betrayal of Christendom," the sack of Christian Constantinople by Christian Crusaders on the Fourth Crusade in 1204, a "crime against humanity" and "an act of gigantic political folly," as well as a flagrant negation of the teachings of the very One in whose name they had gone forth and whose cross they bore.[16]

By the period of the Reformation, the atmosphere had changed drastically; as one historian has put it, albeit with some exaggeration, "in the sixteenth century the idea of a Crusade falls into oblivion."[17] It is more precise to say, with another scholar, that "the idea of the crusade continued to haunt the imagination of western princes until the seventeenth century."[18] What fell into virtual oblivion was the practical possibility of a Crusade to Palestine to free the Holy Land from the infidel, for now the infidel had become a clear and present danger to Christian Europe itself. In 1453, Constantinople, the capital of the Byzantine empire, which had been the victim of Western Christian aggression in 1204, fell to the Ottoman Turks, who during the next three-quarters of a century threatened central Europe: Belgrade surrendered to them in 1520, Vienna was in danger, and in 1526 at the battle of Mohacs the army of Hungary and its king, Louis II, fell before the superior might of the Turkish armies. Thanks to the recent invention of printing, a vast propaganda literature on the Turkish peril spread over central Europe, with some calling for compromise and appeasement and others for war and even for a revival of the Crusade—directed this time not against the Turks who had taken Palestine, but against the Turks who had pointed a dagger at the very heart of Western Christendom. All of this came at the very time that the Reformation seemed to be pointing its own dagger at Christendom, dividing the Christian forces just when they needed to unite against the common enemy. The coincidence of the two threats was the occasion for the convoking of the diet of the Holy Roman Empire at Augsburg in 1530, where the Augsburg Confession presented the case for the Lutheran Reformation.

That confession made it the official position of the Reformation party that, since "all government in the world and all established rule and laws were instituted and ordained by God," it was perfectly legitimate for Christians to "punish evildoers with the sword" and to "engage in just wars." Specifically, it declared that Emperor Charles V, "His Imperial Majesty, may in salutary and godly fashion imitate the example of David in making war on the Turk."[19] But the parallel between the Holy Roman Emperor and the ancient king of Israel did not make the emperor a theocratic ruler, who governed and waged war in the name of Jesus. The reason given for approving war against the Turk was, therefore, not the Crusade ideal of a holy war against the enemy of the cross of Christ; rather it was that, as the "incumbent of a royal office," Charles V, like King David of Israel, had the right, indeed the obligation, of "the defense and protection of [his] subjects." Luther's treatise of 1526 on the Turkish war took the same position. It was mistaken to preach a Crusade and to urge "the emperor, as guardian of the church and defender of the faith," to take arms against the Turks; on the contrary, taking arms against the Turks would be the duty of the rulers of Europe, "whether they themselves were Christians or not," in keeping with their calling in the world to govern.[20] In its validation of war against the Turks, the mainstream of the Reformation rejected the Crusade ideal but insisted on the just war theory: such a war was legitimate on account of the Jesus who had acknowledged that Pontius Pilate and Caesar possessed an authority that came from God (John 19:11), not on account of the Jesus whose crucifixion under Pontius Pilate had placed authority into the hands of his disciples and his church (Matt. 28:19–20).

Curiously, the nearest analogue to the Crusade ideal in the Reformation era did not come from either Roman Catholicism or mainline Protestantism, but from one of the left-wing leaders of the Radical Reformation, Thomas Muentzer.[21] He was convinced that "Christ the Son of God and his apostles" had established a pure faith, but that it had been corrupted immediately thereafter, so that "the precious Stone Jesus Christ," on whom the church was to have been built, had been "completely trampled" by his false disciples. Muentzer, in what his editor has correctly called "one of the most remarkable sermons of the Reformation Era," preached on 13 July 1524, announced the vengeance of that precious Stone Jesus Christ, which was "about to fall and strike these schemes of [mere] reason and dash them to the ground." For Jesus had warned: "Do not think that I have come to bring peace on earth; I have not come to bring peace, but a sword" (Matt. 10:34). He had, moreover, "commanded in deep gravity, saying: 'Take these enemies of mine and strangle them before my very eyes' (Luke 19:27)." And why did the Prince of Peace, whom Muentzer himself here called "the gentle Son of God," issue such a bloodthirsty command?

> Ah, because they ruin Christ's government for him. . . . Now if you want to be true governors, you must begin government at the roots, and, as Christ commanded, drive his enemies from the elect. For you are the means to this end. Beloved, don't give us any old jokes about how the power of God should do it without your sword. Otherwise may it rust away for you in its scabbard!

The summons of Jesus was a call for nothing less than Christian revolution, a new kind of holy war.[22] Muentzer was captured and put to death the following year; but his spirit would live on, through the radical political apocalypticism of the Fifth Monarchy Men who emerged from English Puritanism in the seventeenth century, and then through the efforts of some twentieth-century Christians in Eastern Europe and in the Third World, for whom Muentzer and other Christian revolutionaries have become, quite literally, church fathers and authentic voices for what one exponent of liberation theology has called "a christology of revolutionary praxis."[23]

Muentzer's theology of holy war ended in the debacle of the Peasants' War; Luther's theory of just war ended in the catastrophe of the Thirty Years' War. Neither holy war nor just war, moreover, constituted a new answer to the dilemma of Jesus and war, as formulated by Comenius: "Is this what was taught by the best of Teachers?" The only truly new answer of the sixteenth and seventeenth centuries to that dilemma (an answer which, they insisted, was actually very old) came, first from Erasmus, then from certain Anabaptists, Quakers, and other peace groups of the Radical Reformation, who bore witness to an understanding of the person and message of Jesus by which holy war was not holy and just war was not just.[24] Although they often invoked arguments from reason and from universal human morality in their attacks on war, it was theology and specifically Christology—a Christology of life and praxis rather than principally a Christology of doctrine—that constituted the heart of their argument.[25]

The foundation of that argument was the definition of the essence of Christianity as "discipleship."[26] "In the ninth chapter of Matthew," the Anabaptists declared in a disputation with the Swiss Reformed at Zofingen, "Christ came to Matthew the tax collector and said to him, 'Follow me' [Matt. 9:9]." Reviving the New Testament call for a drastic break with the past as the condition for authentic discipleship, they rejected such external criteria of discipleship as participation in the outward rituals of the institutional church and recitation of its creedal formulas. These external criteria and so-called means of grace must be subordinated to the person of Jesus; for "Christ himself is the means, whom no one can truly know except by following him in his life." Although there were some striking affinities between Anabaptism and medieval monasticism, as the Protestant critics of both were quick to point out—one of Luther's favorite epithets for the Anabaptists was "the new monks"—such a following of Christ in radical discipleship went even beyond the conception of following that had been at work in the *Imitation of Christ* and other monastic works of devotion. For in the Anabaptist theology of discipleship, Jesus was both example and exemplar: of course an example of how to live a godly life in strict conformity to the demands of the law and will of God, but also an exemplar of the way such a life under God worked itself out concretely in the world. And that way was "the way of the cross," on which the disciple followed Jesus into death and through death into life.[27] Some of the most profoundly stirring documents to come out of the Reformation anywhere are the accounts of the martyrdom of Anabaptists, who, as one of their enemies put it, "marched to the scaffold as though they were going to a dance," because they saw the scaffold and the execution pyre as an opportunity to participate, through the way of the cross, in the life and death and resurrection of Jesus.

The primary imperative of such a definition of discipleship was a total resignation to the will of God in obedience to Jesus and in imitation of him, what Anabaptists came to call "passivity" or "yieldedness." By sharp contrast with the revolutionary activism of a Thomas Muentzer, the evangelical Anabaptists believed themselves to be summoned to a yielded life of total dependence on God, the kind of life Christ himself had lived. They were not to try to reshape the external world and the civil order into a Christian society in conformity with the will of Jesus, but were to become the "little flock" to which Jesus had addressed himself (Luke 12:32), a genuine community of committed disciples and the true church. Therefore, by a sharp contrast with Luther's way of interpreting the secularity of the Christian life, they called upon the true disciples of Jesus to separate themselves drastically from the world and from the worldly life. By means of his doctrine of the two kingdoms, Luther had distinguished between the duties of the Christian as citizen and the duties of the Christian as disciple. Both were necessary, according to Luther's reading of the Gospels; but Jesus in passages like the Sermon on the Mount was talking only about the latter, meanwhile leaving undisturbed the external structures of government and citizenship, such as military service, in which his disciples were to participate fully. On the basis of their own distinction between the kingdom of Christ and the kingdoms of this world, Anabaptists attacked Luther's distinction as an evasion both of the full cost of discipleship and of the way of the cross to which it led: Jesus was the Prince of Peace.

It was into the context of that image of Jesus that the pacifist Anabaptists put their interpretation of war and of the use of force, a succinct statement of which appears in their Seven Articles of 1527, commonly known as the Schleitheim Confession:

> We are agreed as follows concerning the sword: The sword is ordained of God outside the perfection of Christ. It punishes and puts to death the wicked, and guards and protects the good. In the [Old Testament] Law the sword was ordained for the punishment of the wicked and for their death, and the same [sword] is [now] ordained to be used by the worldly magistrates. In the perfection of Christ, however, only the ban is used for a warning and for the excommunication of the one who has sinned, without putting the flesh to death—simply the warning and the command to sin no more.[28]

Despite the conventional accusations against it in the polemics of its opponents, this position is anything but anarchy. Echoing the words of the New Testament which had been the traditional legitimation of government, "Let every person be subject to the governing authorities. For there is no authority except from God, and those that exist have been instituted by God," the Anabaptists acknowledged that God had instituted government, which, as a later verse said, "does not bear the sword in vain" (Rom. 13:1–4). They were not intent on overthrowing the governing authorities, but on supporting them. What they opposed was the idea that the followers of Christ could themselves be magistrates and wield the sword. For government had been instituted "outside the perfection of Christ," and those who now lived "in the perfection of Christ" invoked the disciplinary measures of the ban and excommunication, not the sword, as the means of carrying out the will of God.

It was a similar concept of "the perfection of Christ" that provided the next stage in the history of Christian pacifism. The Society of Friends, in England and then in America, worked out a theologically more elaborate formulation of the case against Christian participation in war. This was the achievement of Robert Barclay, the principal systematic theologian and apologist of the Quaker movement. Barclay was prepared to acknowledge that for "the present magistrates of the Christian world" war was not "altogether unlawful"; for they were still "far from the perfection of the Christian religion." "But," he went on, "for such whom Christ has brought hither, it is not lawful to defend themselves by arms, but they ought over all to trust to the Lord." For they had been led by the Spirit of Christ to see the fundamental inconsistency between warfare and "the law of Christ." True obedience to the law of Christ demanded of the Quakers that they not wage war, but "suffer ourselves to be spoiled, taken, imprisoned, banished, beaten, and evilly entreated, without any resistance, placing our trust only in GOD, that he may defend us, and lead us by the way of the cross unto his kingdom." It did not matter that the majority of those who claimed to be followers of Christ were willing to wield the sword and go to war, because it was not by the way of the majority, but by "the way of the cross" of Jesus, the Prince of Peace, that God would "lead us unto his kingdom."[29]

The image of Jesus as Prince of Peace was not, however, a prominent theme of Christian iconography in the period of the Reformation. The reason for this was, in part, that many of the exponents of Christian pacifism were also critical of the use of images in the church. But it is also intrinsically more difficult to dramatize the figure of Jesus as Prince of Peace. For one *Ninth Symphony* in the nineteenth century, there are dozens of compositions like the *Marche militaire* and the *1812 Overture*. The most effective representations of the Prince of Peace have been achieved by an unintentional irony. Thus an illustration for the last masterpiece of Italian Renaissance literature, Torquato

Engraving from Torquato Tasso's *Jérusalem Délivrée*, Beinecke Rare Book and Manuscript Library, Yale University.

Tasso's *Jerusalem Delivered*, might appear to be a depiction of the catalogue quoted earlier from Comenius's *Angel of Peace:* "spears, swords, wheels, halters, crosses, flames, and headsmen." In fact it carries out the motif of such descriptions of the Crusaders as this:

> Some shirts of mail, some coats of plate put on,
> Some don'd a cuirass, some a corslet bright,
> An hawberk some, and some a habergeon,
> So every one in arms was quickly dight,
> His wonted guide each soldier tends upon,
> Loose in the wind waved their banners light,
> Their standard royal towards heaven they spread,
> The cross triumphant on the Pagans dead.[30]

"The cross triumphant" was sacred to all Christians, pacifists as well as Crusaders. But Christian pacifism saw it as triumphing *over* armor and weapons, not *through* them: Jesus the Prince of Peace had seized the sword by the blade and torn it from the hands of the soldiers, lifting it to the sky hilt-high to make the sign of the cross.

It is noteworthy, in relation to the total history of the images of Jesus, that several of those who attacked the traditional use of the figure of Jesus to justify war were at the same time carrying on a vigorous campaign against the traditional dogmas about the person of Jesus Christ. Some of the Anabaptists, such as David Joris, became Antitrinitarians, and some of the Quaker emphases on reason and the "inner light" did lead to a repudiation of Christian orthodoxy. Those who defended both the doctrine of just war and the doctrine of the two natures in Christ professed to find inconsistency in the practice of invoking, as a divine authority against war, a Jesus Christ to whom meanwhile many of his traditional divine prerogatives were being systematically denied. For if Jesus as Lord did indeed have the absolute right to command such radical obedience, to prohibit even fighting in self-defense, and to abrogate the fundamental demands of state and society, he must be vastly more than many of the simplistic christological formulas of Anabaptists and Quakers confessed him to be.

Such an argument undoubtedly carried a great deal of validity. And yet—the copies of the Gospels being read by both sides contained a parable of Jesus that contrasted saying the right thing and doing the right thing in quite another fashion: "What do you think? A man had two sons; and he went to the first and said, 'Son, go and work in the vineyard today.' And he answered, 'I will not'; but afterward he repented and went. And he went to the second and said the same; and he answered, 'I go, sir,' but did not go. Which of the two did the will of his father?" (Matt. 21:28–31).

15

The Teacher of Common Sense

The true light that enlightens
every man.

During the Age of Reason, the Enlightenment of the seventeenth and eighteenth centuries, the orthodox Christian image of Jesus Christ came in for severe attack and drastic revision. Among the efforts of this period to deal with him, the best known are the early attempts at a biography of Jesus, what Albert Schweitzer (or rather his English translator) called "the quest of the Historical Jesus." But the Enlightenment's quest of the Historical Jesus was made possible, and made necessary, when Enlightenment philosophy deposed the Cosmic Christ.[1]

In 1730 there appeared in London the first volume of *Christianity as Old as the Creation, or, The Gospel, a Republication of the Religion of Nature*, by Matthew Tindal. If we judge by the literally hundreds of replies he evoked, Tindal might seem to have been attacking the gospel of Jesus Christ. In fact he was—or, at any rate, he thought he was—defending it, and in the only way he believed to be open to him now, which was to equate the essence of the gospel with reason and natural religion and to identify the essential Jesus as the Teacher of Common Sense. One of the factors he cited in support of the argument that a new understanding of Jesus had become necessary was the disappearance of miracle as a proof for the uniqueness of his person and the validity of his message. Throughout most of the history of Christianity it had seemed possible to argue on the basis of the supposedly incontestable historical evidence for miracles. Any question about the credibility of the miracle stories in the Bible could be dismissed as, in effect, "a denial either that there is any divine power or that it intervenes in human affairs."[2] Jesus had "procured authority for himself by means of miracles," whose purpose it was "that he should be believed in."[3] Many of the defenders of Christianity were, of course, aware all along of the ambiguity of such proofs, which were an argument in a circle: the historical credibility of the miracle stories was based on the theological doctrine of the divine nature of Jesus, which was in turn validated by the presumed scientific and philosophical possibility of miracles. But the argument in a circle worked, though only so long as the circle remained unbroken. Conversely, once the circle was broken, it was broken in several places— scientific-philosophical, historical, and theological—but not in all of them at the same time. We must look at each of them in turn, and at its implications for the image of Jesus.

Although the perception of Jesus as the Logos and Cosmic Christ had been one of the philosophical sources of modern scientific thought, the scientific thought of the seventeenth and eighteenth centuries gradually eroded it. Isaac Newton provides the most important evidence for this change. The ancient "negative theology" of the Greek fathers persisted in Newton: "As a blind man has no idea of colors," he said at the conclusion of his most famous book, "so we have no idea of the manner by which the all-wise God perceives and understands all things." But he also declared his conviction, as an article of sound natural philosophy, which could "discourse of [God] from the appearances of things," that "this most beautiful system of the sun, planets, and comets" was not to be attributed to some "blind metaphysical necessity," but "could only proceed from the counsel and dominion of an intelligent and powerful Being," who governed all things, "not as the soul of the world, but as Lord over all."[4] There was, he asserted elsewhere, "nothing of contradiction" in acknowledging that as the First Cause, God could "vary the laws of Nature" (thus apparently allowing for the miraculous) and yet at the same time in assuming that the world "once formed . . . may continue by those laws for many ages" (thus apparently precluding the miraculous).[5] In his writings on theology and biblical interpretation Newton accepted as trustworthy the miracle stories of the Bible, especially the accounts of miracles attributed to Jesus, but the miracles did not lead to the orthodox image of the Cosmic Christ. For he rejected the traditional doctrines of the Trinity and the person of Christ as incompatible both with reason and with Scripture, and, like John Milton, taught a subordination of Jesus to the Father that earned for him the epithet "Arian."[6]

It remained only to rule the miracles themselves out of court as inadmissible evidence. "There is not to be found in all history," David Hume asserted, "any miracle attested by a sufficient number of men, of such unquestioned good-sense, education, and learning, as to secure us against all delusion in themselves."[7] Reflecting the Enlightenment habit of undercutting all of historic Christianity by attacking Roman Catholicism, he referred to various alleged miracles, past and present, "Grecian, Chinese, and Roman Catholic," but was silent about the miracles in the Gospels, preferring to consider the miracles reported in the Pentateuch. Asserting that not reason but faith was the foundation of "our most holy religion," he concluded with the argument that faith was itself the greatest miracle, and indeed the only miracle:

> On the whole, we may conclude that the Christian Religion not only was at first attended with miracles, but even at this day cannot be believed by any reasonable person without one. Mere reason is insufficient to convince us of its veracity: And whoever is moved by Faith to assent to it, is conscious of a continued miracle in his own person, which subverts all the principles of his understanding, and gives him a determination to believe what is most contrary to custom and experience.

In such a context the miracles of Jesus had lost all power to prove who he was. For, as Goethe was to have Faust say, "The miracle is faith's most cherished child [*Das Wunder ist des Glaubens liebstes Kind*]," rather than the other way around.[8]

Miracle was, therefore, an issue both for science (usually called natural philosophy) and for history. In Edward Gibbon's examination of five historical causes for the victory of Christianity in the Roman empire, miracles constituted the third cause. Gibbon used the issue of miracles to describe the way "credulity" and "fanaticism" had prevailed in the Christian movement of the first three centuries. "The duty of an historian," he observed a bit archly, "does not call upon him to interpose his private judgment in this nice and important controversy" over whether or not miracles had continued after the apostolic age. And, even more coyly, he closed the chapter with a consideration also of the miracles of the apostolic age, above all the miracles performed by Jesus himself. "How shall we excuse the supine inattention of the Pagan and philosophic world to those evidences which were presented by the hand of Omnipotence, not to their reason, but to their senses?" Gibbon asked. For, he continued, "during the age of Christ, of his apostles, and of their first disciples, the doctrine which they preached was confirmed by innumerable prodigies. . . . The Laws of nature were frequently suspended for the benefit of the church." Then, focusing on the most spectacular miracle of all, he facetiously accused the classical writers of having "omitted to mention the greatest phenomenon to which the mortal eye has been witness since the creation of the globe . . . , the praeternatural darkness of the Passion," when the sun was obscured for three hours on Good Friday while Jesus hung on the cross.[9]

In the same spirit Gibbon forbore to list the commanding moral and religious authority of the figure of Jesus Christ as one of his five "secondary causes of the rapid growth of the Christian church," but cited, as "an obvious but satisfying answer" to the whole question, that the triumph of Christianity (or, as he called it later, the "triumph of barbarism and religion") "was owing to the convincing evidence of the doctrine itself, and to the ruling providence of its great Author." Consideration of that answer, however, lay beyond "the duty of an historian." Instead, he subjected early Christianity to a searching, and in many ways devastating, historical analysis. In later chapters he did discuss the rise and development of the doctrine of the Trinity, including especially the confession that Christ was "one in being with the Father," and the history of the doctrine of the incarnation.[10] But it was only in connection with the theological controversies over the person and the natures of Christ that he said anything significant about the life of Jesus at all, and then he disposed of it in one paragraph:

> The familiar companions of Jesus of Nazareth conversed with their friend and countryman, who, in all the actions of rational and animal life, appeared of the same species with themselves. His progress from infancy to youth and manhood was marked by a regular increase in stature and wisdom; and, after a painful agony of mind and body, he expired on the cross. He lived and died for the service of mankind; . . . the tears which he

shed over his friend and country may be esteemed the purest evidence of his humanity.[11]

Now it may be true, as one twentieth-century scholar has suggested, that calling "the unique attractiveness of the central figure of Christianity as presented in the Synoptic Gospels . . . a primary factor in the success of Christianity" is only "a product of nineteenth-century idealism and humanitarianism."[12] Yet that does not mean that the history of the life and death, the teachings and miracles, the preexistence and exaltation, of Jesus did not figure prominently in the triumph of the Christian movement. But Gibbon the historian was not dealing with that history.

Other historians of Gibbon's time were less hesitant. Indeed, the effort to reconstruct the biography of Jesus from the data in the Gospels was about to become, at the very time when Gibbon published his first volume in 1776, an overriding preoccupation of scholars and other literati in many lands. For in 1778 the German philosopher and literary critic Gotthold Ephraim Lessing published, as the last of seven *Wolfenbüttel Fragments* by an anonymous author, a treatise bearing the title *Concerning the Intention of Jesus and His Teaching.* That publication set off a debate over the authentic message and purpose of Jesus that has continued now for two centuries and shows no sign of relenting. The author of the treatise, as of the six previously published *Fragments,* was Hermann Samuel Reimarus, who at his death had left behind a massive work entitled *Apology for the Rational Worshipers of God.* In it he defended a Deistic philosophy of religion, with many affinities to Tindal's, against the traditional Christian doctrine of Creator and creation, and he insisted that the Jesus of the Gospels "taught no new mysteries or articles of faith or undertook to teach them." For "if Jesus himself had wished to expound this strange doctrine of three different persons in one divine nature . . . , would he have kept silent about it until after his resurrection?"[13] It was not to miracles, which were "unworthy of notice," or to the disclosure of so-called mysteries like the Trinity that the success of Jesus and his message was to be attributed, but to purely natural motives and causes, "a reason which operates and has operated at all times so naturally, that we need no miracle to make everything comprehensible and clear. That is the real mighty wind (Acts 2:2) that so quickly wafted all the people together. This is the true original language that performs the miracles."[14]

The controversy aroused by Lessing's publication of Reimarus belongs, of course, to the history of theology and of New Testament scholarship, but it extended far beyond theological circles and is therefore relevant also to our study of the place of Jesus in the history of culture. A century after Lessing, another German man of letters and, as Leander Keck has called him, "ex-theologian," David Friedrich Strauss, once again focused attention on Reimarus in defense of his own exposition of the concept of "myth" as a means of finding the elusive figure within and behind the Gospel accounts.[15] Strauss's *Life of Jesus,* first published in 1835–36, obtained an international circulation, popular at least as much as academic, when it was translated into English (anonymously) by a scholarly young Englishwoman named Mary Ann Evans, who went on in 1854 to translate Ludwig Feuerbach's *Essence of Christianity* as well; she is better known by her nom de plume of George Eliot.[16] As her biographer notes of her translation of Strauss, "few books of the nineteenth century have had a profounder influence on religious thought in England."[17] And it was the audacity of Reimarus that had prepared the way for Strauss to have that profound influence, first in Germany and then in England and America.

As the thought of Lessing and the interest of George Eliot in Strauss's *Life of Jesus* suggest, the quest of the Historical Jesus was not confined to the German biblical and theological scholars whose names form the table of contents of Albert Schweitzer's *Quest*. Even for the theologians, moreover, as Otto Pfleiderer has noted, "the examination of the literary details of the Gospels" became so dominant "that the interest in the supreme problems of the evangelical history seemed to have been almost lost sight of."[18] But in the latter part of the eighteenth century and the early part of the nineteenth, the quest of the Historical Jesus became at least as much the vocation of other intellectuals than theologians and New Testament scholars. In a search for new ways to understand reality, to validate morality, and to organize society, now that the old orthodoxy had been discredited, they undertook to reinterpret the major classics of Western culture in a manner that would make their abiding message available to a new age. If metaphysical unity with God in the Trinity and miraculous revelation from on high no longer constituted credentials for the message of Jesus, the harmony between his message and the best of human wisdom everywhere could. Where others had perceived in part, he "saw life steadily and saw it whole" (as Matthew Arnold was to say of Sophocles); but his way of doing so stood in continuity with the rest of human experience.

Enlightenment scholars searching for the Historical Jesus were, therefore, engaged at the same time in what might be called the quest of the historical Homer and the quest of the historical Socrates, as well as in a quest of the historical Moses. Less than two decades after the publication of Reimarus's essay on the Jesus of the Gospels, Friedrich August Wolf, one of the pioneers of modern classical scholarship, wrote his *Prolegomena ad Homerum*. In it he argued that Homer was not the name for an individual poetic genius who composed the *Iliad* and the *Odyssey*, but for a multiplicity of sources now collected into those epic poems. Wolf's method bore certain analogies to the techniques being employed by other scholars to identify the multiplicity of sources collected into the Pentateuch, but also to the effort to sort out various strata by sifting through the Gospels. Other scholars of the time were addressing themselves yet once more to the perennial Socratic problem; but, as Jaeger says, "Schleiermacher was the first to express the full complexity of this historical problem in a single condensed question." In a formulation suggestive of the problem of the relation between the Synoptic Gospels and the Gospel of John, to which he was to address himself in his own later *Lectures on the Life of Jesus*, Schleiermacher, translator of Plato into German, asked: "What *can* Socrates have been, in addition to all Xenophon says he was, without contradicting the characteristic qualities and rules of life that Xenophon definitely declares to have been Socratic—and what *must* he have been, to give Plato the impulse and the justification to portray him as he does in the dialogues?"[19]

The parallels between Socrates and Jesus had been drawn in the second and third centuries, as we have seen earlier. And again in the Enlightenment these parallels were, to be sure, of more than purely literary importance. Both Socrates and Jesus were outstanding teachers; both of them urged and practiced great simplicity of life; both were regarded as traitors to the religion of their community; neither of them wrote anything; both of them were executed; and both have become the subject of traditions that are difficult or impossible to harmonize. Yet the study of the parallel went even beyond those striking similarities. For the thinkers of the Enlightenment took Socrates as evidence for the presence, beyond the limits of alleged biblical revelation, of a wisdom and moral power that must have come from the God whom Jesus called Father. If, as the prologue to the Gospel of John asserted, the Logos-Word that became incarnate in Jesus of Nazareth was "the true light that enlightens every man" (John 1:9), whether Jew or Christian, Greek or heathen, Socrates made it extremely difficult to restrict the revealing activity of God—perhaps even the saving activity of God—to the history of the people of Israel and of the church. And if the true God had spoken and acted through Socrates, that meant that divine truth was universal. If it was universal, then both Socrates and Jesus must themselves have taught that it was.

On the other hand, even those who were prepared to concede the force of the parallelism were also concerned to identify the superiority and distinctiveness of the person and teaching of Jesus—if only it were possible to find out what his true person and authentic teachings were, behind the veil of the apostles and evangelists. Joseph Priestley, scientist and scholar, took up the question of disentangling the historical Jesus from the sources about him by writing a long book entitled *The Corruptions of Christianity* and by compiling *A Harmony of the Gospels*. In another work, a longish pamphlet of sixty pages dealing with the similarities and differences between Jesus and Socrates, he strove to do justice to the philosophical greatness and moral stature of Socrates, but came down on the side of the essential superiority of Jesus:

> In comparing the characters, the moral instructions, and the whole of the history, of Socrates and Jesus, it is, I think, impossible not to be sensibly struck with the great advantage of revealed religion, such as that of the Jews and the christians, as enlightening and enlarging the minds of men, and imparting a superior excellence of character. This alone can account for the difference between Socrates and Jesus, and the disciples of each of them; but this one circumstance is abundantly sufficient for the purpose.[20]

For Priestley, Jesus was no longer the Cosmic Christ or the Second Person of the Trinity, but he was a divinely inspired teacher, in a way that even Socrates was not.

Priestley's *Socrates and Jesus Compared*, as well as his other works of theology and biblical scholarship, had a profound influence on a man who was certainly the most eminent of all the many participants in the quest of the historical Jesus (even though Schweitzer does not so much as mention his name): Thomas Jefferson, third president of the United States. Nor was Jefferson's curiosity about the problems of

Jesus and the Gospels merely one of the seemingly infinite number of scholarly and scientific hobbies in which his capacious and penetrating intellect engaged; rather, Jefferson concerned himself with these problems during most of his adult life. He was convinced, as Daniel Boorstin has noted, that "purified Christianity could promote moral health in the actual setting of eighteenth-century America."[21] Therefore it was simultaneously as a statesman and as a philosopher that he was functioning when he undertook to discover (or rediscover) such a purified Christianity, and the results of his discovery went into his formulation of the American tradition.

Writing in his middle forties, he avowed that "from a very early part of [his] life" he had experienced the "difficulty of reconciling the idea of Unity and Trinity" in traditional Christian doctrine. In his judgment, such doctrines as the Trinity were not needed to account for Jesus of Nazareth, who was "a man, of illegitimate birth, of a benevolent heart, [and an] enthusiastic mind, who set out without pretensions of divinity, ended in believing them, and was punished capitally for sedition by being gibbeted according to the Roman law." Nor was it enough simply to reject the dogmatic and liturgical tradition of orthodox Christianity or to restore the message of the Bible. Jefferson was convinced that the purified Christianity he sought, the authentic message of Jesus, was not to be automatically equated with the total content of the Gospels, and that therefore it was necessary to extract that message from the present form of the texts. Out of that conviction came two separate attempts at what he himself called "abstracting what is really his from the rubbish in which it is buried, easily distinguished by its lustre from the dross of his biographers, and as separable from that as the diamond from the dung hill."[22]

The first such attempt was carried out while Jefferson was president, in February 1804. Working in the White House—as he admitted later, "too hastily"—he completed the task in "2. or 3. nights only at Washington, after getting thro' the evening task of reading the letters and papers of the day." As is evident from the photograph of an early facsimile of its first page, in an imitation of Jefferson's hand, the outcome bore the title *The Philosophy of Jesus of Nazareth*. The subtitle asserted that this had been "extracted from the account of his life and doctrines as given by Mathew, Mark, Luke, & John," and that what he was presenting was "an abridgement of the New Testament for the use of the Indians unembarrassed with matters of fact

The Philosophy

of Jesus of Nazareth
extracted from the account of
his life and doctrines as given by
Mathew, Mark, Luke, & John.

being an abridgement of
the New Testament
for the use of the Indians
unembarrassed with matters of fact
or faith beyond the level of their
comprehension.

Title page of Thomas Jefferson's *Philosophy of Jesus of Nazareth*, holograph facsimile, Thomas Jefferson Papers, University of Virginia Library.

or faith beyond the level of their comprehensions." Whether he actually meant native Americans by the term "Indians" or was referring to his political opponents, he did take it upon himself to clip from two printed copies of the English New Testament those sayings which he recognized to be authentic, since they were, as he himself said, "easily distinguished" from the "rubbish" of the Gospel writers.

Long after leaving the presidency, Jefferson returned to his New Testament research and, probably in the summer of 1820, completed work on a much more ambitious compilation, entitled *The Life and Morals of Jesus of Nazareth Extracted textually from the Gospels in Greek, Latin, French & English.* The text is in four parallel columns in the four languages, pasted together in the order that Jefferson had outlined in a preliminary table of contents. What is omitted is in many ways even more revealing than what is included. Both the beginning and the end of the Gospel story have disappeared. The prologue of the Gospel of John is gone, and so are the accounts of the annunciation, the virgin birth, and the appearance of the angels to the shepherds. The account closes with a conflation of the first half of John 19:42 with the second half of Matthew 27:60: "There laid they Jesus and rolled a great stone to the door of the sepulchre, and departed." There is no mention of the resurrection. In *The Philosophy of Jesus*, Luke 2:40 appears in full, "And the child grew, and waxed strong in spirit, filled with wisdom; and the grace of God was upon him." But in *The Life and Morals of Jesus of Nazareth*, Jefferson took the trouble to expunge, in all four languages, the final words, "and the grace of God was upon him."[23] As the editor of Jefferson's version of the Gospel puts it, rather gently but no less effectively, "Although many distinguished biblical scholars have been daunted by the challenge of disentangling the many layers of the New Testament, the rationalistic Jefferson was supremely confident of his ability to differentiate between the true and the false precepts of Jesus."[24]

The Jesus who emerged from this method of differentiating between the true and the false was the Teacher of Common Sense, or, in Jefferson's words, "the greatest of all the Reformers of the depraved religion of his own country." The content of his message was a morality of absolute love and service, which was not dependent either upon the dogmas of the Trinity and the two natures in Christ or finally even upon the claim that he had a unique inspiration from God, but authenticated itself to his hearers by its intrinsic worth. But as one study of Jefferson has noted, Jefferson has "a concept of self-evident truths that accords well with his general training, his known reading and recommendations, and the language he used both in and of the Declaration [of Independence]"; but the "truths" he enumerated as "self-evident" were at once "more specific" and "more confusing" than those being propounded as such by some of his contemporaries.[25] Evidently, one source both of the specificity and of the confusion was his understanding of the "philosophy" and "morals" contained in the message of Jesus as the Teacher of Common Sense. Many of these elements of the Enlightenment image of Jesus are tersely summarized in the well-known letter of Jefferson's colleague Benjamin Franklin, writing a few weeks before his death to Ezra Stiles, president of Yale College:

> As to Jesus of Nazareth, my opinion of whom you particularly desire, I think the system of morals and religion, as he left them to us, the best the world ever saw or is likely to see; but I apprehend it has received various corrupting changes, and I have, with most of the present dissenters in England, some doubts as to his divinity, tho' it is a question I do not dogmatize upon, having never studied it, and think it needless to busy myself with it now, when I expect soon an opportunity of knowing the truth with less trouble. I see no harm, however, in its being believed, if that belief has the good consequence, as probably it has, of making his doctrines more respected and better observed.[26]

It is probably correct to suggest that "few other Americans of his time could have said" this,[27] but for Franklin and Jefferson that message of common sense was enough, and *Poor Richard's Almanak* can be read as a compilation of it. But for many others, it was either too much or too little—or perhaps both.

16
The Poet of the Spirit

You are the fairest of the sons of men; grace is poured upon your lips.

When Shakespeare had Hamlet say, "There are more things in heaven and earth, Horatio, / Than are dreamt of in your philosophy,"[1] he could have been anticipating the rebuke issued by much of nineteenth-century thought and literature to its predecessors of the eighteenth century: by reducing mystery to reason and by flattening transcendence into common sense, the rationalism of the Enlightenment had dethroned superstition only to enthrone banality. What the nineteenth century substituted for such rationalism was, in René Wellek's words, the "attempt, apparently doomed to failure and abandoned by our time, to identify subject and object, to reconcile man and nature, consciousness and unconsciousness by poetry which is 'the first and last of all knowledge.' "[2] Wellek was defining Romanticism, in response to Lovejoy's effort to show that "the word 'romantic' has come to mean so many things that, by itself, it means nothing."[3] For our present purposes we may characterize as "Romantic" the effort of various nineteenth-century writers and thinkers to go beyond the quest of the Historical Jesus to a Jesus who—(to use Wellek's formula) by identifying subject and object and by reconciling man and nature, consciousness and unconsciousness—could be called the Poet of the Spirit.

As if to announce the end of the eighteenth century, the leading German interpreter of this Romantic version of faith in Christ, Friedrich Schleiermacher, quoted in the preceding chapter, issued his *On Religion. Speeches to Its Cultured Despisers* in 1799.[4] He went on, in 1806, to publish a kind of Platonic dialogue about Christ entitled *Christmas Eve Celebration* and, in 1819, to become "the first person to lecture publicly on the topic of the life of Jesus," making this the subject of academic lectures at the University of Berlin five times between 1819 and 1832, although the book to come out of student notes on the lectures did not appear until 1864.[5] Schleiermacher's most abiding achievement was a systematic theology entitled *The Christian Faith* and published in 1821–22.[6] Among English writers, probably the most profound as well as the most important of the transmitters of German Romanticism was Samuel Taylor Coleridge, who died in the same year as Schleiermacher.[7] Coleridge's *Aids to Reflection* of 1825 and his posthumously published *Confessions of an Inquiring Spirit* articulated in philosophical and theological prose some of the ideas to which he gave voice in his poetry, especially after 1810 or so, as he found himself moving closer to historic Christian beliefs. Coleridge was, in turn, a major force in the intellectual and spiritual development of Ralph Waldo Emerson, who belonged to the next generation and who was probably the most influential thinker in nineteenth-century America.[8] While acknowledging Lovejoy's corrective suggestion "that we should learn to use the word 'Romanticism' in the plural,"[9] we may nevertheless perhaps be permitted the generalization that each of these three—a German, an Englishman, and an American—stands in his own individual way as a spokesman for the literary and philosophical spirit of the Romanticism of the nineteenth century, and that each of them sought the incarnation of that spirit in the person of Jesus.

Like the rationalists, they all found it impossible to accept the Gospel stories of the miracles of Jesus as literal historical truth. Rather than explaining them away, however, they endeavored to incorporate them into a more comprehensive world view.[10] As Coleridge put it, "what we now consider as miracles in opposition to ordinary experience" would, with further insight, be seen "with a yet higher devotion as harmonious parts of one great complex miracle, when the antithesis between experience and belief would itself be taken up into [the] unity of intuitive reason."[11] Both the eighteenth-century attack of the Enlightenment on the notion of miracles as violations of natural law and the theological apologetics in defense of miracles had missed the point; for on both sides, in the phrase of Emerson's first book, published in 1836, "the savant becomes unpoetic," through the failure to realize "that a guess is often more fruitful than an indisputable affirmation, and that a dream may let us deeper into the secret of nature than a hundred concerted experiments."[12]

In this search for a "unity of intuitive reason" that would go beyond the antitheses between nature and miracle or between experience and belief, Jesus was, they recognized, the crucial problem and, they believed, the source for a solution to the problem as well. What has been called "Coleridge's ever-changing attitude toward Christ" was the endeavor to break out of the dilemmas formulated by the eighteenth century.[13] Similarly, in his lectures on the *Life of Jesus*, Schleiermacher discarded as not very helpful "the contrast between the supernatural and the natural that we include in the term 'miracle' on the basis of scholastic terminology."[14] Miracles were important as a "sign" and "mighty work," in which not the suspension of the laws of nature, but the "significance" was the primary component. Confronted by the Gospel accounts of the miracles, therefore, the biographer of Jesus had to relate them to the central themes of his life and work:

> The more the deed can be understood as a moral act on the part of Christ and the more we can establish a comparison between Christ's way of accomplishing a given result and that employed by other people, the more we can comprehend the acts as genuine constituents of the life of Jesus. The less we can understand them as moral acts on Christ's part and the less at the same time we can discover analogies, the less we shall be able to form a definite idea of the account and understand the facts on which it is based.[15]

On that basis Schleiermacher felt able to classify the miracle stories under various categories and to deal with the historical content in each of them.

The central content of the biography of Jesus, in Schleiermacher's *Life*, was the "development" in him of a "God-consciousness" that was, in comparison with the God-consciousness of others, on the one hand, "perfect" and therefore unique in degree, but, on the other hand, not fundamentally different in kind.[16] Understandably, the discussion of this theme follows immediately upon a consideration of the problems inherent in the orthodox dogma of the two natures, divine and human, and the treatment of the God-consciousness of Jesus may be seen as a substitute for that dogma. Thus the *Life of Jesus* formed a transition in Schleiermacher's own development from the somewhat dithyrambic picture of Jesus in the last of his *Speeches on Religion* of 1799 to the fully articulated and far more subtle portrait in *The Christian Faith* of 1821–22. In the *Speeches* Schleiermacher insisted that what was distinctive about Jesus was neither "the purity of his moral teaching" nor even "the individuality of his character, the close union of high power with touching gentleness," both of which were present in every great religious teacher; but "the truly divine element is the glorious clearness to which the great idea he came to exhibit attained in his soul": namely, "that all that is finite requires a higher mediation to be in accord with the Deity, and that for man under the power of the finite and the particular, and too ready to imagine the divine itself in this form, salvation is only to be found in redemption."[17] This Poet of the Spirit was thus the fulfillment of the theme announced near the opening of the *Speeches:*

> As a human being I speak to you of the sacred secrets of humanity according to my views—of what was in me as with youthful enthusiasm I sought the unknown, of what since then I have thought and experienced, of the innermost springs of my being which shall for ever remain for me the highest, however I be moved by the changes of time and humanity.[18]

By the time he wrote *The Christian Faith* two decades later, Schleiermacher had come to define Jesus as the "archetype [*Urbild*]" of authentic humanity in its relation to, and consciousness of, God: in Jesus Christ, he said there, "the archetype must have become completely historical . . . and each historical moment of this individual must have borne within it the archetypal."[19]

Because such "God-consciousness" and divine inspiration had been manifested with special force in artists and poets, the aesthetic experience provided the most appropriate categories for interpreting the figure of Jesus. In his early work on the life and teachings of Jesus, *The Spirit of Christianity and Its Fate,* Hegel defined "truth" as "beauty intellectually represented," and he therefore saw "the spirit of Jesus" as "a spirit raised above morality."[20] Jesus had, of course, been an inspiration to artists, poets, and musicians since the beginnings of Christianity. What sets much of the nineteenth century apart from that universal tradition is the effort to make this poetic and artistic understanding of him supersede the dogmatic, the moral, and even the historical. William Blake's powerful poem, *The Everlasting Gospel*, which he never finished, resembled other attempts of the time to rediscover the authentic Jesus who had been buried under tradition and dogma: Blake's Jesus, as the embodiment of what he calls the "poetic," denounced in his words and violated in his deeds the conventionalities of gentle and genteel religion. This was the restatement of an essentially apocalyptic picture of Jesus—the very feature of the message of the Gospels on which, along with the miraculous, the Enlightenment had foundered.[21] In Blake's case, moreover, the phrase "poetic and artistic understanding" of Jesus takes on special meaning, because Blake created a series of portraits of Jesus in which the antithesis between nature and supernature is transcended. Thus in *Christ Appearing to the Apostles after the Resurrection*, painted just before the transition from the eighteenth century to the nineteenth, the light surrounding the central figure clearly belongs to another order of reality than the natural, and yet the wounds in the hands and the side of Christ are there to prove the identity between the Risen One and the Historical Jesus, whom the disciples had known as part of the natural world. Because of the wounds and because of "the opposition between the one young apostle who regards the risen Christ with adoration while the others bow before Him as if He were an idol," it is, as Martin Butlin suggests, "tempting to see this more specifically as showing Doubting Thomas."[22] And, it may be added, Doubting Thomas had in many ways become the patron saint of the Enlightenment.

For it was a hasty and superficial conclusion from the scientific discovery of the natural world to suppose that now all mystery had been exorcised from it. If the mystery of faith did not make sense to the Doubting Thomases among the children of the eighteenth century, then perhaps the mystery of beauty could. In a famous (and sometimes ridiculed) passage that has been called "an image impatient with all possibility of loss . . . less an image than a promise of perpetual repetition,"[23] Emerson articulated that mystery of beauty:

> Standing on the bare ground—my head bathed by the blithe air and uplifted into infinite space—all mean egotism vanishes. I become a transparent eyeball; I am nothing; I see all; the currents of the Universal Being circulate

through me; I am part or parcel [particle] of God. . . . I am the lover of uncontained and immortal beauty.[24]

For, as he went on to say a little later, "The ancient Greeks called the world *kosmos*, beauty. Such is the constitution of all things, or such the plastic power of the human eye, that the primary forms, as the sky, the mountain, the tree, the animal, give us a delight *in and for themselves*." Thus Emerson sought, as he said in one of his earliest lectures, to "look upon Nature with the eye of the Artist," for in that way he could "learn from the great Artist whose blood beats in our veins, whose taste is upspringing in our own perception of beauty."[25] The presence, within and beneath human consciousness, of a sense of the mystery of beauty constituted Emerson's version of what the medieval scholastics had called the *analogia entis*, the analogy of being between Creator and creature, which now had become an aesthetic *analogia Naturae*, an analogy of Nature.

More even than it had in Schleiermacher's lectures on the life of Jesus or in the Romanticism of the young Hegel's treatment of Christian beginnings, the sort of aestheticism articulated by Emerson shaped the presentation of the biography of Jesus published in 1863 by Emerson's French contemporary, Ernest Renan, which has been called, perhaps a bit hyperbolically, "the most famous and enduring work upon the subject ever written."[26] More than sixty thousand copies of the book were sold in the first six months. Renan's *Vie de Jésus* was a celebration of what he himself called "the poetry of the soul—faith, liberty, virtue, devotion," as this had been voiced by Jesus, the Poet of the Spirit.[27] "This sublime person," he said, "who every day still presides over the destiny of the world, we may call divine," not in the sense in which that word had been employed by the orthodox dogma of the two natures, but because "his worship will constantly renew its youth, the tale of his life will cause endless tears, his sufferings will soften the best hearts."[28] Renan was writing as a historian; he had been appointed a professor in the Collège de France in 1862, although he was forced to resign his professorship in 1864. As a historian, however, he invoked the aesthetic mystery as an antidote to the ravages of a rationalistic historical skepticism. It was, he urged, necessary for the historian to understand how a faith "has charmed and satisfied the human conscience," but equally necessary not to believe it any longer, since "absolute faith is incompatible with sincere history." But he consoled himself with the belief that "to abstain from attaching one's self to any of the forms which captivate the adoration of men, is not to deprive ourselves of the enjoyment of that which is good and beautiful in them."[29] So it was to be with Jesus.

Many of the efforts to cast the person of Jesus in such a mold, including Renan's, came to grief on the moral question. Try though they did, they could not bring together the True, the Good, and the Beautiful, or connect their fundamental category of an aesthetic appreciation of Jesus to the prophetic earnestness that had been unmistakably present in his summons to discipleship. For Emerson, the crisis came in the conflict over slavery during the decades before the outbreak of the Civil War, a time that his biographer, echoing the title of the first volume of Winston Churchill's history of World War II, has called "The Gathering Storm."[30] He had attempted, in the first of the *Essays: Second Series* of 1844, entitled "The Poet," to bring together the True, the Good, and the Beautiful. "The Universe," he said there, "has three children, born at one time." "Theologically," he continued, they had been called "the Father, the Spirit and the Son," but "we will call [them] here the Knower, the Doer and the Sayer." "These stand respectively," he explained, "for the love of truth, for the love of good, and for the love of beauty." "The three are equal," he added in an obvious allusion to a trinitarian dogma that he rejected. It was the task of the poet to be the sayer and the namer, and to represent beauty. In that task he stood in continuity with God. "For the world is not painted or adorned, but is from the beginning beautiful; and God has not made some beautiful things, but Beauty is the creator of the universe." As Jesus was the Poet of the Spirit, so now the poet was to be the new Second Person of the Trinity, through whom the Beauty that was the creator of the universe would shine through, manifesting its essential unity with Truth and Goodness. But at the end of the essay Emerson lamented: "I look in vain for the poet whom I describe. . . . Time and nature yield us many gifts, but not yet the timely man, the new religion, the reconciler, whom all things await."[31] Emerson closed his poem, "Give All to Love," published in his *Poems* of 1847,[32] with the lines:

Heartily know,
When half-gods go,
The gods arrive.

But in place of the "half-god" Jesus who had gone, no "god," no new Poet of the Spirit, had arrived to unite the Good, the True, and the Beautiful.

Nor was it only the morality of Jesus that could not be accommodated in the Romantic reaction to the Enlightenment. Despite the valiant efforts of both Schleiermacher and Renan, the Historical Jesus did not quite suit its categories. As Karl Barth put it, "Jesus of Nazareth fits extremely badly into this theology. . . . The historical in religion, the objective element, the Lord Jesus, is a problem child [*Sorgenkind*] to the theologian, a problem child that ought throughout to be accorded respect and that somehow does receive respect, but a problem child nevertheless."[33] In this criticism Barth was echoing the comments of David Friedrich Strauss, who noted that although the title of Schleiermacher's lecture course was *The Life of Jesus*, in fact "he uses the name 'Christ' virtually throughout" rather than "Jesus."[34] The same criticism was repeated by Albert Schweitzer.[35] Strauss was objecting in part to Schleiermacher's effort, especially in *The Christian Faith*, to combine a critical historical study of the Jesus of the Gospels with an affirmative attitude toward the Christ of church dogma, a task that Strauss regarded as impossible and essentially dishonest. But also for Karl Barth, who carried out that very task in a way unmatched by anyone else in the twentieth century, the Romantic portrait of Jesus, as represented by Schleiermacher, was a brilliant failure.

In turn, however, Barth was hostile to the enterprise of apologetics at work in Strauss and in Schleiermacher's *Speeches On Religion*, whose subtitle makes clear that it was addressed "to the cultured among [religion's] despisers." For the sake of that appeal to the cultured despisers, the Schleiermacher of the *Speeches* was prepared to cut and trim, to adjust and omit, even if this meant overlooking or distorting central elements of the Christian tradition. "Even the distinctive artistic style of the *Speeches* is to be understood as 'apologetic' in this [reductionistic] sense," Barth charged, "in which Schleiermacher—as he himself said once, more as one playing music than as one presenting arguments—accommodated himself to the language" of his hearers. Barth concluded:

As an apologist for Christianity, he played upon it as a virtuoso does upon his violin, [selecting] those tones and ways of playing that, even if they did not have to sound delightful, could at least sound acceptable, to his hearers. Schleiermacher does not speak as a responsible servant of the matter [of Christian revelation], but, in true virtuoso style, as a free master of it.[36]

And the Historical Jesus, the "problem child," was, for Barth, the crucial instance of this tendency.

From within the privileged sanctuary of the church and of its dogmatic theology, one may certainly raise serious questions about the foreshortening of the doctrinal perspective on the person of Jesus Christ in such reductionistic apologetics. But the appeal of these portraits of Jesus to large sections of the populace in the nineteenth century appears incontestable, especially at a time when the traditional Christ of church and of dogma no longer spoke to them. Romanticism, in the sense of the word being employed here, arose at least in part out of the very crisis of faith connected with the quest of the Historical Jesus. In its concrete performance as an outlook on the past and as a method for understanding the past, moreover, the Romanticism of the nineteenth century demonstrated that it had an antenna far more sensitive to the signals of that past than the Rationalism that sought to lay exclusive claim to the title "historical." For example, it is difficult to see how our present awareness of the culture and thought of the Middle Ages could have developed as it did if it had not been for the pervasive force of Romanticism, just at the time when medieval studies came into prominence as a field of study. In 1845, Philip Schaf, a leading example of Romanticism in American theology, published his *Principle of Protestantism*, which articulated his theory of historical development and included the Reformation in the theory.[37] In the same year, John Henry Newman, who is sometimes associated with Romanticism, published his own epoch-making *Essay on Development*, which has played a major part in both the "rediscovery of tradition" and the "recovery of tradition."[38] Romanticism was able to do far greater justice than much of modern Existentialism to the depth and complexity of the past and thus to make that past live—at least for audiences that shared Romantic presuppositions.

On graduation evening, Sunday, 15 July 1838, Ralph Waldo Emerson, at the invitation of the senior class of the Harvard Divinity School, delivered an address that was to scandalize New England and bar him from returning to Harvard for almost thirty years.[39] In it he attacked "historical Christianity" for having "dwelt . . . with noxious exaggeration about the *person* of Jesus" when, in truth, "the soul knows no persons." Instead of urging that "[you] live after the infinite Law that is in you, and in company with the infinite Beauty which heaven and earth reflect to you in all lovely forms," it demanded that "you must subordinate your nature to Christ's nature; you must accept our interpretations, and take his portrait as the vulgar draw it." That was a violation of the imperative to "every man to expand to the full circle of the universe," with "no preferences but those of spontaneous love."

But it was also a violation of the authentic portrait of Jesus. "His doctrine and memory" had suffered a grave "distortion" already in his own time, and even more in "the following ages." The tropes in which he spoke were taken literally, and "the figures of his rhetoric have usurped the place of his truth." The church could not tell the difference between prose and poetry, and those who professed to be his orthodox followers threatened their theological adversaries, saying, "This was Jehovah come down out of heaven. I will kill you, if you say he was a man." Of course "he spoke of miracles," but only because "he felt that man's life was a miracle . . . and he knew that this daily miracle shines as the character ascends." In the mouths of the theologians and prelates, however, "the word Miracle . . . gives a false impression; it is Monster," instead of being "one with the blowing clover and the falling rain." The outcome of such a distortion was conventional Christian preaching. "I once heard a preacher," Emerson said, "who sorely tempted me to say I would go to church no more. Men go, thought I, where they are wont to go, else had no soul entered the temple in the afternoon." Such preachers, he said, "do not see that they make his gospel not glad, and shear him of the locks of beauty and the attributes of heaven."

How different was the true message of Jesus as Poet of the Spirit. "A true conversion, a true Christ, is now, as always, to be made by the reception of beautiful sentiments." Those beautiful sentiments were not confined to the Jesus of the Gospels, but they had achieved their pinnacle there—precisely because they were universal:

> Jesus Christ belonged to the true race of the prophets. He saw with open eye the mystery of the soul. Drawn by its severe harmony, ravished with its beauty, he lived in it, and had his being there. Alone in all history he estimated the greatness of man. One man was true to what is in you and

me. He saw that God incarnates himself in man, and evermore goes forth anew to take possession of his World. He said, in this jubilee of sublime emotion, "I am divine. Through me, God acts; through me, speaks. Would you see God, see me; or see thee, when thou also thinkest as I now think."

Therefore, Emerson went on to say, "it is the office of a true teacher to show us that God is, not was; that He speaketh, not spake." Otherwise, "the true Christianity—a faith like Christ's in the infinitude of men—is lost." He concluded by expressing the hope that "that supreme Beauty which ravished the souls of those Eastern men" of the Bible "shall speak in the West also," showing "that the Ought, that Duty, is one thing with Science, with Beauty, and with Joy." Therefore, he urged the neophyte minister of Jesus Christ, "Yourself a newborn bard of the Holy Ghost, cast behind you all conformity, and acquaint men at first hand with Deity." For that was to be truly faithful to the person and message of Jesus, Poet of the Spirit.

But the poetic treatment of the person of Jesus could also move in quite another direction, not to a denial of the historic faith of Orthodoxy about him but to an affirmation of it. One of the most effective examples is the scene in Dostoevsky's *Crime and Punishment* in which Raskolnikov demanded that Sonia read to him the story of the resurrection of Lazarus.[40] He had kissed her foot, explaining: "I did not bow down to you, I bowed down to all the suffering of humanity." Then he picked up the Russian New Testament and asked her to find the account of Lazarus. "Read!" he cried out to her plaintively, and then repeated it more urgently, but she hesitated. Gradually he understood that she combined a reluctance to read it to him with "a tormenting desire to read and to read to him," and that made him even more insistent. As she read the verses of the eleventh chapter of the Gospel of John, it was as though she were "making a public confession [*ispoviedovala*]." At first, Sonia's reading of the Gospel story "passionately reproduced the doubt, the reproach and censure" of those who had refused to accept Christ. But when she came to the miracle of the raising of Lazarus, she was "cold and trembling with ecstasy [*drozha i cholodeja*], as though she were seeing it before her very eyes." As the candle guttered, it cast its dying light on "the murderer and the harlot who had so strangely been reading together the holy book," whom Dostoevsky clearly sees as this new Magdalene and this new Lazarus. And the result was that Raskolnikov knew he must confess to her his murder of the old pawnbroker. When he finally did, she told him what he must do: "Go at once, this very minute.... Kiss the earth which you have defiled!" Precisely because Sonia knew that the Gospel story was true, it was through the history of Jesus' miracle of the raising of Lazarus that Raskolnikov came to an authentic aware- ness of himself and to a sense of kinship with the earth, to what René Wellek, in his definition of Romanticism quoted earlier, calls a rec- onciliation of man and nature, consciousness and unconsciousness, subject and object. The full poetic meaning of this reconciliation and identification with Christ becomes evident from an unused entry in Dostoevsky's notebook for the novel:[41]

> Now, kiss the Bible, kiss it, now read.
> [Lazarus come forth.]
> [And later when Svidrigaylov gives her money]
> "I myself [was] a dead Lazarus, but Christ resurrected me."
> N.B. Sonia follows him to Golgotha, forty steps behind.

And that Christ, too, was the Poet of the Spirit.

17

The Liberator

There is neither Jew nor Greek,
there is neither slave nor free,
there is neither male nor female;
for you are all one in Christ Jesus.
For freedom Christ has set us free;
stand fast, therefore, and do not
submit again to a yoke of slavery.

It is sometimes difficult to see in the Jesus of both Rationalism and Romanticism just why he was ever crucified, so accommodated had his image become to the spirit of the times. For example, one of the most widely read books ever written in the English language, Charles Monroe Sheldon's *In His Steps*, first published in 1896, was an idealized description of the success in business and in society that awaited an American community in which everyone decided to follow seriously in the footsteps of Jesus. Surely an example of such eminent practicality, a teacher of such convincing rationality, a figure of such incandescent beauty ought to have appealed to the first century as much as to the eighteenth or nineteenth.

Yet the same nineteenth-century Russian writer whose narrative in *Crime and Punishment* of Sonia and Raskolnikov reading together the Gospel story of the raising of Lazarus gave such vivid expression to the perception of Jesus as Poet of the Spirit also expressed, perhaps more profoundly than anyone before or since, the meaning of Jesus the Liberator, as one whom the first century—or any other century of human history—was bound to reject. Dostoevsky did this in Ivan Karamazov's vision of the Grand Inquisitor.[1] Christ returned to earth and was welcomed by the people as he blessed them with his presence and his miracles. But once again he was arrested—this time by orders of the Grand Inquisitor, the cardinal-archbishop of Seville and defender of the faith—and confronted by this spokesman for an institutional Christianity that had finally succeeded in correcting all the mistakes he made while he was on earth. In the well-known woodcut by William Sharp, the two stand in dramatic contrast. The gaunt form of the aged Inquisitor, in clerical garb, is illumined, as he faces Jesus the Prisoner. The face of Jesus is not visible, for he is turned toward the Inquisitor with his back to the viewer; yet it is the darkened figure of the Prisoner, not the illumined figure of the Inquisitor, that dominates the picture. For Jesus the Prisoner was in fact Jesus the Liberator, as the Inquisitor acknowledged when he rehearsed the three questions that Satan, "the wise and dread spirit, the spirit of self-destruction and non-existence," had addressed to Jesus during the temptation in the wilderness. "For in those three questions the whole subsequent history of mankind is, as it were, brought together into one whole, and foretold, and in them are united all the unresolved historical contradictions of human nature."

The first of Satan's questions, "If you are the Son of God, command these stones to become loaves of bread" (Matt. 4:3), presented the choice between turning the stones into bread, so that "mankind will run after thee like a flock of sheep, grateful and obedient," and "some promise of freedom which men in their simplicity and their natural unruliness cannot even understand"; "for nothing has ever been more insupportable for a man and a human society than freedom." Jesus chose to be the Liberator rather than the Bread King, but in that he was mistaken. The freedom he offered was only for the elite. Ever since that mistake, his followers had been coming to the powers of the earth in both church and state, to "lay their freedom at our feet, and say to us, 'Make us your slaves, but feed us.'" When the Inquisitor had finished his commentary on the temptation of Jesus,

> he waited some time for his Prisoner to answer him. . . . But [Jesus] suddenly approached the old man in silence, and softly kissed him on his bloodless aged lips. That was all his answer. The old man shuddered. His lips moved. He went to the door, opened it, and said to him: "Go, and

William Sharp, woodcut, *The Grand Inquisitor*, from Fyodor Dostoevsky's *Brothers Karamazov* (Modern Library edition).

come no more. . . . come not at all, never, never!" And he let Him out into the dark alleys of the town. The Prisoner went away.

And, Dostoevsky (or, at any rate, Ivan Karamazov) implies, he never came back again.

Alongside the conventional portraits of Jesus as the pillar of the status quo in state and church, there had been a continuing tradition of describing him, in his own time and in every age that was to follow, as the Liberator. So it apparently was that many of his own contemporaries had seen him, as the one who challenged every social system and called it to account before the judgment of God. But it was above all in the nineteenth and twentieth centuries that the first-century Prophet who had preached the justice of God as it was directed against all the oppressors of humanity became Jesus the Liberator. And Jesus the Liberator became—and in our time has become and is—a political force that overthrows empires, even so-called Christian empires. The charter and the agenda of liberation in Jesus Christ were formulated in what has been called the Magna Charta of Christian liberty, the epistle of Paul to the Galatians: "There is neither Jew nor Greek, there is neither slave nor free, there is neither male nor female; for you are all one in Christ Jesus. . . . For freedom Christ has set us free; stand fast, therefore, and do not submit again to a yoke of slavery."[2] Neither Jew nor Greek; neither slave nor free; neither male nor female—each in its historical turn, these three captivities have originally been justified in the name of Christ the Creator and Lord as belonging to the natural order and to natural law, but they have finally been challenged, and have eventually been overcome, in the name of Jesus the Liberator.

From the seventeenth to the nineteenth century, the most persistent test case for the complicated dilemma of the relevance of Jesus the Liberator to the social order was the debate over slavery.[3] Both sides appealed to the text of the Bible and the authority of the person of Jesus. Both sides, as Abraham Lincoln said in the Second Inaugural of 4 March 1865, "read the same Bible, and pray to the same God; and each invokes his aid against the other." As he pointed out there, moreover, "it may seem strange that any men should dare to ask a just God's assistance in wringing their bread from the sweat of other men's faces." But he added, quoting the commandment of Jesus in the Sermon on the Mount, "let us judge not, that we be not judged" (Matt. 7:1). It was above all his awareness that "since man is finite he can never be absolutely sure that he rightly senses the will of the infinite God" that made "Abraham Lincoln in a real sense the spiritual center of American history."[4] To an abolitionist like James Russell Lowell, editor of the *Anti-Slavery Standard* and distinguished New England man of letters, the authority of Jesus for the situation was less equivocal.[5] Facing the implications of the war with Mexico for the future of slavery, he spoke out against the injustice both of slavery and of the war, in a poem of 1845 that was to become, for the next hundred years and more, a battle hymn of the Social Gospel:

> Once to every man and nation
> Comes the moment to decide,
> In the strife of truth with falsehood,
> For the good or evil side;
> Some great cause, God's new Messiah,
> Offering each the bloom or blight,
> And the choice goes by for ever
> 'Twixt that darkness and that light.
>
> By the light of burning martyrs
> Jesus' bleeding feet I track,
> Toiling up new Calvaries ever
> With the cross that turns not back;
> New occasions teach new duties,
> Time makes ancient good uncouth;
> They must upward still, and onward,
> Who would keep abreast of truth.

On the one hand, therefore, Robert Sanderson, an Anglican bishop in the seventeenth century, had declared that Christians "must not acknowledge any our supreme Master, nor yield our selves to be wholly and absolutely ruled by the will of any . . . but only Christ our Lord and Master in heaven." But on the other hand, he could, in the very same sermon, reject any interpretation of the supreme lordship of Christ over all earthly masters that proceeded "as if Christ or his Apostle had any purpose . . . to slacken those sinews and ligaments . . . which tie into one body . . . those many little members and parts, whereof all humane societies consist," and that included the sinews of slavery.[6]

The juxtaposition of those two statements in the same sermon about what it meant, and what it did not mean, to call Jesus the Liberator would be easy to duplicate over and over from the literature of the debate over slavery. The tension they represent was not unique to the modern period, however, for it seems to have been present in the Gospel portraits of Jesus themselves. Among those who claimed to be followers of Christ there had long been an uneasiness about the institution of slavery. They recognized that because of his coming "slavery had been deprived of any claim to be an inner necessity derived from the structure of human nature."[7] Augustine articulated this uneasiness when he declared it to have been the original intention of the Creator "that his rational creature should not have dominion over anything but the irrational creation—not man over man, but man over the beasts." Slavery, therefore, was not a natural institution created by God, but was a result of the fall of the human race into sin.[8] Yet in a fallen world, where it was necessary to accept the imperfections of all human institutions, slavery, too, had to be tolerated, and the authority of Christ the Liberator could not be invoked to justify overthrowing it by revolutionary force. The most compelling testimony for such social conservatism was found in the epistle of Paul to Philemon. In it the same apostle who announced the Magna Charta "There is neither slave nor free" informed Philemon, a slaveholder, that he was sending Onesimus, a runaway slave, back to him, in order "to do nothing without your consent"; but he expressed the hope that Philemon "might have him back for ever, no longer as a slave but more than a slave, as a beloved brother," which John Knox takes to mean that Onesimus might become a Christian evangelist.[9] Although, in Bishop Lightfoot's words, "the word 'emancipation' seems to be trembling on his lips,"[10] Paul declined to compel Philemon to set Onesimus free as a matter of Christian duty (Philem. 14–16), and he did not address (one way or the other) the general question of the Christian attitude toward slavery as an institution.

Those who continued to find that institution tolerable could thus lay claim to the letter of what the New Testament had said: certainly it was not, strictly speaking, against the law, either in the Old Testament or in the New, to have ownership of another human being.[11] As on the question of paying taxes to Caesar (Matt. 22:21), so here, the New Testament appeared to have taken it for granted that there would be slavery in the society. It had even used it as an analogy for the relation of the believer to the lordship of Christ, as well as for the relation of the sinner to the lordship of the devil.[12] It was, consequently, no more legitimate to employ the sayings of Jesus as a weapon against slavery than it was to use his language about the kingdom of

God as the basis for denouncing all earthly kingdoms as usurpations. Yet the spirit of the epistle to Philemon, if not the letter, did call the institution of slavery into question, and new occasions did teach new duties. Even though the church "allowed [the institution of slavery] to endure," therefore, it "was fully conscious of the inconsistency between this institution and the inner freedom and equality which was the Christian ideal."[13] It was only a matter of time—though, in the event, a long time indeed—before the recognition of that inconsistency between the toleration of slavery and the proclamation of Jesus as Liberator produced decisive action.

The rediscovery of Jesus the Liberator was not confined to the debate over slavery, nor to British and American thought. Perhaps the most widely celebrated such rediscovery in the nineteenth century was that of Lev Tolstoy. In his novel *Resurrection*, whose uncensored version was published two decades later than *The Brothers Karamazov*, the same contrast between the Liberator and an inquisitor appears, once again in a prison, where a visitor "was startled to see a large picture of the Crucifixion, hanging in an alcove. 'What's that here for?' he wondered, his mind involuntarily connecting the image of Christ with liberation and not with captivity."[14] The message of Tolstoy's *Resurrection* was that the teachings of Jesus were intended to be taken literally. The final chapter of the novel was a commentary on portions of the Gospels, above all on the commandments of the Sermon on the Mount, in which the protagonist "pictured to himself what this life might be like if people were taught to obey these commandments." The excitement and the ecstasy that came over him, "as happens to vast numbers who read the Gospels," convinced him that "it is man's sole duty to fulfil these commandments, that in this lies the only reasonable meaning of life." In that realization, "it was as though, after long pining and suffering, he had suddenly found peace and liberation."[15]

"When the novel *Resurrection* appeared in 1899," a scholarly monograph by the Soviet literary historian G. I. Petrov has observed, "it was the occasion for displeasure and embarrassment in the government and in the higher circles of the church."[16] Tolstoy's radical Christianity drew the excommunication of the Russian Orthodox Church, but his reinterpretation of the message of Jesus also drew the devoted attention of many thousands from both within and beyond Russia as well as Orthodoxy. They made pilgrimages to Yasnaya Polyana to visit the prophet of a new Christianity, and they wrote to him from all over the world. Even George Bernard Shaw corresponded with him about his own "theology," although Tolstoy found offensive Shaw's flippancy in treating the gospel, since "the problem about God and evil is too important to be spoken of in jest."[17] In his novels, as Isaiah Berlin has put it, "Tolstoy perceived reality in its multiplicity, as a collection of separate entities round and into which he saw with a clarity and penetration scarcely ever equalled." But in his philosophy and theology, "he believed only in one vast, unitary whole," which he finally formulated as "a simple Christian ethic divorced from any complex theology or metaphysic . . . , the necessity of expelling everything that does not submit to some very general, very simple standard: say, what peasants like or dislike, or what the gospels declare to be good," two standards that were often the same for Tolstoy.[18] "Do not resist one who is evil. But if any one strikes you on the right cheek, turn to him the other also" (Matt. 5:39): Tolstoy's radical views about the literal application of these words of Jesus seemed to most prophets of liberation and champions of the oppressed to be the height of impracticality, a capitulation to injustice, indeed "the opium of the masses."

One exception was a young Indian-born barrister in South Africa, who came under the powerful influence of Tolstoy's religious and ethical philosophy. Tolstoy's book *The Kingdom of God Is within You*, he was to write later, "overwhelmed me. It left an abiding impression on me. Before the independent thinking, profound morality, and the truthfulness of this book, all [other Christian] . . . books . . . seemed to pale into insignificance."[19] He went on to found a Tolstoyan commune in South Africa in 1910, the year of Tolstoy's death. Tolstoy wrote a letter (in English) to his admirer in South Africa on 7 September 1910, just two months before he died. Except for short personal notes to friends and family, it was to be his final epistle, almost a religious-philosophical last will and testament:

> The longer I live, and especially now when I feel keenly the nearness of death, I want to tell others what I feel so particularly keenly about, and what in my opinion is of enormous importance, namely what is called non-resistance, but what is essentially nothing other than the teaching of love undistorted by false interpretations. . . . This law has been proclaimed by all the world's sages, Indian, Chinese, Jewish, Greek and Roman. I think it has been expressed most clearly of all by Christ. . . . The whole of Christian civilisation, so brilliant on the surface, grew up on [an] obvious, strange,

sometimes conscious but for the most part unconscious misunderstanding and contradiction [of the authentic teachings of Jesus the Liberator]. . . . For 19 centuries Christian mankind has lived in this way. . . . There is such an obvious contradiction that sooner or later, probably very soon, it will be exposed and will put an end either to the acceptance of the Christian religion which is necessary to maintain power, or to the existence of an army and any violence supported by it, which is no less necessary to maintain power.[20]

"Your British, as well as our Russian" government, with their nominal allegiance to the lordship of Jesus Christ, would have to face this contradiction and its consequences.

The name of Tolstoy's Indian disciple and correspondent in South Africa was Mohandas K. Gandhi. His philosophy of what Erik Erikson has aptly termed "militant non-violence" was a blending of elements from traditional Hinduism, which he had initially rejected but on which he eventually looked more favorably, and elements from Christianity, or more specifically from the teachings of Jesus. Tolstoy's interpretations had helped him to understand the authentic message of Jesus, within and behind the traditional Christianity he and his Indian countrymen had learned from the missionaries. And so "a gathering of economists found themselves lectured to ('perhaps you will treat my intrusion as a welcome diversion from the trodden path') on—Jesus."[21] By the time Gandhi died a martyr on 30 January 1948, history had fulfilled Tolstoy's dying prophecy. "Your British" and "our Russian" empires, both of which had claimed to embody Christian values in their governments, had been overthrown by forces claiming to be champions of liberation and of nonviolence, though certainly not of traditional Christian belief in the message of Jesus the Liberator.

Yet Gandhi continued to have many disciples for his gospel of nonviolence in the spirit of Jesus the Liberator. They were to learn that following in the footsteps of Jesus the Liberator, and in the footsteps of Mahatma Gandhi, might temporarily lead them, as it had Gandhi himself, to triumphant processions like the one on Palm Sunday (Matt. 21:1-11). But eventually it would take them to the confrontations with the establishment that immediately followed the triumph.[22] And there would be some whose path of following Jesus the Liberator (to borrow Sheldon's title) "in his steps" took them the full distance from Palm Sunday to Good Friday, as the way of triumph became the way of the cross and the imitation of Christ took the form of being quite literally, in the words of the New Testament, "made conformable unto his death."[23] One of these was Martin Luther King, Jr., who, like Gandhi, was martyred by an assassin's bullet, on 4 April 1968.

Radical conformity to the life of Jesus, and even to his death, and revolutionary obedience to his imperatives were not alien to the particular traditions out of which Martin Luther King came. Both as a black American and as an American Baptist who believed himself to stand as well in the spiritual lineage of the sixteenth-century Continental Anabaptists, he was descended from forebears who had historically always been a despised minority and who had often been obliged to learn the "cost of discipleship" by suffering oppression and even death. Like many Protestant leaders, he came from a family of ministers, and in later years he would often recall having heard the stories and sayings of the Gospels in church and home long before he learned to read them in school. His eventual decision as an undergraduate to follow his father and his grandfather into the Christian ministry took him to theological seminary and then to graduate school. His academic studies developed in him the theological, philosophical, and moral principles that were to mold his life, shape his message, determine his public career, and bring him to his death.

While many of the books he studied as a seminarian and graduate student were the standard titles that most Protestant students of theology at that time were reading—his dissertation dealt with the doctrine of God in the thought of Paul Tillich and Henry Nelson Wieman—one name stands out on his reading list that was absent from most of the others: Mohandas K. Gandhi, whose death in 1948 coincided with Martin Luther King's matriculation in the seminary. Gandhi, while employing the instruments of nonviolence in his battle for the liberation of India from colonialism under the British empire, had expressed the hope that it would be through American blacks "that the unadulterated message of nonviolence will be delivered to the world." One influential black Christian in America who owed much to Gandhi was Howard Thurman.[24] Thurman reached through the philosophy of Gandhi, but beyond it, to the message of Jesus, upon which Gandhi had drawn, to portray Jesus as the Liberator especially of those who had been denied opportunity and fulfillment. But it was Mordecai Johnson, another leading black preacher and thinker, whose sermon at Crozer Theological Seminary in Philadelphia brought the young theological student face to face with the thought of Gandhi as an eminently workable contemporary system. Johnson, he recalled, aroused in him the conviction that Gandhi was "the first person in history to live the love ethic of Jesus above mere interaction between individuals." Years later, in his last book, he was still citing Gandhi against the "nihilistic philosophy" and hatred that threatened to make his revolution "bloody and violent." "What was new about Mahatma Gandhi's movement in India," King declared, "was that he mounted a revolution on hope and love, hope and nonviolence."[25]

That interpretation of the teaching of Jesus as a love ethic that repudiated violence and went beyond individualism represented the intellectual and moral foundation of King's thought and action. For it had to be action as well as thought. The Sermon on the Mount, which he had studied in the seminary as a biblical text, became for him in the mature years of his ministry a textbook for social and political activism. As he would later reminisce,

> When I went to Montgomery as a pastor, I had not the slightest idea that I would later become involved in a crisis in which nonviolent resistance would be applicable. I neither started the protest nor suggested it. I simply responded to the call of the people for a spokesman. When the protest began, my mind, consciously or unconsciously, was driven back to the Sermon on the Mount, with its sublime teachings on love, and to the Gandhian method of nonviolent resistance.[26]

Gandhi and the Sermon on the Mount were his continuing inspiration. The accents of the Sermon on the Mount, as he had learned through these experiences to interpret it, ring out in all his speeches and public documents. The most profound of these documents is probably his "Letter from Birmingham Jail," completed on 16 April 1963, in which he voiced the prophetic hope that "one day the South will know that when these disinherited children of God sat down at lunch counters, they were in fact standing up for what is best in the American dream and for the most sacred values in our Judeo-Christian heritage."[27]

This sounded naive to all of his critics and even to some of his supporters, as well as to the main body of the scholarly and theological interpreters of the teachings of Jesus and the Sermon on the Mount, who had by this time achieved something of a consensus that the message of Jesus was a "consistent eschatology." But King's interpretation of the Sermon on the Mount was in fact a carefully thought out and highly sophisticated strategy. In 1959, he and his wife, Coretta Scott King, made a pilgrimage to India, the land of Gandhi, where they saw some of the concrete results that had been attained by the "naive" Mahatma. Through "militant nonviolence" Gandhi had accomplished a liberation that the repeated Indian rebellions before him, going back to the Sepoy Mutiny of 1857 and beyond, had been unable to attain. "I left India," King reported, "more convinced than ever before that nonviolent resistance is the most potent weapon available to oppressed people in their struggle for freedom." "It was," he added, speaking of Gandhi's historic achievement, "a marvelous thing to see the results of a nonviolent campaign."[28]

In his own series of nonviolent campaigns over the next decade, Martin Luther King put that philosophy to the test. Even many of his followers, both black and white, urged that the time for nonviolence had passed, that the message of liberation in the Sermon on the Mount could not succeed as a "weapon available to oppressed people in their struggle for freedom." Repeatedly he acknowledged that he was finding their arguments increasingly persuasive, their impatience more appealing, their strategies of direct action more tempting. Yet each time he ended up reaffirming his fundamental commitment to the practicality of the teachings of the Sermon on the Mount as a political program for the liberation of American blacks. At the heart of this program was the vision of human society as a "beloved community."[29] He described this community at length especially in his book *Stride toward Freedom*.[30] It was to be a society in which—within the standard triad of justice, power, and love—the historic definition of justice would gradually become a reality through the moderation of power by love. He knew it would not happen all of a sudden, and he was realistic enough to recognize that there would be many individuals whom the evangelical imperatives of love would not change; only law, and the enforcement of law, could do that. But he had learned from Gandhi that "mere interaction between individuals" was not, despite centuries of Christian interpretation, the deepest meaning of "the love ethic of Jesus." Rather, the love ethic would have to penetrate and reform the structures of society itself and, through those structures, create a context of love and justice to which, through power, even the recalcitrant would have to conform.

When an eminent scholar of black literature in America was asked why Martin Luther King had not become a Marxist and why those who followed him had accepted his philosophy of nonviolence, he unhesitatingly replied: "Because of the overpowering force of the figure of Jesus." That was also the reason in many cases for the positive response, painfully slow in coming though it was, that King's message called forth in white Christians. Obviously there remained a large group who did not respond that way, and Martin Luther King, Jr., became their victim, as he had long known he might. But in his death he carried out what he knew in his life, that he had been called to follow in the footsteps of Another. And so, when he accepted the Nobel Peace Prize in December 1963, he repeated, yet one more time, the commands and the promises of Jesus in the gospel of liberation as enunciated in the Sermon on the Mount:

> When the years have rolled past and when the blazing light of truth is focused on this marvelous age in which we live, men and women will know and children will be taught that we have a finer land, a better people, a more noble civilization, because these humble children of God were willing to "suffer for righteousness' sake."

Despite all its ambiguity, theological no less than political, such a reading of the message of Jesus continues to inspire the campaign for human liberation. Especially in the Third World, Jesus the Liberator is being pitted against all the Grand Inquisitors, whether sacred or secular. But now he is seen as inverting his original statement (Matt. 4:4) to read that man shall not live by the word of God alone but by bread as well, as sanctioning not only militant nonviolence but direct action, as not only blessing a spiritual poverty that awaits supernatural goods in the life to come but leading the poor of this world to natural goods in this life and in this world. This is what Casalis calls a "christology of revolutionary praxis."[31] The contrast between this picture of Jesus the Liberator and earlier pictures of Jesus the Liberator may perhaps become visible if we compare the two versions in the New Testament of one of the Beatitudes. As the advocates of a nonpolitical interpretation of Christ the Liberator have always pointed out, the more familiar version in the Gospel of Matthew reads, "Blessed are the poor in spirit, for theirs is the kingdom of heaven" (Matt. 5:3). Yet the theology of liberation is based on the reminder that in the Gospel of Luke Jesus cries out, "Blessed are you poor . . . , but woe to you that are rich!" (Luke 6:20, 24).[32] But if Dostoevsky's legend of the Grand Inquisitor was the most profound portrayal of Jesus the Liberator, it was the American War between the States that evoked not only Lincoln's recognition of the ambiguity in citing Jesus as an authority for specific political action, but also the most stirring summons to live and die in the name of Jesus the political Liberator. In February 1862, Julia Ward Howe, drawing upon Romantic imagery of Jesus, published "The Battle Hymn of the Republic":

> In the beauty of the lilies Christ was born across the sea,
> With a glory in his bosom that transfigures you and me;
> As he died to make men holy, let us die to make men free,
> While God is marching on.

18

The Man Who Belongs to the World

Both in Jerusalem, and in all Ju-
daea, and in Samaria, and unto
the uttermost part of the earth.

 Nazareth was what is known in colloquial English as a
hick town, an insignificant village. It almost sounds like
a proverbial saying when in the Gospel of John Nathanael
asks (John 1:46), "Can anything good come out of Nazareth?" Thus Jesus of Nazareth was a villager and a provincial. Whatever may be the historical status of the story
of his flight to Egypt as an infant with his parents, he never as an
adult traveled beyond the borders of the Levant. As far as we can
tell, he did not command either of the world languages of his time,
Latin and Greek, although both are said by the Gospel of John to
have appeared in the inscription on his cross (John 19:20). The only
reference to his having written anything in any language, when he
stooped to write with his finger on the ground, comes in a passage
of dubious textual authenticity, which most manuscripts include
somewhere in the Gospel of John (John 8:6, 8). He spoke of how "the
rulers of the Gentiles lord it over them, and their great men exercise
authority over them" (Matt. 20:25), but as of a phenomenon belonging
to a world far removed from his own. And even when, in an appearance after the resurrection, he is represented by the author of the
Acts of the Apostles as having referred to the outside world, it was
as a provincial might, dividing the world into the immediate environs

and everything that was elsewhere: "Ye shall be witnesses unto me both in Jerusalem, and in all Judaea, and in Samaria—and unto the uttermost part of the earth."[1] Therefore his cosmopolitan detractors in the Roman empire were able to sneer that he had put in his appearance "in some small corner of the earth somewhere," and not (to borrow a modern phrase that seems appropriate) out here in the real world.[2]

Jesus of Nazareth may have been a provincial, but Jesus Christ is the Man Who Belongs to the World. By a geographical expansion shattering anything that either his cosmopolitan detractors within paganism or, for that matter, the author of the Book of Acts within Christianity could have imagined, his name has moved out far from that "small corner of the earth somewhere" and has come to be known "unto the uttermost part of the earth." In the words of the paraphrase of Psalm 72 by Isaac Watts,

> Jesus shall reign where'er the sun
> Does his successive journeys run,
> His kingdom stretch from shore to shore
> Till moons shall wax and wane no more.
> People and realms of every tongue
> Dwell on his love with sweetest song.[3]

When that hymn was published in 1719, the most dramatic growth in the extension of his influence ever known was just beginning. Because of that quantum increase, the best-known history of Christian expansion in English devoted three of its seven volumes to the nineteenth century alone, calling it *The Great Century*.[4] The sun never sets on the empire of Jesus the King, the Man Who Belongs to the World.

Not coincidentally, the great century of Christian missionary expansion was also in many ways the great century of European colonialism.[5] As in past centuries of Christian conversion, the missionary and the military sometimes went hand in hand, each serving the purposes of the other, and not always in a manner or a spirit consonant with the spirit of Christ. The medieval method of carrying on Christian missions was often to conquer the tribe in warfare and then to subject the entire enemy army to baptism at the nearest river.[6] That pattern continued to appear in modern missions, despite the many differences between their methods. Consequently, although Jesus himself had lived in the Near East, it was as a religion of Europe that his message came to the nations of the world and the islands of the sea—a religion of Europe both in the sense of a religion *from* Europe and, often, a religion *about* Europe as well. Indeed, at the end of the "great century" and on the eve of the First World War, the provocative aphorism was coined, apparently by Hilaire Belloc: "The Faith is Europe and Europe is the Faith."[7]

The identification of Europe and "the faith" implied, on the one hand, that those who accepted European economic, political, and military domination and who adopted European civilization thereby came under pressure to undergo conversion to the European faith in Jesus Christ. It likewise implied, however, that faith in Jesus Christ must be on European terms, take them or leave them, and that the forms it took—organizational, ethical, doctrinal, liturgical—must be, with as much adaptation as necessary but as little adaptation as possible, the ones it had acquired in its European configuration.

Although it has become part of the conventional wisdom in much of contemporary anticolonialist literature, both Eastern and Western, it is an oversimplification to dismiss the missions as nothing more than a cloak for white imperialism. Such an oversimplification ignores the biographical, religious, and political realities running through the history of Christian missions during the "great century" and long before, as missionaries have, in the name of Jesus, striven to understand and learned to respect the particularity of the cultures to which they have come. It should be noted, in addition, that there was historically a sharp difference on this count between the missionary methods of the Eastern and the Western churches. When Constantine-Cyril and Methodius came as Christian missionaries to the Slavs in the ninth century, they translated not only the Bible, but the Eastern Orthodox liturgy into Slavonic.[8] By contrast, when Augustine had come to the English in 597, he had brought with him not only the message of the gospel and the authority of the See of Rome, but the liturgy of the Latin Mass, and he had made the acceptance of this a condition of conversion to faith in Christ.[9] While Greek-speaking missionaries like Cyril and Methodius did not teach their Slavic disciples to read Greek, Western missionaries had to provide the nations they converted with the rudiments of Latin and the means of learning it. In the Carolingian period, "the use of Latin was everywhere and irrevocably narrowed down to liturgy and the written word," and Latin became a "purely artificial language." Nevertheless, it was also the "sole medium of intellectual life" and could become again, incidentally to the process and quite unintentionally, a way of access to the heritage of pre-Christian Roman culture and classical Latin literature.[10]

The most celebrated instance of the Christian understanding and respect for a native culture, however, was in the work of a Roman Catholic rather than of an Eastern Orthodox missionary, the Jesuit Matteo Ricci, in China. He has been called by a modern English historian of Chinese culture "one of the most remarkable and brilliant men in history."[11] The first generation of Jesuits, under the leadership and inspiration of Francis Xavier, made the mission to China a major item on their agenda. But in carrying out the mission, the Jesuits had followed the medieval pattern of the Western church, introducing the Roman Catholic liturgy of the Mass, forbidding any of the Chinese vernaculars in worship, and enforcing the use of Latin. With Ricci's arrival at Macau in 1582, that strategy underwent drastic revision. Ricci adopted the monastic habit of a Buddhist monk, then the garb of a Confucian scholar, and became a renowned authority both in the natural sciences and in the history and literature of China.

This erudition enabled him to present the person and message of Jesus as the fulfillment of the historic aspirations of Chinese culture, in much the way that Jesus had been presented by the early fathers as the culmination of the Greco-Roman faith in the Logos and by the New Testament as the fulfillment of the Jewish hope for the Messiah. The Chinese, Ricci maintained, "could certainly become Christians, since the essence of their doctrine contains nothing contrary to the essence of the Catholic faith, nor would the Catholic faith hinder them in any way, but would indeed aid in that attainment of the quiet and peace of the republic which their books claim as their goal."[12] Already in his lifetime and even more in the years of the "rites controversy" over the legitimacy of "accommodationism" that followed his death in 1610, Ricci was accused of having compromised the uniqueness of the person of Christ. But the upsurge of interest in his work has made it clear, on the basis of such theological works in Chinese as *The True Meaning of the Lord of Heaven* of 1603, that Ricci was and remained an orthodox Catholic believer, whose very orthodoxy it was that impelled him to take seriously the integrity of Chinese traditions.[13] Although with a less dramatic involvement in native thought and culture than Ricci's, both Roman Catholic and Protestant missionaries in the nineteenth century often managed to combine a commitment to evangelization in the name of Jesus with a deep (and ever deepening) respect for the native culture and indigenous traditions of the nations to which they had been sent.

As in the past, Christian missions in the nineteenth and twentieth centuries have involved many social changes as well as changes in religious affiliation. Perhaps the most important of these changes for the future cultural development of the nations was the close association between the missions and the campaign for world literacy. A monument to the importance of that achievement for the history of the Slavs is the very alphabet in which most Slavs write, which is called Cyrillic, in honor of Saint Cyril, the ninth-century "apostle to the Slavs," who, with his brother Methodius, is traditionally given credit for having invented it, using Greek uncial script, plus some letters from Hebrew, because of the complexity of Slavic phonemes. Not only among the Slavs in the ninth century, but also among the other so-called heathen in the nineteenth century, the two fundamental elements of missionary culture for more than a millennium have therefore been the translation of the Bible, especially of the New Testament, and education in the missionary schools. In one after another of the nations of Africa and of the South Seas, Christian missionaries found, upon arriving, that none of the native languages had been committed to writing, and that therefore it was necessary, for the sake of the translation of the word of God, to reduce one or more of those languages to written form. In many cases, therefore, the first efforts ever at a scientific understanding of the language, by native or foreigner, came from Christian missionaries. They compiled the first dictionaries, wrote the first grammars, developed the first alphabets. Thus it came about that the first important proper name to have been written in many of these languages must have been the name of Jesus, with its pronunciation adapted to their distinctive phonic structure, just as it had been in all the languages of Europe. The Protestant missionary Bible societies, especially the British and Foreign Bible Society and the American Bible Society, owed their origins to Christian missions in the nineteenth century. During the nineteenth and twentieth centuries, they have put at least the Gospels, and sometimes the rest of the New Testament and of the entire Bible, into more than a thousand additional languages, which averages out to more than five new languages per year.[14]

The schools founded by Protestant missionary societies and by Roman Catholic religious orders have been closely associated with this enterprise and often functioned as the centers for both the translation of the Gospels and the linguistic study undergirding it.[15] At the same time, they taught the children of Christian converts, and any other children who would come, the Western language and the Western-Christian culture of the church that had sent the missionaries. This often led to an ambivalence about the native culture, which the teachers in the missionary schools wanted to master in the name of Christ, and felt obliged to exorcise also in the name of Christ. Because the indigenous legends and practices were seen as permeated with the spirit and the superstition of heathenism, such schools did not regard it as part of their mission to propagate them; and yet they had to learn them, if not always to teach them, in order to teach the message of Jesus. In the memoirs of Asian and African leaders who were graduates from these schools it has become almost obligatory, as part of an attack upon white Christian colonialism, to express bitterness and recrimination about the loss of native roots that came as a by-product of missionary education and of imperialist schools both in the mission field and in the home country. Jawaharlal Nehru, for example, was educated at Harrow and Cambridge, becoming, in his own eloquent English phrase, "a queer mixture of the East and West, out of place everywhere, at home nowhere" and sensing a profound alienation between himself and the religion of the common people of India—an alienation from which he never quite recovered.[16] Nehru could have been speaking for several generations in many nations, some of them committed Christians and others merely deracinated Asians or Africans, who were "out of place everywhere, at home nowhere." Thus it was with a grim literalness that there was fulfilled, in the life of entire cultures and not only of individual families, the alienation described by the saying of Jesus in the Gospels: "I have come to set a man against his father, and a daughter against her mother, and a daughter-in-law against her mother-in-law; and a man's foes will be those of his own household" (Matt. 10:35–36).

So it was that Jesus was seen as a Western figure, and in the early religious art of the "younger churches" he often continued to be represented as he had been in the evangelical and pietist literature of the missionary movements in Europe, England, and America. Beginning already with Ricci and even earlier, however, Christian art in the mission field recognized the need to present the figure of Jesus

Monika Liu Ho-Peh, *The Stilling of the Tempest*, probably 1950s.

in a form that was congenial to his new audience. Ricci, therefore, adapted to his purposes in China a picture from the engravings prepared by one Anthony Wierix, representing Christ and Peter after the resurrection (John 21), which he altered to depict Peter's walking on the water (Matt. 14).[17] A similar theme appears in *The Stilling of the Tempest* by Monika Liu Ho-Peh, an artist with a Chinese surname and a Christian name taken from that of Augustine's mother. Here a Chinese Jesus, standing in the prow of the boat, rebukes the waves and commands, "Peace! Be still!" (Mark 4:39), as his terrified Chinese disciples—most of them bearded, as in Western art, but with Oriental features—strain at the oars and tug at the flapping sails. The dangers of a storm at sea were familiar to the missionaries and to their congregations, and a miracle that demonstrated the sovereignty of Jesus over the forces of nature spoke to their condition.

Yet evangelicals and pietists, too, early recognized, sometimes far more explicitly in the mission field than at home, that it was not enough to bring pictures of Jesus, even pictures of Jesus with native features, or words about Jesus, even words about Jesus in the native vernaculars, to the non-Christian world. It had not been enough in the days of Jesus, either, and so he had come as a healer and not only as a teacher. Similarly, the mission of his followers in the second and third centuries had been one of help and healing, not of evangelization alone. For the word "salvation"—*sotēria* in Greek, *salus* in Latin and its derivative languages, *Heil* in German and its cognate languages—meant "health." As Harnack has noted,

> Into this world of craving for salvation the preaching of Christianity made its way. Long before it had achieved its final triumph by dint of an impressive philosophy of religion, its success was already assured by the fact that it promised and offered salvation—a feature in which it surpassed all other religions and cults. It did more than set up the actual Jesus against the imaginary Aesculapius of dreamland. *Deliberately and consciously it assumed the form of "the religion of salvation or healing," or "the medicine of soul and body," and at the same time it recognized that one of its chief duties was to care assiduously for the sick in body.*[18]

That trenchant description of the full range of the gospel of salvation through Jesus could apply as easily to the nineteenth and twentieth centuries as to the second and third. In the third century, Origen described Jesus, "the Logos and the healing power [*therapeia*] within him," as "more powerful than any evils in the soul."[19] And the closing chapter of the New Testament depicted the city of God, with the throne of Jesus Christ the Lamb of God and the tree of life, and explained that "the leaves of the tree were for the healing of the nations" (Rev. 22:2).

In an age in which the healing of the nations from the ravages of hunger, disease, and war has become the dominant moral imperative, Jesus the Healer has come to assume a central place. It was an emblem of the central place of Jesus when, under the terms of the Geneva Convention of 1864 for the Amelioration of the Condition of the Wounded and Sick of Armies in the Field, the international organization created to carry out that moral imperative took the name "Red Cross Society"; its symbol, based on a reversal of the colors of the Swiss flag, is a red cross on a white background. Yet the connection between evangelization in the name of Jesus and the mission of help and healing has also been an issue for debate, especially in the twentieth century. This debate, too, comes as a commentary on the literal meaning of a word in the Gospels: "Whosoever shall give you a cup of water to drink in my name, because ye belong to Christ, verily I say unto you, he shall not lose his reward."[20] It has almost seemed that in every epoch there were some who were primarily interested in naming the name of Christ, clarifying its doctrinal and theological meaning, and defending that meaning against its enemies—but who named the name without giving the cup of water. Yet it has seemed possible for others to give the cup of water, to provide the healing, and to improve the social lot of the disadvantaged—but to do so without explicitly naming the name of Christ. Does that saying of Jesus mean that each of these ways of responding to his summons is only a partial obedience to this dual command? In the answer to this question, much of the debate over the primary responsibility of Christ's disciples in the modern world has concentrated on the disjunction between the two components of the imperative.

A growing feature of the debate has been the stress on cooperation rather than competition between the disciples of Jesus and those who follow other ancient Teachers of the Way. Those followers of Jesus who advocate such cooperation insist that they are no less committed to the universality of his person and message than are the advocates of the traditional methods of conquest through evangelization. But the universality of Jesus, they have urged, does not establish itself in the world through the obliteration of whatever elements of light and truth have already been granted to the nations of the world. For whatever the proximate and historical sources of that truth may have been, its ultimate source is God, the same God whom Jesus called Father; else the confession of the oneness of God is empty. Criticism of many of the elements of historic Christianity, especially of its dogmatism and cultural imperialism, led to the suggestion that it had much to learn, as well as much to teach, in its encounter with other faiths. Jesus was indeed the Man Who Belongs to the World, but he was this because he made it possible to appreciate more profoundly the full scope of the revelation of God wherever it had appeared in the history of the world, in the light of which, in turn, his own meaning and message acquired more profound significance. In the paradoxical formula of Archbishop Nathan Söderblom's Gifford Lectures of 1931, "the uniqueness of Christ as the historical revealer, as the Word made flesh, and the mystery of Calvary," which are an "essentially unique character of Christianity," compel the affirmation that "God reveals himself in history, outside the Church as well as in it."[21] The most complete statement of that position was the thought-provoking and massive report, *Re-thinking Missions: A Layman's Inquiry after One Hundred Years*, published in 1932 by a Commission of Appraisal representing seven American Protestant denominations.

Having carried out an extensive survey of world missions, particularly in Asia and in Africa, the authors of this "laymen's inquiry" reviewed, in seven volumes of data, the state of evangelization and Christian world service, recommending far-reaching revisions not only of specific strategy but of underlying philosophy. They concluded that the stress upon the particularity of Jesus and the absoluteness of his message had been, though perhaps necessary, a temporary element in the program of the missions. As one historian of missions has summarized the position of *Re-thinking Missions*,

> The task of the missionary today, it was maintained, is to see the best in other religions, to help the adherents of those religions to discover, or to rediscover, all that is best in their own traditions, to cooperate with the most active and vigorous elements in the other traditions in social reform and in the purification of religious expression. The aim should not be conversion—the drawing of members of one religious faith over into another or an attempt to establish a Christian monopoly. Cooperation is to replace aggression. The ultimate aim, so far as any can be descried, is the emergence of the various religions out of their isolation into a world fellowship in which each will find its appropriate place.[22]

So drastic a revision of the traditional Christian understanding that "there is salvation in no one else than [Jesus], for there is no other name under heaven [than the name of Jesus] given among men by which we must be saved" (Acts 4:12) would inevitably evoke vigorous discussion and extensive controversy, especially coming as it did just when the theology of Karl Barth was emphasizing again the uniqueness of Jesus and the centrality of his claims.

Such proposals for the redefinition of the universality of Jesus came also at a time when scholars in the West were giving new attention to the languages and cultures of other religious traditions. Not surprisingly, many of those scholars have had ties, of family or education or both, to Christian missions. Sons and daughters of Protestant missionaries, as well as many of the missionaries themselves, took the lead in explaining Eastern cultures to Europe and America. The researches into scholarly linguistics that had originally been the necessary preparation for the translation of the Gospels into more than a thousand tongues now became a bridge that carried Western travelers in the opposite direction as well. In 1875, the eminent German-born Indologist Friedrich Max Müller, professor at Oxford, began the publication of the monumental *Sacred Books of the East*, which eventually came to fifty-one volumes. This series opened up the riches of the Eastern religious sages, particularly those of India, to readers who could not study the original sources. At about the same time, in connection with the World's Columbian Exposition held at Chicago in 1893 to commemorate the four-hundredth anniversary of Columbus's discovery of the New World, there was held a world parliament of religions, whose purpose it was to draw the religious implications of the discovery that the human race was not exclusively European and therefore not exclusively Christian, but global and universal. Despite the phenomenal successes of Christian missions during the nineteenth and twentieth centuries, it seems incontestable that the percentage of Christians in the total world population is continually declining, and therefore it seems inconceivable that the Christian church and the Christian message will ever conquer the population of the world and replace the other religions of the human race. If Jesus is to be the Man Who Belongs to the World, it will have to be by some other way.

Perhaps the most remarkable document to come out of this deepening sense of a new universalism was not *Re-thinking Missions* of

1932, but a decree published a third of a century later, on 28 October 1965, the Declaration on the Relationship of the Church to Non-Christian Religions, *Nostra aetate*, of the Second Vatican Council. In a series of succinct but striking paragraphs, the decree described the religious quest and the spiritual values at work in primitive religion, in Hinduism, in Buddhism, and in Islam; and in a historic affirmation the council declared:

> The Catholic Church rejects nothing which is true and holy in those religions. She looks with sincere respect upon those ways of conduct and of life, those rules and teachings which, though differing in many particulars from what she holds and sets forth, nevertheless often reflect a ray of that Truth which enlightens all men (John 1:9). Indeed, she proclaims and must ever proclaim Christ, "the way, the truth, and the life" (John 14:6), in whom men find the fullness of religious life, and in whom God has reconciled all things to Himself.[23]

The two passages from the Gospel according to John quoted in the decree clearly identify the issue. For it is in that Gospel that Jesus speaks of himself as "the way, the truth, and the life" and says that no one comes to the Father except through him. And yet that same Gospel provided the epigraph for the universalism of the Enlightenment's portrait of Jesus; for the Gospel of John declares in its prologue that the Logos-Word of God, incarnate in Jesus, enlightens everyone who comes into the world. By citing the authority of both passages, the Second Vatican Council sought to affirm universality and particularity simultaneously and to ground both of them in the figure of Jesus.

A special issue at the Second Vatican Council and throughout Christianity, especially since the Second World War, was the relation between Christianity and its parent faith, Judaism. The Holocaust took place in what had been nominally Christian territory; moreover, the record of the churches in opposing it was not the noblest page in Christian history. Among both Roman Catholics and Protestants in Germany there were those who, as the New Testament says about the apostle Paul's involvement in the martyrdom of Stephen, were "consenting to the death" of the Jews (Acts 8:1), and many more who were (as it seems now, by hindsight) blindly insensitive to the situation. The Second Vatican Council "deplores," it declared, "the hatred, persecutions, and displays of anti-Semitism directed against the Jews at any time and from any source," which would appear to include the official sources of the church's past.[24] And it condemned any attempt to blame the death of Jesus "upon all the Jews then living, without distinction, or upon the Jews today," insisting that "the Jews should not be presented as repudiated or cursed by God."

This rethinking of the relation between Christianity and Judaism was partly the consequence of the worldwide horror over the Holocaust, but partly it also came through a deepening of Christian understanding and reflection. The result was the most basic Christian reconsideration of the status of Judaism since the first century. Ironically, the years of Nazi anti-Semitism and the Holocaust in Germany had also been the years in which Christians developed the new awareness of the Jewishness of Jesus, the apostles, and the New Testament, an awareness that receives expression in the language of the Vatican Council. It was in 1933, the beginning of the Nazi era in Germany, that there appeared, also in Germany, the first volume of one of the most influential biblical reference works of the twentieth century, the multivolume *Theological Dictionary of the New Testament* edited by Gerhard Kittel.[25] Probably the most important scholarly and theological generalization to be drawn from the hundreds of articles in the Kittel *Dictionary* has been that the teaching and language of the New Testament, including the teaching and language of Jesus himself, cannot be understood apart from their setting in the context of Judaism. It was once again in the Gospel of John, despite the hostility of some of its language about Jews, that Jesus, speaking as a Jew to a non-Jew, was described as saying: "We [Jews] worship what we know, for salvation is from the Jews" (John 4:22). Directly he went on to say, in the very next verse: "But the hour is coming, and now is, when the true worshipers [which, of course, refers to both Jews and Gentiles] will worship the Father in spirit and truth." Once again the theme is universality-with-particularity, as both of these are grounded in the figure of Jesus the Jew.

By a curious blend of these currents of religious faith and scholarship with the no less powerful influences of skepticism and religious relativism, the universality-with-particularity of Jesus has thus become an issue not only for Christians in the twentieth century, but for humanity. The later chapters of this book show that as respect for the organized church has declined, reverence for Jesus has grown. For the unity and variety of the portraits of "Jesus through the centuries" has demonstrated that there is more in him than is dreamt of in the philosophy and Christology of the theologians. Within the church, but also far beyond its walls, his person and message are, in the phrase of Augustine, a "beauty ever ancient, ever new,"[26] and now he belongs to the world.

Notes

INTRODUCTION: THE GOOD, THE TRUE, AND THE BEAUTIFUL

1. Athanasius, *Discourses against the Arians* 1.10.36.
2. Albert Schweitzer, *The Quest of the Historical Jesus*, trans. William Montgomery (1956; New York: Macmillan, 1961), p. 4; translation herein revised.
3. Alfred North Whitehead, *Science and the Modern World* (1925; New York: Mentor Editions, 1952), pp. 49–50.
4. Fernand Braudel, *The Mediterranean and the Mediterranean World in the Age of Philip II*, trans. Sian Reynolds, 2 vols. (New York: Harper and Row, 1972), 1:168.
5. Arthur O. Lovejoy, *The Great Chain of Being: A Study of the History of an Idea* (Cambridge, Mass.: Harvard University Press, 1936), p. 6.
6. John Calvin, *Institutes of the Christian Religion* 3.2.34, ed. John Thomas McNeill, 2 vols. (Philadelphia: Westminster Press, 1960), 1:581.
7. See, for example, Athanasius, *On Luke 10:22*; Gregory of Nyssa, *Against Eunomius* 2.4. See also p. 41.
8. Jaroslav Pelikan, *Historical Theology: Continuity and Change in Christian Doctrine* (New York: Corpus Books, 1971), pp. 33–67: "The Evolution of the Historical."
9. Jaroslav Pelikan, *The Christian Tradition: A History of the Development of Doctrine*, 4 vols. to date (Chicago: University of Chicago Press, 1971–), 1:1.
10. Werner Elert, *Der Ausgang der altkirchlichen Christologie* (Berlin: Lutherisches Verlagshaus, 1957), pp. 12–25: "Christusbild und Christusdogma."
11. See Jaroslav Pelikan, *Fools for Christ: Essays on the True, the Good, and the Beautiful* (Philadelphia: Muhlenberg Press, 1955).
12. On this image in relation to analogous ones at Ravenna, see Spiro K. Kostof, *The Orthodox Baptistery of Ravenna* (New Haven: Yale University Press, 1965), pp. 67–68.
13. Gregory of Nyssa, *Against Eunomius* 2.10; Augustine, *On the Trinity* 6.10.11.
14. Augustine, *Tractates on the Gospel of John* 22.8.
15. Agnes von Zahn-Harnack, *Adolf von Harnack*, 2d ed. (Berlin: Walter de Gruyter, 1951), pp. 181–88.
16. Adolf Harnack, *What Is Christianity?* trans. Thomas Bailey Saunders (1900; New York: Harper Torchbooks, 1957), p. 1; translation herein revised. Quotation is from

John Stuart Mill, *On Liberty*, chap. 2, in *The English Philosophers from Bacon to Mill*, ed. Edwin A. Burtt (New York: Modern Library, 1939), p. 967.

1. THE RABBI

1. For a brief but helpful review of the problem, see Matthew Black, "The Recovery of the Language of Jesus," *New Testament Studies* 3 (1956–57): 305–13; also his longer monograph, *An Aramaic Approach to the Gospels and Acts*, 3d ed. (Oxford: Clarendon Press, 1967).
2. Acts 6:1; 9:29.
3. Mark 15:34; the version in Matt. 27:46 differs somewhat, and the textual variants of the transliterations in both passages differ still further.
4. See, in general, Eric M. Meyers and James F. Strange, *Archeology, the Rabbis, and Early Christianity* (Nashville: Abingdon Press, 1981).
5. The exceptions occur in Matt. 23:7–8 and in John 3:26.
6. Rudolf Bultmann, *The History of the Synoptic Tradition*, trans. John Marsh (New York: Harper and Row, 1963), pp. 125–26.
7. Matt. 22:23–33; Matt. 22:15–22; Mark 10:17–22; Matt. 18:1–6.
8. See, for example, William Oscar Emil Oesterley, *The Gospel Parables in the Light of Their Jewish Background* (New York: Macmillan, 1936).
9. Justin Martyr, *First Apology* 65.4.
10. Matt. 5:21–48; italics mine.
11. Howard Clark Kee, *Miracle in the Early Christian World: A Study in Sociohistorical Method* (New Haven: Yale University Press, 1983), p. 188.
12. Mark 7:34; 5:41.
13. Acts 3:22–23; 7:37; Clement of Alexandria, *The Tutor* 1.7.
14. Pelikan, *Christian Tradition* 2:209–10, 238–40.
15. John 1:41; 4:25.
16. 1 Cor. 16:22; *Didache* 10.6.
17. Gregory Dix, *Jew and Greek. A Study in the Primitive Church* (New York: Harper and Brothers, 1953), p. 109.
18. See Peter C. Hodgson, *The Formation of Historical Theology* (New York: Harper and Row, 1966).
19. Krister Stendahl, *Paul among Jews and Gentiles* (Philadelphia: Fortress Press, 1976), p. 4; italics in original.
20. Robert L. Wilken, *John Chrysostom and the Jews* (Berkeley and Los Angeles: University of California Press, 1983), p. 162.

2. THE TURNING POINT OF HISTORY

1. Charles Norris Cochrane, *Christianity and Classical Culture: A Study of Thought and Action from Augustus to Augustine* (Oxford: Clarendon Press, 1944), p. 456.
2. Erwin Panofsky, *The Life and Art of Albrecht Dürer*, 4th ed. (Princeton: Princeton University Press, 1955), pp. 56–57.
3. Rev. 21:6; 1:8.
4. Two of the most profound attempts to address that problem are Amos Wilder, *Ethics and Eschatology in the Teaching of Jesus*, rev. ed. (New York: Harper, 1950), and Rudolf Otto, *The Kingdom of God and the Son of Man*, trans. Floyd V. Filson and Bertram Lee Wolff (London: Lutterworth, 1938).
5. Matt. 10:23; Matt. 24:34; Mark 13:30; Luke 21:32.
6. Schweitzer, *Quest of the Historical Jesus*, p. 360.

7. Jaroslav Pelikan, "The Eschatology of Tertullian," *Church History* 21 (1952): 108–22.
8. Tertullian, *On Spectacles* 30; *On Prayer* 29.
9. Tertullian, *Apology* 39; italics mine.
10. Ps. 96:10; italics mine. Justin, *Dialogue with Trypho* 73.1; Venantius Fortunatus, *Carmina* 2.7.
11. Irenaeus, *Proof of the Apostolic Preaching;* Cyprian, *Testimonies.*
12. Augustine, *City of God* 16.43; 17.20; 17.4.
13. Augustine, *City of God* 17.16; Eusebius, *Ecclesiastical History* 1.3.14–15.
14. Augustine, *City of God* 17.20–23.
15. Augustine, *City of God* 17.5–6.
16. Pelikan, *Christian Tradition* 1:25–26.
17. Fred L. Horton, Jr., *The Melchizedek Tradition: A Critical Examination of the Sources to the Fifth Century A.D. and in the Epistle to the Hebrews* (Cambridge: Cambridge University Press, 1976).
18. Eusebius, *Ecclesiastical History* 1.19; Augustine, *City of God* 17.4; John Calvin, *Institutes of the Christian Religion* 2.15, McNeill ed., 1:494–503.
19. Peter Brown, *Augustine of Hippo. A Biography* (London: Faber and Faber, 1969), pp. 299–312.
20. Eph. 1:10; Gal. 4:4.
21. *Epistle to Diognetus* 9.
22. Luke 2:1; 3:1; Eusebius, *Ecclesiastical History* 1.5.2.
23. Augustine, *City of God* 2.18–19.
24. Augustine, *City of God* 1.30.
25. Augustine, *City of God* 4.3–4.
26. Sallust, *Catilina* 7; Augustine, *City of God* 5.12–13.
27. Augustine, *City of God* 4.33; 5.1; 5.11.
28. Augustine, *City of God* 16.10; 12.18.
29. Augustine, *City of God* 12.13; Origen, *Against Celsus* 4.67.
30. Augustine, *City of God* 7.32.
31. Christopher Dawson, "St. Augustine and His Age," in *St. Augustine,* ed. Martin C. D'Arcy (New York: Meridian Books, 1957), p. 69.
32. See *Oxford English Dictionary,* s.v. "crucial."
33. Augustine, *On the Creed* 9.
34. Martin Werner, *Die Entstehung des christlichen Dogmas* (Bern: Paul Haupt, 1941), pp. 112–13. See also p. 50.
35. Eusebius, *The Preparation of the Gospel* 1.3.6–7.
36. I have adapted here some of the material in my book *The Finality of Jesus Christ in an Age of Universal History* (London: Lutterworth, 1965), pp. 48–56.
37. Eusebius, *Ecclesiastical History* 1.4.6.
38. C. F. Georg Heinrici, *Das Urchristentum in der Kirchengeschichte des Eusebius* (Leipzig: Verlag der Dürr'schen Buchhandlung, 1894), p. 21.
39. Eusebius, *Ecclesiastical History* 4.26.7, quoting Melito of Sardis.
40. Eduard Schwartz, *Zur Geschichte des Athanasius* (Berlin: Walter de Gruyter, 1959), p. 286, n. 3.
41. See p. 112.
42. Karl Holl, "Die schriftstellerische Form des griechischen Heiligenlebens," *Gesammelte Aufsätze zur Kirchengeschichte,* 3 vols. (1928; reprint, Darmstadt: Wissenschaftliche Buchgesellschaft, 1964), 2:249–69.
43. Athanasius, *Life of Antony* 7.
44. Athanasius, *Life of Antony* 1–2.

45. Johannes Quasten, *Patrology*, 3 vols. to date (Westminster, Md.: Newman Press, 1951–), 3:43.
46. Judith H. Anderson, *Biographical Truth: The Representation of Historical Persons in Tudor-Stuart Writing* (New Haven: Yale University Press, 1984), pp. 21–22.
47. See the translation and helpful table prepared by Archibald Robertson, *Nicene and Post-Nicene Fathers of the Church* 4:502–03.
48. Bruno Krusch, *Studien zur christlichen-mittelalterlichen Chronologie: Die Entstehung unserer heutigen Zeitrechnung*, 2 vols. (Berlin: Akademie der Wissenschaften, 1938), 2:59–87.

3. THE LIGHT OF THE GENTILES

1. Reinhold Niebuhr, *The Nature and Destiny of Man*, 2 vols. (New York: Charles Scribner's Sons, 1941–43), 2:6.
2. Ignatius, *Ephesians* 10.1; 1.2.
3. Luke 2:32; Prosper of Aquitaine, *The Call of All Nations* 2.18.
4. Augustine, *City of God* 18.47.
5. Judith Baskin, *Pharaoh's Counsellors: Job, Jethro, and Balaam in Rabbinic and Patristic Tradition* (Chico, Calif.: Scholars Press, 1983).
6. Vergil, *Eclogues* 4.5–52.
7. Compare Isa. 61:17 (Rev. 21:1); Phil. 3:20; Isa. 53:5; Gen. 3:15; Isa. 7:14; Isa. 9:6.
8. Constantine, *Oration to the Saints* 19–21.
9. Jerome, *Epistles* 53.7. Augustine, *City of God* 10.27; Augustine, *Epistles* 137.3.12.
10. Domenico Comparetti, *Vergil in the Middle Ages*, trans. E. F. M. Benecke (London: George Allen and Unwin Ltd., 1966), p. 98, n. 6.
11. Dante, *Purgatorio* 22.70–73.
12. Vergil, *Aeneid* 6.99.
13. Origen, *Against Celsus* 7.56; 7.53.
14. Theophilus, *To Autolycus* 2.9; Lactantius, *Divine Institutes* 1.6.
15. Clement of Alexandria, *Exhortation to the Greeks* 2.
16. Constantine, *Oration to the Saints* 18.
17. Augustine, *City of God* 18.23.
18. Justin Martyr, *I Apology* 20; Clement of Alexandria, *Exhortation to the Greeks* 8.27.4.
19. A. Rossi, "Le Sibille nelle arti figurative italiane," *L'Arte* 18 (1915): 272–85.
20. Charles de Tolnay, *The Sistine Ceiling*, vol. 2 of his *Michelangelo* (Princeton: Princeton University Press, 1945), pp. 46, 57.
21. Clement of Alexandria, *Tutor* 1.2.
22. Clement of Alexandria, *Exhortation* 10.110.
23. Eric Osborn, *The Beginning of Christian Philosophy* (Cambridge: Cambridge University Press, 1981), p. 219.
24. Osborn, *Beginning of Christian Philosophy*, p. 219.
25. Clement of Alexandria, *Stromata* 1.5; Gal. 3:24.
26. Henry Chadwick, *Early Christian Thought and the Classical Tradition* (New York and Oxford: Oxford University Press, 1966), p. 40.
27. Clement of Alexandria, *Stromata* 5.9; italics mine.
28. Clement of Alexandria, *Stromata* 5.14.
29. Raymond Klibansky, *The Continuity of the Platonic Tradition during the Middle Ages*, 2d ed. (Millwood, N.J.: Kraus International Publications, 1982).
30. Plato, *Timaeus* 28–29; all translations of *Timaeus* by Francis Macdonald Cornford, *Plato's Cosmology* (London: Routledge and Kegan Paul, 1937).
31. Clement of Alexandria, *Stromata* 5.14.

32. Clement of Alexandria, *Stromata* 5.13.84, quoting *Timaeus* 40 and Luke 10:22.
33. Clement of Alexandria, *Stromata* 5.14.
34. Compare Henri de Lubac, *Histoire et esprit. L'intelligence de l'Ecriture d'après Origène* (Paris: Aubier, 1950), pp. 144–45.
35. John 3:14–15; Augustine, *Tractates on the Gospel of John* 12.11.
36. Justin Martyr, *I Apology* 55; *Dialogue with Trypho* 86.
37. Iris Murdoch, *The Fire and the Sun: Why Plato Banished the Artists* (Oxford: Clarendon Press, 1977), p. 87.
38. Plato, *Timaeus* 36B.
39. Justin Martyr, *I Apology* 60.
40. Hugo Rahner, "Odysseus am Mastbaum," *Zeitschrift für katholische Theologie* 65 (1941): 123–52; an English summary appears in his *Greek Myths and Christian Mystery*, trans. Brian Battershaw (New York: Harper and Row, 1963), pp. 371–86.
41. Homer, *Odyssey* 12.158–64, trans. Richmond Lattimore (New York: Harper and Row, 1967); italics mine.
42. Justin Martyr, *II Apology* 10; Tertullian, *Apology* 4.
43. Tertullian, *To the Nations* 1.10.
44. Homer, *Odyssey* 12.219–21.
45. Clement of Alexandria, *Exhortation* 12.118.4.
46. Karl Krumbacher, *Geschichte der byzantinischen Literatur*, 2d ed. (Munich: C. H. Beck, 1897), pp. 529–30, 538.
47. Josef Wilpert, *I sarcofagi cristiani antichi*, 2 vols. (Rome: Pontificio istituto di archeologia cristiana, 1919), vol. 1, pl. 24.
48. Quoted in Rahner, *Greek Myths and Christian Mystery*, p. 381; translation herein slightly revised.
49. David Lerch, *Isaaks Opferung christlich gedeutet: Eine auslegungsgeschichtliche Untersuchung* (Tübingen: J. C. B. Mohr, 1950).
50. George Leonard Prestige, *God in Patristic Thought* (London: SPCK, 1956), pp. 117–24.
51. Deut. 18:15–22; Clement of Alexandria, *Tutor* 1.7.
52. Adolf von Harnack, "Sokrates und die alte Kirche," *Reden und Aufsätze*, 2 vols. (Giessen: Alfred Töpelmann, 1906), 1:27–48; Geddes MacGregor, *The Hemlock and the Cross: Humanism, Socrates, and Christ* (Philadelphia: Lippincott, 1963).
53. Justin Martyr, *I Apology* 5, 46; *II Apology* 10.
54. 2 Tim. 1:10; Jaroslav Pelikan, *The Shape of Death: Life, Death, and Immortality in the Early Fathers* (New York: Abingdon Press, 1961).
55. Clement of Alexandria, *Stromata* 5.14.
56. Plato, *Republic* 2.360–61; translation, except for the final quotation, is my own.
57. Gilbert Murray, *Five Stages of Greek Religion* (Boston: Beacon Press, 1951), p. 157, and his footnote on the Greek verb *anaschindyleō*.
58. Acts 17:23; Clement of Alexandria, *Stromata* 5.12.

4. THE KING OF KINGS

1. Augustine, *On the Psalms* 76.7.
2. Justin Martyr, *I Apology* 31.
3. Irenaeus, *Against Heresies* 5.26.2; 5.33–34 (quoting Papias).
4. Irenaeus, *Against Heresies* 5.35.1; Justin Martyr, *Dialogue with Trypho* 80; see Richard Patrick Crosland Hanson, *Allegory and Event* (Richmond, Va.: John Knox Press, 1959), pp. 333–56.
5. Justin Martyr, *Dialogue with Trypho* 135.

6. *Martyrum Scillitanorum Acta* 6, in *The Acts of the Christian Martyrs*, ed. Herbert Musurillo (Oxford: Clarendon Press, 1972), pp. 86–89.
7. *Martyrdom of Polycarp* 8–9.
8. *Martyrdom of Ignatius* 2.
9. Justin Martyr, *I Apology* 11; 51; 17.
10. Tertullian, *Apology* 30–32; 1 Tim. 2:2.
11. Irenaeus, *Against Heresies* 5.24.1; Rom. 13:1, 4, 6.
12. Tertullian, *On Idolatry* 15; Matt. 22:21.
13. 1 Cor. 8:4–6; see the comments of Augustine, *City of God* 9.23.
14. See above all William Hugh Clifford Frend, *Martyrdom and Persecution in the Early Church: A Study of a Conflict from the Maccabees to Donatus* (Oxford: Blackwell, 1965).
15. *Epistle to Diognetus* 7, 5; italics mine.
16. Vergil, *Aeneid* 1.279.
17. Tertullian, *Apology* 21.
18. Jacob Burckhardt, *Die Zeit Constantins des Grossen* (Vienna: Phaidon, n.d.), p. 242.
19. Hermann Doerries, *Constantine the Great*, trans. Roland H. Bainton (New York: Harper Torchbooks, 1972), pp. 229–30.
20. Ramsay MacMullen, *Constantine* (New York: Dial Press, 1969), p. 111.
21. Lactantius, *On the Manner in Which the Persecutors Died* 44; *Divine Institutes* 4.26–27; *Epitome* 47.
22. Eusebius, *Life of Constantine* 1.24–31.
23. Eusebius, *Ecclesiastical History* 9.9.10–11.
24. Eusebius, *Life of Constantine* 1.6–7.
25. Adolf Harnack, *Grundrisz der Dogmengeschichte*, 4th ed. (Tübingen: J. C. B. Mohr, 1905), p. 192.
26. For a fuller exposition of the issues and alternatives, see Pelikan, *Christian Tradition* 1:172–225.
27. Theodoret, *Ecclesiastical History* 1.11–12.
28. Socrates, *Ecclesiastical History* 1.9.
29. Eusebius, *Life of Constantine* 3.20, 64–65.
30. Eusebius, *Life of Constantine* 2.56–60.
31. Hermann Doerries, *Constantine and Religious Liberty*, trans. Roland H. Bainton (New Haven: Yale University Press, 1960), p. 110.
32. Eusebius, *Life of Constantine* 3.15.
33. Eusebius, *Ecclesiastical History* 10.9.4.
34. Frank Edward Brightman, "Byzantine Imperial Coronations," *Journal of Theological Studies* 2 (1901): 359–92.
35. Gen. 14:18; Ps. 110:4; Heb. 7:1–17.
36. C. Lepelley, "S. Léon . . . et la cité romaine," *Revue des sciences religieuses* 35 (1961): 130–50.
37. Matt. 16:18–19; see Pelikan, *Christian Tradition* 4:81–84.
38. See Walter Ullmann, *Medieval Papalism: The Political Theories of the Medieval Canonists* (London: Methuen, 1949).

5. THE COSMIC CHRIST

1. Alfred North Whitehead, *Science and the Modern World* (1925; New York: Mentor Books, 1952), p. 13.
2. Ferdinand Hahn, *Christologische Hoheitstitel: Ihre Geschichte im frühen Christentum* (Göttingen: Vandenhoeck und Ruprecht, 1963).
3. Gregory of Nazianzus, *Orations* 36.11.

4. Goethe, *Faust* 1224–37.
5. Gregory T. Armstrong, *Die Genesis in der alten Kirche* (Tübingen: J. C. B. Mohr, 1962).
6. Gregory of Nyssa, *On the Making of Man* 25.2.
7. See pp. 40–42 above.
8. Jaroslav Pelikan, "Creation and Causality in the History of Christian Thought," in *Issues in Evolution*, ed. Sol Tax and Charles Callender (Chicago: University of Chicago Press, 1960), pp. 329–40.
9. Pelikan, *Christian Tradition* 1:35–37; 3:290–91.
10. Gregory of Nyssa, *On the Making of Man* 24.
11. Basil of Caesarea, *Hexaemeron* 1.2; 3.8. Gregory of Nyssa, *On the Making of Man* 8.4.
12. Basil of Caesarea, *Hexaemeron* 6.1; 9.2.
13. Basil of Caesarea, *Hexaemeron* 9.6; Gen. 1:26 (italics mine); Heb. 1:2–3.
14. Hilary of Poitiers, *On the Trinity* 2.6.
15. Prov. 8:22 (italics mine); Athanasius, *Discourses against the Arians* 2.18–82.
16. Augustine, *Confessions* 11.3.5–11.9.11.
17. In Plato's *Theaetetus* 203 the word occurs twice, once in each of these senses.
18. Epiphanius of Salamis, *Against All Heresies* 51.3; Gregory of Nyssa, *The Great Catechism* 1.
19. Gregory of Nazianzus, *Theological Orations* 3.17.
20. Gregory of Nyssa, *On the Making of Man* 16.2; 5.2 (John 1:1; 1 Cor. 2:16; 2 Cor. 13:3).
21. Gregory of Nazianzus, *Theological Orations* 4.20.
22. Tertullian, *On the Flesh of Christ* 5.
23. Tertullian, *On Prescription against Heretics* 7.
24. Gregory of Nazianzus, *Theological Orations* 2.6.
25. Basil of Caesarea, *Hexaemeron* 1.6.
26. Basil of Caesarea, *Hexaemeron* 6.5–7.
27. Gregory of Nyssa, *On the Making of Man* 8.8.
28. Gregory of Nyssa, *Against Eunomius* 2.3.
29. Gregory of Nazianzus, *Theological Orations* 4.17.
30. Jaroslav Pelikan, *Development of Christian Doctrine: Some Historical Prolegomena* (New Haven: Yale University Press, 1969), pp. 129–31; Hilary, *On the Trinity* 4.14.
31. Basil of Caesarea, *Hexaemeron* 2.2.
32. Gregory of Nazianzus, *Orations* 38.10–11.
33. Basil of Caesarea, *On the Holy Spirit* 7; Col. 1:15–17.
34. Rom. 4:17; Athanasius, *The Incarnation of the Word* 42.
35. Athanasius, *Discourses against the Arians* 3.63; *Defense of the Nicene Definition* 3.11.
36. Athanasius, *Discourses against the Arians* 1.23; 3.19–20 (Eph. 3:14–15).
37. Athanasius, *Discourses against the Arians* 1.25.
38. Athanasius, *Against the Heathen* 45.
39. Athanasius, *To the Bishops of Egypt* 15.
40. Athanasius, *Against the Heathen* 41.
41. Athanasius, *Discourses against the Arians* 2.63 (Col. 1:17; Rom. 8:21).
42. Athanasius, *Against the Heathen* 7–8.
43. Athanasius, *The Incarnation of the Word* 5.
44. Gregory of Nyssa, *On the Making of Man* 5.2; 30.34.
45. Cf. Pelikan, *Christian Tradition* 1:344–45; 2:10–16.
46. Clement of Alexandria, *Exhortation to the Greeks* 1.8.4; Athanasius, *The Incarnation of the Word* 54.3.
47. Gregory of Nyssa, *On the Making of Man* 16.2.

48. Gregory of Nyssa, *Sermons on the Song of Songs* 13.
49. Basil of Caesarea, *Hexaemeron* 1.3; 3.6.
50. Gregory of Nyssa, *On the Making of Man* 23.1, 5.
51. Gregory of Nyssa, *On the Making of Man* 22.5.
52. Gregory of Nazianzus, *Orations* 39.13; 45.26.
53. Erich Auerbach, " 'Sermo Humilis' and 'Gloria Passionis,' " in *Literary Language and Its Public in Late Latin Antiquity and in the Middle Ages*, trans. Ralph Manheim (New York: Pantheon, 1965), pp. 27–81.
54. Augustine, *Confessions* 7.18.24–25.

6. THE SON OF MAN

1. From the vast literature, see Carl H. Kraeling, *Anthropos and Son of Man* (New York: Columbia University Press, 1927).
2. So, for example, in Ps. 8:4 (cf. Heb. 2:6–9), and above all in Ezekiel, where it appears some ninety times as a designation for the prophet himself.
3. For a very early instance of the parallel, see Ignatius, *Epistle to the Ephesians* 20.2.
4. "Pastoral Constitution on the Church in the Modern World: *Gaudium et Spes*" 22, in *The Documents of Vatican II*, ed. Walter M. Abbott (New York: America Press, 1966), p. 220.
5. Adolf von Harnack, *The Mission and Expansion of Christianity in the First Three Centuries*, trans. James Moffatt, 2 vols. (London: Williams and Norgate, 1908), 1:108.
6. See the discussion of this by Augustine, *Tractates on the Gospel of John* 12.13.
7. Blaise Pascal, *Pensées* 526, 431.
8. F. D. E. Schleiermacher, *The Christian Faith*, trans. H. R. Mackintosh and J. S. Stewart (Edinburgh: T. and T. Clark, 1928), p. 98.
9. Augustine, *Enchiridion* 108.
10. Gregory of Nyssa, *On the Making of Man* 16.2.
11. On Augustine's view of image and renewal, cf. Gerhart B. Ladner, *The Idea of Reform: Its Impact on Christian Thought and Action in the Age of the Fathers* (Cambridge, Mass.: Harvard University Press, 1959), pp. 185–203.
12. Augustine, *Retractations* 1.25.68; 2.24.2.
13. Augustine, *Reply to Faustus the Manichean* 24.2.
14. Augustine, *On the Trinity* 1.10.21.
15. Augustine, *Ten Homilies on the First Epistle of John* 4.5–6; 10.6; *Tractates on the Gospel of John* 82.4; *Confessions* 10.43.68.
16. Augustine, *The Teacher* 38.
17. Augustine, *Soliloquies* 2.7.
18. Augustine, *On the Trinity* 12.15.24; *Confessions* 7.18.24–25.
19. William S. Babcock, "The Christ of the Exchange: A Study in the Christology of Augustine's *Enarrationes in Psalmos.*" Ph.D. diss., Yale University, 1971.
20. Augustine, *Tractates on the Gospel of John* 36.1–2.
21. Augustine, *On the Trinity* 12.4.4.
22. Dorothy Leigh Sayers, *The Mind of the Maker* (New York: Harcourt, Brace, 1941), pp. 33–41.
23. Augustine, *Confessions* 13.11.12.
24. Augustine, *On the Trinity* 9.2.2.
25. Augustine, *On the Trinity* 10.11.17–12.19.
26. Augustine, *On the Trinity* 7.4.7; 15.12.43–44.
27. Ronald Steel, *Walter Lippmann and the American Century* (Boston: Little, Brown, 1980), pp. 390–91.

28. On the *Confessions,* see especially Peter Brown, *Augustine of Hippo,* pp. 158–81, and the literature cited there.

29. Augustine, *Confessions* 6.6.9.

30. See Georg Nicolaus Knauer, *Die Psalmenzitate in Augustins Konfessionen* (Göttingen: Vandenhoeck und Ruprecht, 1955).

31. Albert C. Outler, "Introduction" to Augustine, *Confessions* (Philadelphia: Westminster Press, 1955), p. 17.

32. Augustine, *Confessions* 2.7.15.

33. Augustine, *Confessions* 5.1.1; 7.21.17; 4.12.19.

34. One of the most notable of these apostrophes is found at the end of book 10, *Confessions* 10.43.68–70.

35. Augustine, *Confessions* 3.1.1.

36. T. S. Eliot, "The Waste Land," 307–11, in *Collected Poems 1909–1935* (New York: Harcourt, Brace, 1936).

37. Compare C. Klegeman, "A Psychoanalytic Study of the *Confessions* of St. Augustine," *Journal of the American Psychoanalytic Association* 5 (1957): 469–84.

38. Augustine, *On the Good of Marriage* 8; Matt. 19:12; 1 Cor. 7:1–5; E. R. Dodds, *Pagan and Christian in an Age of Anxiety* (Cambridge: Cambridge University Press, 1965), pp. 29–30.

39. Augustine, *On Marriage and Concupiscence* 1.21.23–1.22.24; *On Continence* 22–23. (The Latin translation of Eph. 5:25–32 has "sacrament" for "mystery.")

40. Augustine, *Confessions* 2.4.9–2.10.18.

41. Oliver Wendell Holmes, Jr., to Harold J. Laski, 5 January 1921, *Holmes-Laski Letters: The Correspondence of Mr. Justice Holmes and Harold J. Laski, 1916–35,* ed. Mark DeWolfe Howe, 2 vols. (Cambridge, Mass.: Harvard University Press, 1953), 1:300.

42. Milton, *Paradise Lost* 1.1–5.

43. Augustine, *Confessions* 13.26.39–40.

44. Augustine, *On the Spirit and the Letter* 6.9.

45. Augustine, *On Marriage and Concupiscence* 2.12.25.

46. Augustine, *On Nature and Grace* 7.8.

47. Augustine, *On the Spirit and the Letter* 1.1.

48. Augustine, *On the Forgiveness of Sins* 2.13.18.

49. Augustine, *Against Two Letters of the Pelagians* 3.5.14–15.

50. Augustine, *On Perfection in Righteousness* 21.44; 12.29.

51. John 10:17–18; Augustine, *Tractates on the Gospel of John* 47.11–13; *On the Psalms* 89.37.

52. See Pelikan, *Christian Tradition* 1:286–90.

53. Gal. 4:4; Irenaeus, *Against Heresies* 3.22.1.

54. Augustine, *Enchiridion* 14.48.

55. Augustine, *On the Grace of Christ and Original Sin* 2.25.29; Ps. 51:5.

56. Augustine, *On Nature and Grace* 36.42; italics mine.

57. Pelikan, *Christian Tradition* 4:38–50.

58. See p. 38 above.

59. Basil of Caesarea, *Hexaemeron* 9.6; Etienne Gilson, *L'esprit de la philosophie médiévale,* 2d ed. (Paris: Librairie Philosophique J. Vrin, 1944), pp. 218–19.

60. See p. 242, n. 53 above.

7. THE TRUE IMAGE

1. Origen, *Against Celsus* 7.65–67; Arnobius, *The Case against the Pagans* 1.38–39.

2. Irenaeus, *Against Heresies* 4.16.4.

3. Lactantius, *Divine Institutes* 2.2–4.
4. Acts 17:24; Arnobius, *Case against the Pagans* 6.3–5.
5. Tertullian, *On Idolatry* 4; Clement of Alexandria, *Exhortation to the Greeks* 4.
6. Origen, *Against Celsus* 7.65.
7. Gregory of Nyssa, *Epistles* 2.
8. Carl H. Kraeling, *The Synagogue*, 2d ed., foreword by Jaroslav Pelikan (New York: KTAV Publishing House, 1979), p. 384.
9. Harold R. Willoughby, review of *The Synagogue*, by Carl H. Kraeling. *Journal of Near Eastern Studies* 20 (January 1961): 56.
10. Kraeling, *Synagogue*, p. 399.
11. For a perceptive essay, see Hans von Campenhausen, "The Theological Problem of Images in the Early Church," in *Tradition and Life in the Church*, trans. A. V. Littledale (Philadelphia: Fortress Press, 1968), pp. 171–200.
12. For some suggestive ideas, see Gervase Mathew, *Byzantine Aesthetics* (New York: Viking Press, 1964).
13. Col. 1:15; Clement of Alexandria, *Exhortation to the Greeks* 10.
14. Vladimir Lossky, *In the Image and Likeness of God*, trans. John Erickson and Thomas E. Bird, introd. John Meyendorff (Tuckahoe, N.Y.: Saint Vladimir's Seminary Press, 1974), p. 136.
15. Whitehead, *Science and the Modern World*, pp. 49–50.
16. On the fourth-century consideration of the problem, see Georges Florovsky, "Origen, Eusebius, and the Iconoclastic Controversy," *Church History* 19 (1950): 77–96.
17. Eusebius, *Epistle to Constantia*, quoting Phil. 2:7.
18. Nicephorus, *Greater Apology for the Holy Images* 12.
19. See pp. 52–53 above.
20. Nicephorus, *Refutation of the Iconoclasts* 1.15.
21. John of Jerusalem, *Against Constantinus Cabalinus* 4.
22. Nicephorus, *Refutation of the Iconoclasts* 2.3.
23. Theodore of Studios, *Refutation of the Poems of the Iconoclasts* 1.10.
24. Pelikan, *Christian Tradition* 1:263–66.
25. John of Jerusalem, *Against Constantinus Cabalinus* 4.
26. John of Damascus, *On the Images* 3.2.
27. Nicephorus, *Refutation of the Iconoclasts* 3.38.
28. Nicephorus, *Refutation of the Iconoclasts* 1.42; 2.1.
29. Theodore of Studios, *Refutation of the Poems of the Iconoclasts* 1.7.
30. John 4:24; cf. Origen, *On First Principles* 1.1.4.
31. Nicephorus, *Refutation of the Iconoclasts* 3.18.
32. Nicephorus, *Refutation of the Iconoclasts* 3.19.
33. Theodore of Studios, *Refutation of the Poems of the Iconoclasts* 1.16.
34. John of Damascus, *On the Images* 3.26.
35. What follows is a summary and interpretation especially of John of Damascus, *On the Images* 1.9-13; 3.18–23.
36. Basil, *On the Holy Spirit* 18.45.
37. Pseudo-Dionysius the Areopagite, *On the Divine Names* 1.5.
38. Justin Martyr, *Dialogue with Trypho* 62.
39. Augustine, *On the Trinity* 7.6.12.
40. Origen, *Against Celsus* 7.65. See p. 41 above.
41. Gregory of Nazianzus, *Theological Orations* 2.31.
42. John of Damascus, *On the Images* 1.
43. John of Damascus, *On the Images* 3.8.
44. Pelikan, *Christian Tradition* 2:10–16.

45. Evgenii Nikolaevich Trubetskoi, *Icons: Theology in Color*, trans. Gertrude Vahar (New York: Saint Vladimir's Seminary Press, 1973).

46. Cf. Ernst Kitzinger, "The Cult of Images before Iconoclasm," *Dumbarton Oaks Papers* 7 (1954): 85–150.

47. André Grabar, *Early Christian Art: From the Rise of Christianity to the Death of Theodosius*, trans. Stuart Gilbert and James Emmons (New York: Odyssey Press, 1968), "Catalogue," p. 15.

48. Clement of Alexandria, *Tutor* 3.7.

49. See Augustine, *Confessions* 4.13.20.

50. Augustine, *Confessions* 10.27.38.

51. Augustine, *On Christian Doctrine* 2.1.1–2.

8. CHRIST CRUCIFIED

1. See the highly revealing Emmaus pericope, Luke 24:13–35, summarizing the "Gospel of the forty days."

2. Shakespeare, *Macbeth* 1.4.7.

3. Isa. 53:5; Acts 8:26–39; cf. also Matt. 8:17.

4. Tertullian, *The Chaplet* 3; Basil of Caesarea, *On the Holy Spirit* 27.66.

5. Julian, *Against the Galileans* 194D, Loeb Classical Library ed., 3:373.

6. Nicholas Monsarrat, *The Cruel Sea* (1951; New York: Giant Cardinal ed., 1963), p. 319.

7. Gustav Mahler to Anna von Mildenburg, 15 March 1897, in *Selected Letters of Gustav Mahler*, ed. Knud Martner (New York: Farrar, Straus, Giroux, 1979), p. 215.

8. Augustine, *On the Trinity* 7.1.1.

9. *Acts of Andrew and Matthew* 19; *Martyrdom of Nereus and Achilleus* 13.

10. Augustine, *City of God* 22.8.

11. Heriger of Lobbes, *Life of Remaclus* 12.

12. This example and others in J. F. Niermeyer, *Mediae Latinitatis Lexicon Minus* (Leiden: E. J. Brill, 1976), s.v. "crux."

13. Shirley Jackson Case, *The Origins of Christian Supernaturalism* (Chicago: University of Chicago Press, 1946), p. 1.

14. See the careful discussion by Henri Chirat, *New Catholic Encyclopedia*, s.v. "Cross, Finding of the Holy," with full documentation of the several references and legends.

15. Sulpicius Severus, *Chronicle* 2.34.4.

16. Socrates Scholasticus, *Ecclesiastical History* 1.17; italics mine.

17. Cyril of Jerusalem, *Catechetical Lectures* 4.10; 10.19; 13.4.

18. Eusebius, *Life of Constantine* 1.41.

19. John of Damascus, *The Orthodox Faith* 4.11.

20. Gustaf Aulén, *Christus Victor: An Historical Study of the Three Main Types of the Idea of Atonement*, trans. A. G. Hebert, introd. Jaroslav Pelikan (New York: Macmillan, 1969), pp. 4–7.

21. Athanasius, *On the Incarnation* 29.1.

22. William J. O'Shea, *The Meaning of Holy Week* (Collegeville, Minn.: Liturgical Press, 1958).

23. Origen, *Commentary on Matthew* 27:32.

24. Karl Young, *The Drama of the Medieval Church*, 2 vols. (Oxford: Clarendon Press, 1933).

25. Frederic James Edward Raby, ed., *The Oxford Book of Medieval Latin Verse* (Oxford: Oxford University Press, 1959), pp. 74–76.

26. See the prejudiced but succinct account of Max Manitius, *Geschichte der lateinischen*

Literatur des Mittelalters, 3 vols. (Munich: C. H. Beck'sche Buchhandlung, 1911–31), 1:295–96.
27. Tertullian, *Against Marcion* 2.2.
28. Augustine, *Sermons* 44.6.6.
29. Sozomen, *Ecclesiastical History* 1.8.
30. Matt. 27:46; Mark 15:34; Ps. 22:1. See Pelikan, *Christian Tradition* 1:245–46, for some representative statements.
31. Priminius, *Scarapsus* 13.
32. Odo of Cluny, *Occupatio* 5.559–62; Matt. 11:29.
33. John of Damascus, *The Orthodox Faith* 4.11.
34. Luke 22:53; Gregory the Great, *Epistles* 6.2.
35. Gen. 50:20; see the comments of Cassian, *Conferences* 3.11.
36. Compare Augustine, *Against Two Letters of the Pelagians* 3.9.25.
37. Boethius, *The Consolation of Philosophy* 4.6.; Thomas Aquinas, *Summa Theologica* I.q.23.a.4.
38. Abelard, *Sermons* 12.
39. Abelard, *Commentary on Romans* 2; Rom. 8:32.
40. See Pelikan, *Christian Tradition* 3:106–57; 4:23–25, 156–57, 161–63.
41. Gerald Phelan, *The Wisdom of Saint Anselm* (Latrobe, Pa.: Saint Vincent's Archabbey, 1960), pp. 30–31.
42. Anselm, *Why God Became Man* 2.15.
43. Athanasius, *Against the Heathen* 1.

9. THE MONK WHO RULES THE WORLD

1. See, for a second-century example, Irenaeus, *Against Heresies* 4.5.4.
2. See Benedict of Nursia, *Rule* 55.
3. Mervin Monroe Deems, "The Sources of Christian Asceticism," in *Environmental Factors in Christian History*, ed. John Thomas McNeill et al. (Chicago: University of Chicago Press, 1939), pp. 149–66.
4. See the edition and discussion, still useful, by Frederick Cornwallis Conybeare, *Philo: About the Contemplative Life, or the Fourth Book of the Treatise concerning Virtues* (Oxford: Clarendon Press, 1895).
5. Eusebius, *Ecclesiastical History* 2.17.
6. Hugh Jackson Lawlor and John Ernest Leonard Oulton, eds., *The Ecclesiastical History*, by Eusebius, 2 vols. (London: SPCK, 1954), 2:67.
7. Gérard Garitte, *Un témoin important du texte de la Vie de S. Antoine par S. Athanase* (Brussels: Palais des Académies, 1939). See also p. 31 above.
8. Augustine, *Confessions* 8.6.15.
9. See John Compton Dickinson, *The Origins of the Austin Canons and Their Introduction into England* (London: SPCK, 1950), pp. 255–72.
10. Benedict, *Rule* 4; prologue.
11. Owen Chadwick, *The Making of the Benedictine Ideal* (Washington, D.C.: Saint Anselm's Abbey, 1981), p. 22; Benedict, *Rule* 53.
12. Athanasius, *Life of Antony* 2; Matt. 19:21.
13. Athanasius, *Life of Antony* 7.
14. Benedict, *Rule* 2, 5; John 6:38.
15. Athanasius, *Life of Antony* 12.
16. Adolf von Harnack, "Das Mönchtum. Seine Ideale und seine Geschichte," in *Reden und Aufsätze* 1:101.

17. The distinction is trenchantly summarized in Thomas Aquinas, *Summa Theologica* II-1.q.108.a.4.

18. Socrates Scholasticus, *Ecclesiastical History* 1.11.

19. Gregory of Nazianzus, *Orations* 12, on the occasion of his assuming the position of bishop-coadjutor of Nazianzus.

20. *Corpus Iuris Civilis: Codex Justinianus* 1.3.47; *Novellae* 6.1; 123.1.

21. Trullan Synod, canon 48.

22. Symeon of Thessalonica, *On the Priesthood*.

23. Francis Dvornik, *The Photian Schism. History and Legend* (Cambridge: Cambridge University Press, 1948), pp. 63–64; it should perhaps be added that it was not only because he had been a layman.

24. Fyodor Dostoevsky, *The Brothers Karamazov*, bk. 6, "The Russian Monk," chap. 3, "Conversations and Exhortations of Father Zossima"; italics mine.

25. Harnack, "Das Mönchtum," p. 111.

26. Thomas Garrigue Masaryk, *The Spirit of Russia*, 3 vols. (London: George Allen and Unwin, 1967–68), 3:15, 204.

27. The chapters "The Religious Orders" and "Fringe Orders and Anti-Orders" in Richard W. Southern, *Western Society and the Church in the Middle Ages*, vol. 2 of The Pelican History of the Church (Harmondsworth: Penguin Books, 1970), pp. 214–358, occupy nearly half of that small book.

28. See especially Walter Ullmann, *The Growth of Papal Government in the Middle Ages: A Study in the Ideological Relation of Clerical to Lay Power*, 2d ed. (London: Methuen, 1962), pp. 262–309.

29. *Be Not Afraid! André Frossard in Conversation with Pope John Paul II*, trans. J. R. Foster (New York: Saint Martin's Press, 1984), p. 150.

30. Gregory VII to Bishop Hermann of Metz, 15 March 1081, in *Das Register Gregors VII*, ed. Erich Caspar, 2 vols. (Berlin: Weidmann, 1920–23), 2:544.

31. Elizabeth T. Kennan, "The 'De Consideratione' of St. Bernard of Clairvaux in the Mid-Twelfth Century: A Review of Scholarship," *Traditio* 23 (1967): 73–115.

32. See Pelikan, *Christian Tradition* 3:300; 4:71.

33. Lowrie J. Daly, *Benedictine Monasticism. Its Formation and Development through the 12th Century* (New York: Sheed and Ward, 1965), pp. 135–36.

34. Kenneth Scott Latourette, *A History of the Expansion of Christianity*, 7 vols. (New York: Harper and Brothers, 1938–45), 2:17; 3:26.

35. Jaroslav Pelikan, *Spirit versus Structure* (New York: Harper and Row, 1968), pp. 52–56.

36. Benedict, *Rule* 48.

37. Jean Leclercq, *The Love of Learning and the Desire for God: A Study of Monastic Culture*, trans. Catharine Misrahi (1961; New York: Mentor Omega Books, 1962), p. 31.

38. Umberto Eco, *The Name of the Rose*, trans. William Weaver (New York: Harcourt Brace Jovanovich, 1983), p. 491.

39. *Modern Catholic Thinkers*, ed. Aloysius Robert Caponigri (New York: Harper and Brothers, 1960), pp. 495–506.

40. Benedict, *Rule* 4; cf. Colman J. Barry, *Worship and Work* (Collegeville, Minn.: Liturgical Press, 1956), p. 85.

41. Dante, *Paradiso* 11.50.

10. THE BRIDEGROOM OF THE SOUL

1. John Julian, *A Dictionary of Hymnology*, 2d ed. (1907; New York: Dover Publications, 1957), pp. 590–91.

2. Julian, *Dictionary of Hymnology*, p. 1038.
3. It will be evident that I owe much to the discussion of David Knowles, *The English Mystical Tradition* (New York: Harper and Brothers, 1961), pp. 1–38.
4. I am adopting here the definition in my article "Mysticism," *Encyclopaedia Britannica*, 14th ed.
5. Abraham Joshua Heschel, *The Prophets* (New York: Harper and Row, 1963), p. 364; italics in original.
6. Gershom Gerhard Scholem, *Major Trends in Jewish Mysticism* (Jerusalem: Schocken Publishing House, 1941).
7. Jean Daniélou, *Platonisme et théologie mystique: Essai sur la doctrine spirituelle de saint Gregoire de Nysse* (Paris: Aubier, 1944).
8. Acts 17:34; Eusebius, *Ecclesiastical History* 3.4.11; 4.23.3; Hilduin of Saint Denis, *Vita Dionysii*.
9. John Meyendorff, *Christ in Eastern Christian Thought* (Washington, D.C., and Cleveland: Corpus Books, 1969), p. 81.
10. See Jaroslav Pelikan, "Introduction" to *Maximus Confessor*, Classics of Western Spirituality (New York: Paulist Press, 1985), pp. 1–13.
11. Marvin H. Pope, *Song of Songs. A New Translation with Introduction and Commentary*, The Anchor Bible (Garden City, N.Y.: Doubleday, 1977), pp. 18–19.
12. Leclercq, *Love of Learning*, pp. 90–91.
13. See the masterful treatment in Etienne Gilson, *The Mystical Theology of Saint Bernard*, trans. Alfred Howard Campbell Downes (London: Sheed and Ward, 1940).
14. Bernard, *Canticles* 1.4.8.
15. Bernard, *Canticles* 22.1.3.
16. Bernard, *Canticles* 43.3.
17. Bernard, *Canticles* 70.7.
18. Bernard, *Canticles* 2.2.3.
19. Bernard, *Canticles* 2.1.2.
20. Bernard, *Canticles* 20.2.
21. Gregory of Nyssa, *Sermons on the Song of Songs* 6.
22. Etienne Gilson, *The Philosophy of St. Bonaventure*, trans. Illtyd Trethowan and F. J. Sheed (New York: Sheed and Ward, 1938).
23. Bonaventure, *The Soul's Journey into God* 2.13, ed. Ewert Cousins, Classics of Western Spirituality (New York: Paulist Press, 1978), p. 77.
24. Bonaventure, *Journey* 4.2, Cousins ed., p. 88.
25. Bonaventure, *Journey* 6.7, Cousins ed., pp. 108–09.
26. Bernard, *Canticles* 20.6.
27. Bernard, *Canticles* 66.10.
28. Knowles, *English Mystical Tradition*, p. 135.
29. Julian of Norwich, *The Revelations of Divine Love* 83, trans. James Walsh (New York: Harper and Brothers, 1961), p. 206.
30. Julian of Norwich, *Revelations* 72, Walsh ed., p. 186.
31. Julian of Norwich, *Revelations* 27, Walsh ed., pp. 91–92.
32. Robert Herrick, "Eternitie," in *The Oxford Book of English Mystical Verse*, ed. D. H. S. Nicholson and A. H. E. Lee (Oxford: Clarendon Press, 1917), pp. 20–21.
33. Dante, *Purgatorio* 17.96.
34. For a general introduction, marred by an uncritical use of such terms as "passionate hallucinations," see Henry Osborn Taylor, *The Mediaeval Mind. A History of the Development of Thought and Emotion in the Middle Ages*, 4th ed., 2 vols. (London: Macmillan, 1938), 2:458–86.
35. *Acta Sanctorum*, February (Paris: Victor Palme, 1865), 3:308.

36. Mariella Liverani, "Margherita da Cortona: Iconographia," in *Bibliotheca Sanctorum*, 12 vols. (Rome: Istituto Giovanni XXIII nella Pontificia Università Lateranense, 1961–69), 8:772.
37. John Rupert Martin, *Baroque* (New York: Harper and Row, 1977), pp. 102–03.
38. See the detailed account of "Interpretations of the Sublime Song" in Pope, *Song of Songs*, pp. 89–229.
39. Thomas G. Bergin, *Dante* (New York: Orion Press, 1965), p. 46.
40. Julian of Norwich, *Revelations* 58, Walsh ed., pp. 159–60.
41. Friedrich von Hügel, *The Mystical Element of Religion as Studied in Saint Catherine of Genoa and Her Friends*, 4th ed., 2 vols. (London: J. M. Dent and Sons, 1961), 2:309–40.
42. Bonaventure, *Journey* 6.5, Cousins ed., p. 107.
43. Pelikan, *Christian Tradition* 4:63–68.
44. Anders Nygren, *Agape and Eros*, trans. Philip S. Watson (Philadelphia: Westminster Press, 1953), p. 650.
45. Hanson, *Allegory and Event*, p. 283.

11. THE DIVINE AND HUMAN MODEL

1. Most of the relevant texts are collected in *St. Francis of Assisi: Writings and Early Biographies*, ed. Marion Alphonse Habig (Chicago: Franciscan Herald Press, 1972).
2. Pius XI, Encyclical *Rite Expiatis* (30 April l926).
3. Thomas of Celano, *First Life of Saint Francis* 7.16, Habig ed., p. 242.
4. Francis of Assisi, *Rule of 1221* 1, Habig ed., p. 31.
5. Bonaventure, *Major Life of Saint Francis* 1.6, Habig ed., p. 639.
6. Thomas of Celano, *First Life* 9.22, Habig ed., pp. 246–47.
7. Bonaventure, *Major Life* 2.8, Habig ed., pp. 645–46.
8. Thomas of Celano, *First Life* 13.32, Habig ed., p. 254.
9. Thomas of Celano, *First Life* 30.84, Habig ed., p. 299.
10. Bonaventure, *Major Life* 13.3, Habig ed., p. 731.
11. Thomas of Celano, *First Life* 4.98, Habig ed., p. 312.
12. Dante, *Paradiso* 11.107.
13. *Dictionnaire de Théologie Catholique*, 15 vols. (Paris: Libraire Letouzey et Ane, 1903–50), s.v. "stigmatisation."
14. Thomas of Celano, *First Life* 4.95–96, 9.113; Habig ed., pp. 310, 326.
15. Leander E. Keck, "The Poor among the Saints in Jewish Christianity and Qumran," *Zeitschrift für die neutestamentliche Wissenschaft* 57 (1966): 54–78.
16. Francis, *Rule of 1223* 6, Habig ed., p. 61; Heb. 11:13; 1 Peter 2:11.
17. Francis, *Rule of 1221* 9, Habig ed., p. 39; Bonaventure, *Major Life* 7.1, Habig ed., p. 680.
18. Gilbert Keith Chesterton, *Saint Francis of Assisi* (Garden City, N.Y.: Doubleday, 1931), p. 51.
19. Francis, *The Canticle of Brother Sun*, Habig ed., pp. 130–31.
20. Thomas of Celano, *First Life* 19.51, 16.42; Habig ed., pp. 272, 264.
21. Thomas of Celano, *First Life* 30.86, Habig ed., p. 30l.
22. Oscar Cullmann, "The Origins of Christmas," in *The Early Church*, ed. A. J. B. Higgins (Philadelphia: Westminster Press, 1956), pp. 17–36.
23. Thomas of Celano, *Second Life of St. Francis* 151.199, Habig ed., p. 521.
24. Bonaventure, *Major Life* 10.7, Habig ed., p. 711.
25. Bonaventure, *Major Life* 14.4, Habig ed., p. 739.
26. Francis, *Rule of 1221* 8, *Rule of 1223* 6; Habig ed., pp. 38, 60.

27. Alan Gewirth, *Marsilius of Padua and Medieval Political Philosophy* (New York: Columbia University Press, 1951), pp. 78–85, 295–96.

28. Thomas à Kempis, *Imitation of Christ* 1.25 (London: Everyman's Library, 1910), pp. 56–57.

29. A. G. Little, "Paul Sabatier, Historian of St. Francis," in *Franciscan Papers, Lists and Documents* (Manchester: University of Manchester, 1929), pp. 179–88.

30. Thomas of Celano, *First Life* 13.33, Habig ed., p. 255.

12. THE UNIVERSAL MAN

1. Jacob Burckhardt, *The Civilization of the Renaissance in Italy*, trans. Samuel George Chetwynd Middlemore, 2 vols. (1929; New York: Harper Torchbooks, 1958), 1:143 and n. 1; italics in original.

2. Harold Rideout Willoughby, *Pagan Regeneration* (Chicago: University of Chicago Press, 1929), pp. 287–88.

3. Erasmus, *Paracelsis*, in *Christian Humanism and the Reformation: Selected Writings of Erasmus*, ed. John C. Olin (New York: Fordham University Press, 1975), p. 100.

4. Konrad Burdach, "Sinn und Ursprung der Worte Renaissance und Reformation," *Reformation Renaissance Humanismus*, 2d ed. (Berlin and Leipzig: Gebrüder Paetel, 1926), p. 83.

5. *Webster's Third New International Dictionary of the English Language Unabridged*, s.v. "Renaissance" (quoting *Horizon Magazine*).

6. See Pelikan, *Christian Tradition* 2:75–90.

7. Goethe, "Observations on Leonardo da Vinci's celebrated picture of The Last Supper," in *Goethe on Art*, ed. John Gage (Berkeley and Los Angeles: University of California Press, 1980), p. 192.

8. Walter Pater, *The Renaissance. Studies in Art and Poetry: The 1893 Text*, ed. Donald H. Hill (Berkeley and Los Angeles: University of California Press, 1980), pp. 93–95.

9. Leo Steinberg, *The Sexuality of Christ in Renaissance Art and in Modern Oblivion* (New York: Pantheon, 1983), pp. 71–72.

10. *Treasures of the Vatican* (New Orleans: Archdiocese of New Orleans, 1984), p. 57.

11. Charles Trinkaus, *In Our Image and Likeness: Humanity and Divinity in Italian Humanist Thought*, 2 vols. (Chicago: University of Chicago Press, 1970), 2:644–50.

12. Burckhardt, *Civilization of the Renaissance* 1:151; see also 1:147.

13. Dante, *Purgatorio* 30.15.

14. Dante, *Vita Nuova* 24, in Mark Musa, *Dante's "Vita Nuova": A Translation and an Essay* (Bloomington: Indiana University Press, 1973), p. 52.

15. Charles S. Singleton, *An Essay on the "Vita Nuova"* (Cambridge, Mass.: Harvard University Press, 1949), p. 112.

16. Bergin, *Dante*, p. 85.

17. Dante, *Purgatorio* 32.101–02.

18. Dante, *Paradiso* 23.34.

19. Dante, *Paradiso* 23.71–74.

20. Dante, *Paradiso* 23.106–08.

21. Dante, *Paradiso* 23.133–39.

22. Ernst Robert Curtius, *European Literature and the Latin Middle Ages*, trans. Willard R. Trask (Princeton: Princeton University Press, 1973), pp. 372–73.

23. For a careful discussion, see Etienne Gilson, *Dante and Philosophy*, trans. Vaid Moore (New York: Sheed and Ward, 1949), pp. 1–82.

24. Dante, *Paradiso* 32.85–86.

25. Dante, *Paradiso* 33.43; 33.145.
26. Dante, *On World-Government or De Monarchia* 3.8, trans. Herbert W. Schneider (New York: Liberal Arts Press, 1957), p. 64.
27. Dante, *De Monarchia* 1.8, Schneider ed., p. 11.
28. Dante, *De Monarchia* 3.16, Schneider ed., p. 78.
29. Dante, *De Monarchia* 3.15, Schneider ed., p. 77.
30. Ernst H. Kantorowicz, *The King's Two Bodies: A Study in Mediaeval Political Theology* (Princeton: Princeton University Press, 1957), p. 464.
31. Paul Oskar Kristeller, *Renaissance Thought: The Classic, Scholastic, and Humanistic Strains* (New York: Harper Torchbooks, 1961), p. 79.
32. Burckhardt, *Civilization of the Renaissance*, 1:196.
33. Petrarch to Nicholas Sygeros, 10 January 1354, in *Letters from Petrarch*, ed. Morris Bishop (Bloomington: Indiana University Press, 1966), p. 153.
34. Deno J. Geanakoplos, *Greek Scholars in Venice: Studies in the Dissemination of Greek Learning from Byzantium to Western Europe* (Cambridge, Mass.: Harvard University Press, 1962).
35. See Pelikan, *Christian Tradition* 4:76–78.
36. Peter Brown, *Augustine of Hippo*, p. 271.
37. Thomas Aquinas *Summa Theologica* 3.44; Pelikan, *Christian Tradition* 3:212; 4:295.
38. Charles Trinkaus, "Introduction" to Valla in *The Renaissance Philosophy of Man*, ed. Ernst Cassirer et al. (Chicago: University of Chicago Press, 1948), p. 147.
39. Hanna Holborn Gray, "Valla's *Encomium of St. Thomas Aquinas* and the Humanist Conception of Christian Antiquity," in *Three Essays* (Chicago: University of Chicago Press, 1978), pp. 23–40.
40. On all these passages, see Pelikan, *Christian Tradition* 4:308–09.
41. E. Harris Harbison, *The Christian Scholar in the Age of the Reformation* (New York: Charles Scribner's Sons, 1956), p. 85.
42. Erasmus, *The Praise of Folly*, in *The Essential Erasmus*, ed. John Patrick Dolan (New York: New American Library, 1964), pp. 157, 165.
43. Erasmus, *Enchiridion* 2.4, 2.6; Dolan ed., pp. 58, 71.
44. Erasmus, *Enchiridion*, conclusion, Dolan ed., p. 93.
45. Erasmus, *Enchiridion* 1.1, Dolan ed., p. 33.
46. Erasmus, *Enchiridion* 1.2, Dolan ed., p. 38; Luke 10:22.
47. Erasmus, *Enchiridion* 1.3, Dolan ed., pp. 42, 40. See p. 81 above.
48. Erasmus, *Enchiridion* 2.3, Dolan ed., pp. 56–57.
49. Erasmus, *Enchiridion* 1.2, Dolan ed., p. 36.
50. Marjorie O'Rourke Boyle, *Christening Pagan Mysteries: Erasmus in Pursuit of Wisdom* (Toronto: University of Toronto Press, 1981), p. 92.
51. Roland H. Bainton, *Erasmus of Christendom* (New York: Charles Scribner's Sons, 1969), p. 272.

13. THE MIRROR OF THE ETERNAL

1. Martin Luther, *Ninety-Five Theses* 1, in *Luther's Works: American Edition*, ed. Jaroslav Pelikan and Helmut Lehmann, 55 vols. (Saint Louis and Philadelphia: Concordia Publishing House and Fortress Press, 1955–), 31:25.
2. Luther, *Preface to Latin Writings*, in *Luther's Works* 34:336–37.
3. Luther, *Large Catechism* 2.3.65.
4. John Calvin, *Institutes of the Christian Religion* 3.24.5, ed. John Thomas McNeill, 2 vols. (Philadelphia: Westminster Press, 1960), 2:970.

5. *Second Helvetic Confession* 10. For other examples, see Pelikan, *Christian Tradition* 4:167, 230–31, 240–41.

6. Brian A. Gerrish, *The Old Protestantism and the New. Essays on the Reformation Heritage* (Chicago: University of Chicago Press, 1982), pp. 150–59.

7. Calvin, *Institutes of the Christian Religion* 2.9.1, McNeill ed., 1:424.

8. Karl Holl, *The Cultural Significance of the Reformation*, trans. Karl and Barbara Hertz and John H. Lichtblau (New York: Meridian Books, 1959), p. 151.

9. Michael Reu, *Luther's German Bible* (Columbus, Ohio: Lutheran Book Concern, 1934), pp. 180–81.

10. Heinrich Bornkamm, *Luther's World of Thought*, trans. Martin H. Bertram (Saint Louis: Concordia Publishing House, 1958), pp. 273–83.

11. Auerbach, *Literary Language and Its Public*, pp. 45–50.

12. A substantial number of these sermons, on the Gospels of Matthew and of John, can be found in volumes 21–24 of *Luther's Works*.

13. Jaroslav Pelikan, *Luther the Expositor. Introduction to the Reformer's Exegetical Writings* (Saint Louis: Concordia Publishing House, 1959), esp. pp. 89–108.

14. Heinrich Heine, *Religion and Philosophy in Germany*, trans. John Snodgrass (Boston: Beacon Press, 1959), p. 46.

15. Luther, *Preface to the New Testament*, in *Luther's Works* 35:357.

16. See, for only one example among many, *Sermons on the Gospel of John*, in *Luther's Works* 22:37–38.

17. *The Martin Luther Christmas Book*, ed. Roland H. Bainton (Philadelphia: Westminster Press, 1948), p. 38.

18. Luther, *The Sermon on the Mount*, in *Luther's Works* 21:197–98.

19. Calvin, *The Gospel According to St. John 1–10*, trans. Thomas Henry Louis Parker (Grand Rapids: Wm. B. Eerdmans, 1959), pp. 89–103.

20. Luther, *Magnificat*, in *Luther's Works* 21:323.

21. Panofsky, *Life and Art of Albrecht Dürer*, p. 199.

22. Wilhelm Dilthey, *Weltanschauung und Analyse des Menschen seit Renaissance und Reformation*, 7th ed. (Stuttgart: B. G. Teubner, 1964), p. 515.

23. Luther, *Preface to the Wittenberg Hymnal of 1524*, in *Luther's Works* 53:316.

24. Nathan Söderblom, *Kristi Pinas Historia* (Stockholm: Svenska Kyrkans Diakonistyrelses Bokförlag, 1928), pp. 430–31; translation provided by Conrad Bergendoff.

25. Luis de León, *The Names of Christ*, bk. 1, ed. Manuel Durán and William Kluback, Classics of Western Spirituality (New York: Paulist Press, 1984), p. 42.

26. Luis de León, *Names of Christ*, bk. 3, Durán-Kluback ed., pp. 303, 366.

27. Luis de León, *Names of Christ*, bk. 2, Durán-Kluback ed., p. 202.

28. *The Poems of St. John of the Cross*, ed. John Frederick Nims, 3d ed. (Chicago: University of Chicago Press, 1979), pp. 18–19.

29. *Poems of St. John of the Cross*, pp. 40–41.

30. *Poems of St. John of the Cross*, pp. 68–71.

31. Luther, *Sermon on the Mount*, in *Luther's Works* 21:105–09.

32. Calvin, *Institutes of the Christian Religion* 4.20.1, McNeill ed., 2:1486.

33. Calvin, *Institutes of the Christian Religion* 4.20.2, McNeill ed., 2:1487.

34. Calvin, *Institutes of the Christian Religion* 4.20.5, McNeill ed., 2:1490; italics mine.

35. John Thomas McNeill, *The History and Character of Calvinism* (New York: Oxford University Press, 1954), p. 185.

36. See Perry Miller, *Orthodoxy in Massachusetts 1630–1650* (Boston: Beacon Press, 1959), pp. 245–53.

37. H. Richard Niebuhr, *The Kingdom of God in America* (New York: Harper and Brothers, 1937), p. 80.

38. Winthrop S. Hudson, *The Great Tradition of the American Churches* (1953; New York: Harper Torchbooks, 1963), p. 49.

39. See Perry Miller, *Roger Williams: His Contribution to the American Tradition* (New York: Atheneum, 1953), p. 38.

40. Sidney E. Mead, *The Lively Experiment: The Shaping of Christianity in America* (New York: Harper and Row, 1963), pp. 72–89. See pp. 209–10 below.

14. THE PRINCE OF PEACE

1. Luis de León, *Names of Christ*, bk. 2, Durán-Kluback ed., pp. 212–39.

2. John Amos Comenius, *The Angel of Peace* 9, trans. Walter Angus Morison (New York: Pantheon Books, n.d.), p. 39; italics in original.

3. For a helpful examination, see Roland H. Bainton, *Christian Attitudes Toward War and Peace: A Historical Survey and Critical Re-evaluation* (New York: Abingdon Press, 1960).

4. Luther, *Whether Soldiers, Too, Can Be Saved*, in *Luther's Works* 46:95.

5. John Calvin, *Institutes of the Christian Religion* 4.20.11–12, McNeill ed., 2:1499–1501.

6. Luther, *Whether Soldiers, Too, Can Be Saved*, in *Luther's Works* 46:97.

7. Luther, *Temporal Authority: To What Extent It Should Be Obeyed*, in *Luther's Works* 45:87.

8. Luther, *Whether Soldiers, Too, Can Be Saved*, in *Luther's Works* 46:113.

9. Bainton, *Christian Attitudes Toward War and Peace*, pp. 136–47.

10. Augustine, *City of God* 3.14; 12.22.

11. Augustine, *City of God* 19.7.

12. Augustine, *Epistles* 189.2.

13. Thomas Aquinas, *Summa Theologica* 2.2.40.

14. John Courtney Murray, "Remarks on the Moral Problem of War," *Theological Studies* 20 (1959): 40–61, still an indispensable introduction.

15. Steven Runciman, *A History of the Crusades*, 3 vols. (Cambridge: Cambridge University Press, 1951–54), 1:83–92.

16. Runciman, *History of the Crusades* 3:7; 2:287; 3:130.

17. Hans Pfeffermann, *Die Zusammenarbeit der Renaissancepäpste mit den Türken* (Winterthur: Mondial Verlag, 1946), p. 63.

18. Aziz S. Atiya, "The Aftermath of the Crusades," in *A History of the Crusades*, ed. Kenneth M. Setton, 5 vols. (Madison: University of Wisconsin Press, 1955–75), 3:660.

19. *Augsburg Confession* 16.1–2; 21.1.

20. Luther, *On War against the Turk*, in *Luther's Works* 46:186–88.

21. See the balanced account of Eric W. Gritsch, *Reformer without a Church: The Life and Thought of Thomas Muentzer* (Philadelphia: Fortress Press, 1967).

22. Thomas Muentzer, "Sermon before the Princes" in *Spiritual and Anabaptist Writers*, ed. George Huntston Williams (Philadelphia: Westminster Press, 1957), pp. 50–53, 65–66.

23. George Casalis, *Correct Ideas Don't Fall from the Skies: Elements for an Inductive Theology*, trans. Jeanne Marie Lyons and Michael John (Maryknoll, N.Y.: Orbis Books, 1984), p. 114.

24. On the entire movement, see George Huntston Williams, *The Radical Reformation* (Philadelphia: Westminster Press, 1962).

25. Harold S. Bender, "The Pacifism of the Sixteenth-Century Anabaptists," *Church History* 24 (1955): 119–31.

26. Pelikan, *Christian Tradition* 4:313–22.

27. Ethelbert Stauffer, "The Anabaptist Theology of Martyrdom," *Mennonite Quarterly Review* 19 (1945): 179–214.
28. A convenient edition in English is that of Hans J. Hillerbrand, ed., *The Reformation* (New York: Harper and Row, 1964), pp. 235–38.
29. Bainton, *Christian Attitudes Toward War and Peace*, pp. 157–65.
30. Torquato Tasso, *Jerusalem Delivered* 1.72, trans. Edward Fairfax (Carbondale: Southern Illinois University Press, 1962), p. 21.

15. THE TEACHER OF COMMON SENSE

1. See Peter Gay, *The Enlightenment: An Interpretation*, 2 vols. (New York: Alfred A. Knopf, 1966–69), 1:256–321.
2. Augustine, *City of God* 10.18.
3. Augustine, *On the Profit of Believing* 14.32.
4. Isaac Newton, *Mathematical Principles of Natural Philosophy*, bk. 3, "The System of the World," General Scholium.
5. Newton, *Optics*, bk. 3, pt. 1.
6. Edwin A. Burtt, *The Metaphysical Foundations of Modern Science*, 2d ed. (1932; Garden City, N.Y.: Anchor Books, 1954), pp. 283–302.
7. David Hume, *Enquiry concerning Human Understanding*, sec. 10, pt. 2, in *The English Philosophers from Bacon to Mill*, ed. Edwin A. Burtt (New York: Modern Library, 1939), pp. 657–67.
8. Goethe, *Faust* 766.
9. Edward Gibbon, *The History of the Decline and Fall of the Roman Empire*, ed. John Bagnell Bury, 7 vols. (London: Methuen, 1896–1900), 2:28–31, 69–70.
10. Gibbon, *Decline and Fall* 2:335–87; 5:96–168.
11. Gibbon, *Decline and Fall* 5:97–98.
12. Arthur Darby Nock, *Conversion: The Old and the New in Religion from Alexander the Great to Augustine of Hippo* (Oxford: Oxford University Press, 1933), p. 210.
13. Hermann Samuel Reimarus, *Fragments*, trans. Ralph S. Fraser, ed. Charles H. Talbert (Philadelphia: Fortress Press, 1970), pp. 72, 95–96.
14. Reimarus, *Fragments*, p. 269.
15. Leander E. Keck, ed., *The Christ of Faith and the Jesus of History*, by David Friedrich Strauss (Philadelphia: Fortress Press, 1977), p. xxxiii.
16. David Friedrich Strauss, *The Life of Jesus Critically Examined*, 5th ed., introd. Otto Pfleiderer (London: Swan Sonnenschein, 1906).
17. Gordon Haight, *George Eliot: A Biography* (New York: Oxford University Press, 1968), p. 59.
18. Otto Pfleiderer, "Introduction" to English translation of Strauss, *Life of Jesus*, p. xxi.
19. Werner Jaeger, *Paideia: The Ideals of Greek Culture*, trans. Gilbert Highet, 3 vols. (New York: Oxford University Press, 1943–45), 2:21; italics in original.
20. Joseph Priestley, *Socrates and Jesus Compared* (Philadelphia: printed for the author, 1803), p. 48.
21. Daniel J. Boorstin, *The Lost World of Thomas Jefferson* (Boston: Beacon Press, 1960), p. 156.
22. Jefferson to William Short, 31 October 1819, in *Jefferson's Extracts from the Gospels*, ed. Dickinson W. Adams (Princeton: Princeton University Press, 1983), p. 388.
23. Adams, *Jefferson's Extracts*, p. 60; p. 135 and note (p. 300).
24. Adams, *Jefferson's Extracts*, pp. 27–28.

25. Garry Wills, *Inventing America: Jefferson's Declaration of Independence* (New York: Vintage Books, 1979), p. 191.
26. *Benjamin Franklin's Autobiographical Writings*, ed. Carl Van Doren (New York: Viking Press, 1945), p. 784.
27. Henry F. May, *The Enlightenment in America* (New York: Oxford University Press, 1976), pp. 128–29.

16. THE POET OF THE SPIRIT

1. Shakespeare, *Hamlet* 1.5.166–67.
2. René Wellek, "Romanticism Re-examined," in *Concepts of Criticism* (New Haven: Yale University Press, 1963), p. 221.
3. Arthur O. Lovejoy, *Essays in the History of Ideas* (New York: Braziller Press, 1955), p. 232.
4. Friedrich Schleiermacher, *On Religion. Speeches to Its Cultured Despisers*, trans. John Oman (1893; New York: Harper Torchbooks, 1958).
5. Jack C. Verheyden, "Introduction" to Friedrich Schleiermacher, *The Life of Jesus*, trans. S. Maclean Gilmour (Philadelphia: Fortress Press, 1975), p. xi.
6. Schleiermacher, *The Christian Faith*, trans. H. R. Mackintosh and J. S. Stewart (Edinburgh: T. and T. Clark, 1928).
7. Samuel Taylor Coleridge, *The Complete Works*, ed. W. G. T. Shedd, 7 vols. (New York: Harper, 1956).
8. *The Complete Essays and Other Writings of Ralph Waldo Emerson*, ed. Brooks Atkinson (New York: Modern Library, 1940).
9. Lovejoy, *Essays*, p. 235.
10. See J. Robert Barth, *Coleridge and Christian Doctrine* (Cambridge, Mass.: Harvard University Press, 1969), pp. 37–42.
11. Coleridge, *The Friend*, in *Works* 2:468.
12. Emerson, *Nature*, Atkinson ed., p. 37.
13. James D. Boulger, *Coleridge as Religious Thinker* (New Haven: Yale University Press, 1961), p. 175.
14. Schleiermacher, *Life of Jesus*, pp. 190–229.
15. Schleiermacher, *Life of Jesus*, p. 205.
16. Schleiermacher, *Life of Jesus*, pp. 87–122.
17. Schleiermacher, *On Religion*, p. 246.
18. *On Religion*, p. 3.
19. Schleiermacher, *Christian Faith*, chap. 90.
20. Georg Wilhelm Friedrich Hegel, *Early Theological Writings*, trans. T. M. Knox (Chicago: University of Chicago Press, 1948), pp. 196, 212.
21. Harold Bloom, *Blake's Apocalypse*, 2d ed. (Ithaca, N.Y.: Cornell University Press, 1970).
22. *The Paintings and Drawings of William Blake*, ed. Martin Butlin, 2 vols. (New Haven: Yale University Press, 1981), *Text*, pp. 175–76.
23. Harold Bloom, *Figures of Capable Imagination* (New York: Seabury Press, 1976), p. 50.
24. Emerson, *Nature*, Atkinson ed., pp. 6, 9; italics in original.
25. Ralph Waldo Emerson, *Early Lectures*, 3 vols. (Cambridge, Mass: Harvard University Press, 1961–72), 1:73.
26. John Haynes Holmes, "Introduction" to Ernest Renan, *The Life of Jesus* (1864; New York: Modern Library, 1927), p. 23.

27. Renan, *Life of Jesus*, p. 69.
28. Renan, *Life of Jesus*, pp. 392–93.
29. Renan, *Life of Jesus*, p. 65.
30. Gay Wilson Allen, *Waldo Emerson. A Biography* (New York: The Viking Press, 1981), pp. 570–92.
31. Emerson, *Essays: Second Series*, Atkinson ed., pp. 321, 338.
32. *Poems*, Atkinson ed., p. 775.
33. Karl Barth, *Die protestantische Theologie im 19. Jahrhundert* (Zurich: Evangelischer Verlag, 1947), pp. 385, 412–13.
34. David Friedrich Strauss, *The Christ of Faith and the Jesus of History*, trans. Leander E. Keck (Philadelphia: Fortress Press, 1977), p. 37.
35. Schweitzer, *Quest*, p. 67.
36. Barth, *19. Jahrhundert*, pp. 397–99.
37. James Hastings Nichols, *Romanticism in American Theology* (Chicago: University of Chicago Press, 1961), pp. 107–39.
38. Jaroslav Pelikan, *The Vindication of Tradition. The 1983 Jefferson Lecture in the Humanities* (New Haven: Yale University Press, 1984), pp. 3–40.
39. Emerson, *An Address*, Atkinson ed., pp. 67–84; italics in original.
40. Fyodor Dostoevsky, *Crime and Punishment* 4.4.
41. *The Notebooks for "Crime and Punishment,"* ed. Edward Wasiolek (Chicago: University of Chicago Press, 1967), p. 231.

17. THE LIBERATOR

1. Dostoevsky, *The Brothers Karamazov* 5.5.
2. Gal. 3:28; 5:1.
3. For a brief account, see John Francis Maxwell, *Slavery and the Catholic Church* (London: Barry Rose, 1975), esp. pp. 88–125.
4. Mead, *Lively Experiment*, p. 73.
5. See Julian, *Dictionary of Hymnology* 2:1684.
6. David Brion Davis, *The Problem of Slavery in Western Culture* (Ithaca, N.Y.: Cornell University Press, 1966), pp. 199–200.
7. Wilhelm Gass, *Geschichte der christlichen Ethik*, 3 vols. (Berlin: G. Reimer, 1881–87), 1:226.
8. Augustine, *City of God* 19.15.
9. John Knox, *Philemon among the Letters of Paul* (Chicago: University of Chicago Press, 1935), pp. 46–56.
10. J. B. Lightfoot, *Saint Paul's Epistles to the Colossians and to Philemon* (London: Macmillan, 1900), p. 321.
11. Isaac Mendelsohn, *Slavery in the Ancient Near East: A Comparative Study* (New York: Oxford University Press, 1949).
12. Rom. 6:16; John 8:34; 2 Pet. 2:19.
13. Ernst Troeltsch, *The Social Teachings of the Christian Churches*, trans. Olive Wyon, 2 vols. (1931; New York: Harper Torchbooks, 1960), 1:133.
14. Lev Nikolaevich Tolstoy, *Resurrection*, pt. 1, chap. 41.
15. Tolstoy, *Resurrection*, pt. 3, chap. 28.
16. G. I. Petrov, *Otluchenie L'va Tolstogo od Tserkvi* (The separation of Lev Tolstoy from the church) (Moscow: Isdatyelstvo "Znanie," 1978), p. 28.
17. Tolstoy to Shaw, 9 May 1910, in *Tolstoy's Letters*, ed. R. K. Christian, 2 vols. (New York: Charles Scribner's Sons, 1978), 2:700.

18. Isaiah Berlin, "The Hedgehog and the Fox," *Russian Thinkers*, ed. Henry Hardy and Aileen Kelly (New York: Penguin Books, 1978), pp. 51–52.

19. Mohandas K. Gandhi, *An Autobiography: The Story of My Experiments with Truth*, trans. Mahadev Desai (Boston: Beacon Press, 1957), pp. 137–38.

20. Tolstoy to Mohandas K. Gandhi, 7 September 1910, *Letters* 2:706–08.

21. Erik Erikson, *Gandhi's Truth: On the Origins of Militant Non-Violence* (New York: Norton, 1969), p. 281.

22. Matt. 21:12–17; Matt. 23.

23. Phil. 3:10.

24. Howard Thurman, *Jesus and the Disinherited* (New York: Abingdon-Cokesbury Press, 1949).

25. Martin Luther King, Jr., *Where Do We Go from Here: Chaos or Community?* (Boston: Beacon Press, 1968), p. 44.

26. Martin Luther King, Jr., *Stride toward Freedom* (New York: Harper and Brothers, 1958), p. 101.

27. David Levering Lewis, *King: A Critical Biography* (1970; reprint, Baltimore: Penguin Books, 1971), p. 191.

28. Lewis, *King*, p. 105.

29. Kenneth L. Smith and Ira G. Zepp, Jr., *Search for the Beloved Community: The Thinking of Martin Luther King, Jr.* (Valley Forge, Pa.: Judson Press, 1974).

30. King, *Stride toward Freedom*, pp. 102–06, 189–224.

31. Casalis, *Correct Ideas Don't Fall from the Skies*, p. 114.

32. Gustavo Guttierez, *A Theology of Liberation: History, Politics, and Salvation* (Maryknoll, N.Y.: Orbis Books, 1973).

18. THE MAN WHO BELONGS TO THE WORLD

1. Acts 1:8.

2. Eusebius, *Ecclesiastical History* 1.4.2.

3. See Julian, *Dictionary of Hymnology* 1:601, and the account given there of the place of this hymn in the history of missions to the South Seas.

4. Kenneth Scott Latourette, *A History of the Expansion of Christianity*, 7 vols. (New York: Harper and Brothers, 1939–45).

5. Arthur Schlesinger, Jr., "The Missionary Enterprise and Theories of Imperialism," in *The Missionary Enterprise in China and America*, ed. John K. Fairbank (Cambridge, Mass.: Harvard University Press, 1974), pp. 336–73.

6. Karl Holl, "Die Missionsmethode der alten und die der mittelalterlichen Kirche," in *Gesammelte Aufsätze zur Kirchengeschichte*, 3 vols. (1928; reprint, Darmstadt: Wissenschaftliche Buchgesellschaft, 1964), 3:117–29.

7. Hilaire Belloc, *Europe and the Faith* (New York: Paulist Press, 1921), p. viii.

8. Francis Dvornik, *Byzantine Missions among the Slavs* (New Brunswick, N.J.: Rutgers University Press, 1970), pp. 107–09.

9. Venerable Bede, *Ecclesiastical History of the English People* 22.

10. Auerbach, *Literary Language and Its Public*, pp. 120–21.

11. Joseph Needham, *Science and Civilization in China, Introductory Considerations*, 2d ed., 2 vols. (Cambridge: Cambridge University Press, 1961), 1:148.

12. As quoted in Jonathan D. Spence, *The Memory Palace of Matteo Ricci* (New York: Viking Press, 1984), p. 210.

13. I know *True Meaning* only in the anonymous French translation, *Entretiens d'un lettre chinois et d'un docteur européen, sur le vraie idée de Dieu*, in *Lettres édifiantes et curieuses* 25 (1811): 143–385.

14. This material has been gathered in *The Book of a Thousand Tongues*, ed. Eric M. North (New York: Harper and Brothers, 1938).

15. For only one example among many, see P. Yang Fu-Mien, "The Catholic Missionary Contribution to the Study of Chinese Dialects," *Orbis* 9 (1960): 158–85.

16. Jawaharlal Nehru, *Toward Freedom: Autobiography* (Boston: Beacon Press, 1958), pp. 236–50.

17. Spence, *Memory Palace*, pp. 59–92.

18. Harnack, *Mission and Expansion* (see chap. 6, n. 5), p. 108; italics in original.

19. Origen, *Against Celsus* 8.72.

20. Mark 9:41.

21. Nathan Söderblom, *The Living God: Basic Forms of Personal Religion* (Boston: Beacon Press, 1962), pp. 349, 379.

22. Stephen Neill, *A History of Christian Missions* (Baltimore: Penguin Books, 1964), p. 456.

23. *Documents of Vatican II*, pp. 660–68.

24. *Documents of Vatican II*, pp. 666–67.

25. On the ironies of its appearance, see Robert P. Ericksen, *Theologians Under Hitler: Gerhard Kittel, Paul Althaus, and Emanuel Hirsch* (New Haven: Yale University Press, 1985).

26. Augustine, *Confessions* 9.27.38.

Index of Proper Names

Index of Biblical References